"The Will and Determination of the Human Spirit Shines..."
- Jeff Liebsch, *Busan HAPS* Magazine

TRAVELIN' MAN

ACROSS THE SAHARA AND BEYOND

8 Countries, 2 Continents ... 1 Pair of Pants

DENNIS D. FEEHELEY

ParkHampton Press

The opinions expressed in this manuscript are solely the opinions of the author and do not represent the opinions or thoughts of the publisher. The author has represented and warranted full ownership and/or legal right to publish all the materials in this book.

Travelin' Man Across the Sahara and Beyond
8 Countries, 2 Continents...1 Pair of Pants
All Rights Reserved.
Copyright © 2014 Dennis D. Feeheley
v3.0

Cover Photo © 2014 JupiterImages Corportion. Interior Photos by John Feeheley and Dennis D. Feeheley. All rights reserved - used with permission.

This book may not be reproduced, transmitted, or stored in whole or in part by any means, including graphic, electronic, or mechanical without the express written consent of the publisher except in the case of brief quotations embodied in critical articles and reviews.

ParkHampton Press

ISBN: 978-0-578-13419-2

PRINTED IN THE UNITED STATES OF AMERICA

Table of Contents

Praise for Dennis D. Feeheley's debut book v
Chapter 1:   The Decision 1
Chapter 2:   The Americans Land in Paris... Again 10
Chapter 3:   Trains, Tractors and Hitching 15
Chapter 4:   Ride and Hide 30
Chapter 5:   Where Are We? … And How Did We Get Here? 40
Chapter 6:   Rules of the Road 43
Chapter 7:   The Race Is On… 58
Chapter 8:   The Race Continues…With Mario at the Wheel 68
Chapter 9:   Stowaways Across the Mediterranean Sea 78
Chapter 10: Out on the Open Sea with… the Fonz? 82
Chapter 11: At Long Last Africa! 91
Chapter 12: Into the Sahara …. Into the Unknown 100
Chapter 13: Habjib, Tunisia: Long Lost Brothers 117
Chapter 14: The Long Border Walk 129
Chapter 15: Back Tracking 140
Chapter 16: Crossing into Algeria…Finally!
             The Long(er) Border Walk 149
Chapter 17: The All Night Ride 162
Chapter 18: Passing the Point of No Return 174
Chapter 19: Losing the Road 185
Chapter 20: Jeep Surfing in the Sahara Sand 192
Chapter 21: Christmas Sunrise in the Sahara 200
Chapter 22: Back On the Road Again 213
Chapter 23: Danger Ahead - End of the Line? 221
Chapter 24: Guns, Guerrillas and…Gas 227

Chapter 25:	Moving Faster than a Sahara Sand Storm	245
Chapter 26:	The Moroccan Border: Moment of Truth	259
Chapter 27:	Hey Joe! What do You Need?	270
Chapter 28:	A Tight Spot	281
Chapter 29:	Out of Money – Out of Time	290
Chapter 30:	Trading for Money or For our Lives	299
Chapter 31:	No Matter What!	315
Chapter 32:	Rocking and Rolling	326
Acknowledgements		343

Praise for Dennis D. Feeheley's debut book

**TRAVELIN MAN
ACROSS THE SAHARA AND BEYOND
8 COUNTRIES, 2 CONTINENTS ... 1 PAIR OF PANTS**

TRAVELIN MAN IS BOTH ENTERTAINING AND INSPIRING… *Travelin' Man* brings back nostalgia of a time when simple was the norm.… With a desire to seek adventure, the two young American nomads head out with a free spirit to discover what the world has to offer… FEEHELEY'S INSIGHTS INTO VARIOUS CULTURES ARE WITTY

THE WILL AND DETERMINATION OF THE HUMAN SPIRIT SHINES.

Jeff Liebsch - Editor, Busan HAPS Magazine

DENNIS FEEHELEY IS A CONSUMMATE STORY TELLER who weaves a gripping, often harrowing tale…A MUST-READ for anyone who likes suspenseful true stories.

**Gus Swanda - Radio Host; 90.5 eFM
Humorist & Social Commentator**

IN DIRECT AND PRECISE PROSE, 19 YEAR OLD '*TRAVELIN MAN*' DENNIS FEEHELEY RECOUNTS AN EPIC JOURNEY .… from London across northern Africa on little more than a whim for adventure.

A GRITTY QUEST FOR SURVIVAL ACROSS THE SAHARA DESERT… Fueled by a do or die attitude and emboldened by trust in each other … Life and death decisions loom every step of the way… AN EXCITING ROLLER-COASTER RIDE ... I couldn't put it down.

-Kenneth May - MFA, Founder of Poetry Plus+ & Wordz Only, South Korea's premier spoken word events.

> *" Up with the sun, gone with the wind*
> *She always said I was lazy*
> *Leavin' my home, leavin' my friends*
> *Runnin' when things get too crazy*
> *Out to the road, out 'neath the stars*
> *Feelin' the breeze, passin' the cars..."*

'Travelin Man' by Bob Seger
Performed by Bob Seger and The Silver Bullet Band
© 1974 1975 Gear Publishing Company (ASCAP)

CHAPTER 1

The Decision

I awoke early with the rising of the sun. It was still cool on the desert sand floor. From the doorway of the single-room, desert camp I had been sleeping in I could see the sun slowly casting its long shadow, as it broke over the distant horizon. There was nothing but endless waves of desert in every direction for as far as I could see.

It was Christmas morning, 1977. I was 19 years old and I was at a remote Bedouin camp in the vast Sahara Desert of Algeria in northern Africa. I had been traveling for over a month. I was now traveling with my brother John, and we were running desperately low on money.

We had left London about three weeks before on this ill-conceived but incredible adventure, and we had already trekked over 3,000 kilometers traveling by train, ship, jeep, foot, truck, thumb - hitchhiking, camel, tractor and bus across Europe and northern Africa; living on less than $6 a day.

The $6 a day covered everything; food, lodging, transportation and all expenses. But even traveling on only 6 bucks a day it had become painfully clear that we could not make it back to England with the money we had. We were running out of money, and we were way out in the northern region of the Sahara Desert, miles and miles from the nearest town, heading to the Moroccan border.

For days now, as we passed through the few isolated Muslim villages that dotted the Saharan desert landscape, we had been repeatedly told by the locals we encountered that the Algerian-Moroccan border was completely closed to everyone, especially to a couple of American travelers passing through. They kept telling John and me to go back, but by this point turning back was not an option for us. We had passed the point of no return. We had no choice except to continue on.

Adding to our desperation, before we could even hope to get to the border, we would soon somehow have to cross the Sub-Saharan war-zone area controlled by the Policerio guerillas. It was a long-running war between Algeria and Morocco, fighting over a large chunk of land in southern Morocco, and we were heading right into it.

With only a single strip of paved road winding endlessly through the empty desert, there weren't exactly many turns we could make. The choices were go forward - or turn around and go back the same way we came.

The single, desolate road cut through the barren desert connecting the small villages. There would be maybe 100-200 kilometers of just desert for as far as you could see in every direction and then a small, speck of a village would come into sight. Then another 100 kilometers or so of nothing but desert, before another village would appear on the distant horizon.

John and I were told the war zone area we were heading toward was closed off to everything and everyone, except to those bringing in supplies for the soldiers – the Poliserio guerillas. But we had no choice except to continue forward towards the Moroccan border since going back to England the way we came was much farther than going ahead. We had long since passed the point of no return.

Our situation was getting increasingly desperate and dangerous. It had become painfully apparent that we didn't have enough money to get back and that any money we spent now was money we would have to somehow make back later to keep going.

This was over 30 years ago in 1977; long before the days of fax machines, cell-phones, the Internet, bank ATMs, videos recorders, home computers, GPS Systems and globalization. Traveling was truly an adventure. Particularly, the way John and I traveled in those days; very, very little money, with a small backpack, and little or no information. You really could get "lost" out in the world, completely out of touch with everything and everyone you left behind. Much of the world then was completely unknown to me with very few and limited forms of communication.

The world was just this immense, fascinating place out there waiting to be discovered and explored. I loved that sense of discovery...Not knowing what the new day would bring or what challenges faced me, and what I would find on the road ahead. I always, for as long as I could remember, had this tremendous desire to roam and travel.

THE DECISION

I thrived on that sense of adventure and discovery...

But as I awoke that Christmas morning of 1977 and looked out over the endless, empty miles of the Sahara Desert, I was not thinking about the wonders of discovery and adventure. Instead, I was seriously thinking about what in the world I had gotten myself into...and how would I ever make it back to England, where I was attending university.

John and I were lost out in the Sahara with nothing but unbroken waves of Saharan Desert sand in every direction for as far as we could see...We were still a few thousand kilometers away from England...We were desperately low on money and had less than $85 dollars each...We had long passed the point of no return and were heading directly into the guerilla war zone area...I had not showered or even washed once in the past weeks...I had eaten almost nothing but bread and Coca-Cola for most of the trip...I had had the 'runs' for several days now and felt sick every time I ate...There was no means of contacting home...I had one pair of pants and only enough clothes in my backpack so that I could wear everything I had at one time. I never carried a sleeping bag or much clothes when I traveled because anytime you're not wearing it – you're carrying it. And I hated carrying it!

At 19 years of age, I was facing a rather serious and dangerous situation. But it was also a unique challenge and I was young and determined, and with my brother John we were filled with the fearlessness, or some might say inexperience, of youth...probably more inexperience than fearlessness.

How John and I came to be in the middle of Algeria, lost out in the remote Sahara Desert at a Bedouin camp, heading into a guerilla war zone with almost no money, no maps or food, and especially how we made it back proved to be the adventure of a lifetime...

ככככ

It all started a few weeks earlier on a cool, early December evening at historic Victoria Train Station in central London. Track number 4 to be exact. John and I had not seen each other for the prior few months, but the last time we were together we had made a plan to take a trip somewhere warm during the winter semester break. I had started my freshman year of college at the magnificent Harlaxton University in Lincolnshire, England and the trip was planned for the long winter semester vacation.

The "extensive" travel plans we made the last time we were together consisted of me asking John, "Where should we go during the winter break."

TRAVELIN' MAN ACROSS THE SAHARA AND BEYOND

John replied, "Well, Europe will be cold in December."
I said, "Africa should be warm in December."
John said, "Yeah, let's go there. It'll be warm."
I said, "Ok, let's go there."

That was it. That was the total extent of our planning. We set a date to meet about 3 months later at Victoria Station in London at 4:00 PM in early December at the end of platform 4. We were both supposed to have about $700 for the trip, at least that's what we were *supposed to* have

With $700 each for over a month's travel covering about 5,000 kilometers, we thought it would be very, very tight but do-able. The money would have to cover everything; trains, ships, food, buses, lodgings, visas, shots, assorted paperwork, unexpected expenses and rip-offs.

We can't forget rip-offs, now can we? I have been ripped-off in almost every conceivable manner during my travels in about 53 countries throughout the world. If you think 53 countries sounds like a lot – my brother John has been to over 60.

I say "about" 53 countries because it depends how I count them. The world has changed so much since I started my international travels…So much. For example, East and West Germany were 2 very different countries when I traveled through them. One was communist, the other was free. Now they are one. On the contrary, when I traveled through Czechoslovakia in 1984 it was a single country. Now it's two.

The ways I have been ripped-off have been both countless and imaginative. Sometimes impossible to defend against no matter how careful you are. For example, I never use something, or eat or drink something before I know the price and it's agreed to. If not, once you eat, drink or use something, any price can be demanded and it's too late to go back. You have no recourse except to pay.

But I'm happy and thankful to say that for every time I was ripped off or someone was a danger to me, I had ten other experiences where people helped me or went out of their way to show me tremendous kindness. The number of times that people helped me out, sometimes in critical situations as in this travel adventure, far outshines any of the negative experiences of my travels.

So at the pre-appointed hour, on the pre-appointed day, at the pre-appointed location, John and I did indeed meet at Victoria Station in London at the end of platform 4. I wasn't sure if John would really be there. Actually, I wasn't sure if I would be there either, as I had already been traveling to

THE DECISION

various other corners around the globe for about two weeks immediately preceding our meeting. But we both did show up right on schedule, although not prepared as we planned.

It was great to see John as he suddenly appeared among the hustling crowds at the station, just as we had agreed months earlier. As I said, at this time I had just turned 19 years old and was on my freshman-year winter break from Harlaxton University.

My brother John was the ripe old age of 21 and already an experienced traveler. I was basically following in his footsteps. I owe a great debt to John as he was the older brother, and paved the way for a lot of what I did when I was young.

Prior to meeting up this day, John had already done a great deal of traveling across the globe the year before, and I had soon followed taking my own trips across Europe, to the Soviet Union and elsewhere. By the time we each reached the young age of 21, John and I had individually traveled to over 30 countries around various areas of the world…sometimes traveling together and often alone.

While John and I had some qualities in common such as a strong work ethic and an adventurous spirit, our characters and appearances were somewhat different. John was about 5'10, slightly stocky with brown hair, blue eyes and somewhat light features. Whereas I was a couple of inches taller, leaner, had darker hair, brown eyes and dark features, especially when I grew a beard, which I usually did when I traveled.

My brother was a very outgoing guy, often joking, very friendly and enjoyed talking a lot. He would talk and joke with just about anyone without any hesitation. I, on the other hand, am quiet by nature and generally more private. I'm quite easygoing and friendly, but very focused and determined when it comes to things that are important to me. As my female friends used to say at the time – John was the friendly jokester and prankster…I was the strong, silent type who always had a lot of girls around.

When I was younger and still today, I've always loved playing sports. When I was a young kid I played competitive sports year-round, and continued playing at the college level in England, where I played basketball and rugby. John, however, was always more into hunting and fishing and other outdoor activities; activities that I took an interest in mainly because of him.

When we were young kids, John would often drag me out to go fishing or hunting at 4:00 or 5:00 in the morning because that's "when the fish were biting" or "the deer were moving." It always seemed to me that the fish were only biting when it was an ungodly early hour, or when it was raining, or cold or storming, never on a bright sunny afternoon.

I was always off playing baseball, or basketball, or golf, or football, or going dirt bike riding or swimming. I loved all kinds of competitive sports as a kid and played sports every chance I could.

But John was a true outdoorsman and being the older brother, he would cajole, threaten, joke or do whatever it took to get me out on the lake or in the woods for fishing and hunting. I'm glad he did. I came to enjoy it and it was a great experience for me. Our personalities tended to complement each other, and I always really enjoyed being around my brother on our various adventures together. We got along very well.

Our first real travel adventure had been when I was 16 and John was 18, during summer vacation from high school when we took a couple months and drove with our cousin Brian across America; from Michigan to California, down to Mexico and back. I didn't know it at the time, but it was to be the first of many travel adventures for us, sometimes together and often individually.

When I met up with John at Victoria Station this early December day in 1977, I was eagerly looking forward to starting off on our trek to Africa together. I expected to have a great trip, but in reality I had no idea what kind of true travel adventure and challenges we were in for, but I would find out soon enough.

After briefly saying hello and getting re-acquainted, John and I quickly took stock of our situation for the trip. We didn't spend a lot time with small talk, we got right to it.

John asked me, "So how much money you got for the trip?"

I hemmed and hawed a bit saying, "Well, I don't have as much as we planned."

"Ok…So, how much do you got?"

"Well," I replied. "I hoped to have more but, you know, uhh, I've already been traveling for the past couple weeks. I just traveled to the Soviet Union and then…uhh…as soon as I got back I took a trip to the Canary Islands with 3 girls from school. It took some of the money I saved. I just flew back to England yesterday."

"With 3 girls, huh? Why am I not surprised… So you just got back yesterday?" John asked.

"Yeah."

"So…you've already been traveling for a few weeks. Huh??"
"Yeah."
"OK. That's interesting…So how much do you got?"

Actually, I hardly had any money at all since I had very little to begin with and I already been traveling for a couple of weeks. About 2 weeks earlier when my freshman fall school semester at Harlaxton University in Lincolnshire, England had finished, I had flown from London to the Soviet Union for about a week-long trip to Moscow with several other university classmates. This was during the Cold War and it was an exceptional opportunity I couldn't pass up. It turned out to be a fascinating experience.

Before returning from the trip to Moscow, my girlfriend Jan talked me into going to the Canary Islands with her and two other female friends Linda and Betts, who were also students from Harlaxton. I absolutely could not afford the trip, but it still didn't exactly take much to talk me into going. They had already booked it, and I couldn't pass up the chance to spend some fun in the sun on a beautiful island.

So after returning to London from Moscow, we spent one night sleeping on some benches at Luton Airport, and then the next day flew to Tenerife and Las Palmas for about a week in the sun. After a great trip to the Canary Islands, we all flew back to England, where we spent another night sleeping at Luton Airport on some benches. It was the second time sleeping there and I was right at home.

Early the next morning I took a bus with Jan from Luton Airport across London to Heathrow Airport for her flight back to America. We had been students together at Harlaxton University during the previous semester, which was the first semester of my freshman year of college. Harlaxton University was a magical place, with students from many countries around the world studying and living together in the mysterious Hartlaxton Manor which sits up on a hill outside the small country town of Grantham. After studying there for a semester, Jan was now leaving England and returning to The States, while I was staying on in England to continue my studies at Harlaxton after my travels during the winter break.

That morning at Heathrow Airport I said a heartfelt goodbye to Jan at her boarding gate. It was a dramatic farewell, reminding me of airport scenes out of a movie…Actually, much of my young life at that time reminded me of scenes out of movies.

◄ TRAVELIN' MAN ACROSS THE SAHARA AND BEYOND

Immediately after saying goodbye at Luton Airport, I hopped a bus and traveled across London again to meet my brother John a couple of hours later at Victoria Station to start the trip to Africa. It was a short bus trip, but I was filled with lots of thoughts of saying farewell and seeing Jan off, while also looking forward to the great adventure ahead with John.

It was the ending of one adventure that I had since the first day I arrived at Harlaxton, and the beginning of an incredible travel adventure with my brother...

Standing out on platform 4 at Victoria Station with the crowds pushing by us, John and I continued discussing our funds for the trip. After telling John of my previous trips to Moscow and The Canary Islands, I finally admitted, "All I have is 97 British Pounds." (about $160) Not the $700 I was supposed to have for the month-long trip to Africa. Not even close. Not by a long shot.

John looked disappointed. I was hoping maybe, somehow, he had more than his $700 share for the trip. Not likely.

So I asked him, "How much do you got?"

"Oh, well, I have my return flight ticket from London to the US." He replied. "I need to use it by next month...January 3rd it expires."

"January 3rd?"

"Yep. If I don't get back by the 3rd, I lose the ticket. So I definitely need to be back in London from our trip by the 3rd."

"Yeah, OK...But how much money do you have?" I asked again.

"Well, ahh...I have $185."

"That's it? 185 bucks? Nothing else? How are we going to travel all the way across Europe and Africa, *and* make it back with that kind of money?" I asked alarmed.

"Who knows? But, hey, look who's talking – It's more than you have."

I couldn't argue with that.

So that was it. That was our situation. It was early December, 1977. I was 19 years old. John was 21. We were at Victoria Station in London, several thousand miles from our home in Michigan. I had about 5 weeks before I could return to school at Harlaxton University in Lincolnshire, and John had a return ticket from London to the US that had to be used by January 3rd. We had a total between us of about $340 and a little change...which we would somehow have to travel all the across Western Europe, cross the

Mediterranean Sea, trek all the way across northern Africa and part of the Sahara Desert, *and* make it back to England with.

So what did we do??

We left the train station and spent some time walking out around Piccadilly Circus in London talking about our predicament. It was a short walk. We quickly decided what we would do…We would go for it. We would cross Europe and go to Africa.

Why? Well, it would be warm there.

How? Not a clue…other than very cheaply.

CHAPTER 2

The Americans Land in Paris... Again

That fateful decision marked the beginning of our trip and an amazing adventure that would cover; A month on the road, over 5,000 kilometers traveled across 8 countries and portions of two continents, one ship ride across the English Channel; three separate crossings by ship of The Strait of Messina, The Mediterranean Sea and the Strait of Gibraltar; over a couple thousand kilometers of hitch-hiking, more than a dozen train trips, and over 1,500 kilometers of rugged travel through the northern region of The Sahara Desert.

All accomplished with $345 between the two of us. For those of you who are mathematically challenged like me - That's less than $175 each. But we had made our decision and there was no turning back.

Not having enough money was the first of many mistakes and blunders on our adventure but it didn't hold us back. We just had an unrelenting, fearless attitude of no retreat. Grit it out and do what you got to do to keep moving forward…Improvise, use your wits and nerve, make do, and keep carrying on to survive on the road. That's the traveling code we lived by and in some cases almost died by. But I was young, with a strong sense of my youth and a passion to discover and explore the world.

I knew it was my time.

So with our decision made John and I immediately started off from London. We found out about a 12 hour overnight budget train and ship leaving from Victoria Station at about 11:50 PM that would take us across the English Channel and then get us all the way to Paris, France.

THE AMERICANS LAND IN PARIS... AGAIN

Looking at the train schedule board, John said to me, "Let's get the overnight ticket. It'll get us all the way to Paris."

"But it's 10 pounds. ($16) That's a lot of money." I replied.

"Yeah, but it'll cover a night's sleep for us and get us across the Channel."

"But 10 quid!" I repeated.

"Yep, but even if we hitch, we still gotta cross the Channel somehow. We can't swim it"

"We can always try," I said with a grin. "Alright. Let's get the tickets."

So we got the tickets for the midnight Train to Dover – Ship across the English Channel to Dunkirk - Train to Paris. The ticket would give us a place to sleep that first night while making distance on the train and ship. It cost us the 10 Pounds, which was a lot of money for us. I was already down to 150 bucks and we hadn't even left Victoria station yet.

A short while after 11:00PM our train was ready for boarding. So with our backpacks firmly on our back, our very limited money and non-existent supplies, we climbed on the midnight train and set out for France, Africa, The Sahara and beyond…

We were off.

As our train pulled out of Victoria Station that night and we started our trip, I felt a slight sense of urgency, knowing in the back of my mind that with the funds we had, it was something of a race against the clock, as well as distance. We had to keep on the move, so that we didn't burn money without gaining mileage. Our money would only last so many days and we had to make as many miles as we could each day to make it back…

The train took us from London across southeastern England to the coastal city of Dover, arriving in the early morning. The train was crowded, but we were lucky enough to find some seats. I didn't sleep much on the train. I was quite tired, but I was so fired up about starting our trip that I didn't really notice.

When we arrived in Dover, it was dark and cold as we left the train and were herded into a small, brightly lit customs building near the shipping docks. After clearing customs to exit England, we then boarded the ship that was to take us the 22 miles across the English Channel. That night was my third crossing of the English Channel by ship.

Over the years, I've probably made over a dozen crossings of the English Channel by ship, usually from Dover, but also from Folkstone. I always enjoyed those crossings - since crossing the Channel usually meant I was just starting some new trip or adventure, or else it meant I was returning to England for university after finishing some trip somewhere.

I have a great deal of affection for England with its rich history, and many wonderful memories of my time there. For three years it was a second home to me during my youth and college days. Returning to England, and seeing from a distance the white cliffs of Dover appear over the water's edge was always heartwarming for me. It's one of my favorite sights in all of England.

While I stood out on deck as our ship headed out across the Channel that night, I watched the white cliffs disappear behind us with a feeling of great anticipation of what lay ahead, beyond the other side of the Channel. It was an incredible feeling of freedom, adventure and exploration. I was heading into the unknown. And I loved it.

The ship ride across the Channel was cold and windy, with some rough seas, not a real comfortable ride. John and I couldn't find any seats so we ended up sleeping on the floor with our backpacks, and for a while out on the ship's deck until it became too cold. Without us getting much sleep, the crowded ship rocked though the rough waters until we arrived at the shores of France in the port city of Dunkirk in the early morning hours.

"Man that was some cold ship ride, wasn't it?" I said to John.

"Yep. Sure was." John replied, "Not too comfortable. Pretty rough seas"

"It'll be good when we get to Africa. Should be nice and warm."

"That's for sure."

"So how long do you think it'll take us to get there?" I asked.

"I have no idea.' John replied. "We have a lot of ground to cover before we even get close. We'll just have to take it a day at a time and see what comes our way."

And that's exactly what we did for the rest of the trip. We never discussed anything long-term. We just focused day to day on the obstacles immediately in front of us, tried to keep moving forward and do what we had to do. We had an unrelenting belief that we would somehow find a way to overcome any obstacle or danger we encountered each day. We never planned or looked ahead beyond what we had to do that day.

That attitude carried us through some real tough times and made for some interesting travel and experiences along the way. But it also led us into a lot of mistakes and danger, and caused a lot of back tracking, which you will soon see.

THE AMERICANS LAND IN PARIS... AGAIN

After getting off the ship, we cleared French customs without a problem and were put on a train that would take us on the last leg of our trip from Dunkirk to Paris. The train ride was uneventful, and I did manage to get some sleep before we rolled into Paris

Upon arriving in Paris the following morning, we had the phone number of a middle aged Parisian couple, named the Erams, who were family friends. We had known them when they lived in Michigan. Their son was the same age as our younger brother Winston, and they used to play together as children.

After some difficulty finding and using a French phone, we gave the Eram's a call and they immediately invited us to their home. We took the subway across town and did a lot of walking, following the directions Mr. Eram gave us over the phone. It took us a while, but we did find it.

We met them at their well-furnished, fashionable flat near the center of Paris. Mr. Eram was in his late 40's, very nicely dressed with that world weary but handsome look so many French men seemed to have. His wife was very petite and charming. They were both very kind people.

Their apartment was a richly and elegantly designed older building with a beautiful view overlooking some small Parisian streets and shops. The Eram's gave John and me a comfortable room to use for the duration of our stay. It was one, of only two times, on the entire trip that we actually had a real bed and place to sleep.

During our stay in Paris, our French friends were very hospitable to us. They took us for an interesting afternoon boat trip down the Sienna River through the heart of Paris. Winding along the waterway through the heart of the city, it gave me a pretty good feel for the history and architecture.

Mr. and Mrs. Eram also drove us to the Arc de Triumph and one evening took us sightseeing throughout the city. It was a wonderful tour and very informative.

The second night we were in Paris, we visited with Mr. Eram's in-laws for dinner at their flat. They prepared and served us a delicious home-cooked, four course French meal. It was a wonderful meal. John even had seconds and, with some encouragement, third helpings of the meal. This seemed to make him quite popular with our French hosts. John really enjoys his food, and French food was no exception.

After the dinner we sat talking in the furnished study with Mr. Eram's father-in-law, who spoke quite good English, as did all their family members. He was a kind man, very interested in our trip and seemed somewhat envious of us.

While talking with us, he said to John and me, "Tell me about your travel route. Maybe I can help you plan a good route through France."

John answered, "Our travel route? Well…ah, we don't have a travel route."

"Oh. OK." He answered, surprised. "Well, then let me see your maps and I'll take a look. Maybe give you some ideas."

This time I answered," Well, ahh, we don't have any maps."

"You don't have maps? Not any map?" Mr. Eram's father-in-law asked even more surprised.

I sheepishly answered, "No. No maps."

Mr. Eram's father-in-law then got up and briskly walked over to a back room and pulled out some old maps for us. He gave us a dusty map of France and of Italy, as well as an old, wrinkled map of northern Africa he had. It was very considerate of him since we had no maps of all. We thanked him for his consideration and later returned to Mr. Eram's flat for our second and last night in Paris.

The maps of France and Italy he gave us only lasted us for a short portion of our trip through Europe, and the map of Africa disappeared well before we ever made it to Africa. It was never used.

We stayed 2 1/2 days with the Eram's and had a very enjoyable, expense-free time, including several delicious home-cooked French meals. I spent only $1 during the two days in Paris as the Erams were very kind and would never allow us to pay for anything.

During my traveling days out on the road, I would often visit people I had met or knew from other countries. I have an address book of over 100 people from over 40 countries, that I had met on the road and exchanged addresses with. I would often look people up when I was traveling. I still have the original, little address book with all the names and addresses. This was long, long before the internet. I always remembered, though, what my mother told me about visiting people on my travels, "Never stay for more than 3 days. For three days you are a guest, stay any longer and you are a nuisance." It was good advice. On my travels I always followed that rule. Both my mother and my father have always been a source of good advice for me.

So after 2 great days in Paris with the Erams, John and I made our plans to head out and get back on the road.

CHAPTER 3

Trains, Tractors and Hitching

We headed out early at day break the following morning to continue our trek across Europe towards Africa. We slowly made our way through the city area of Paris to get to the highway that would take us down to the city of Dijon, and on southward to Italy and Africa. Paris is a big city and, even though it was quiet on the streets during the early morning, we had some difficulty locating the correct roadway heading south out of town. We ended up spending a couple of frustrating hours walking and taking a subway ride across town before reaching the right road to start hitching out of the city.

Once we were on the roadway we found a good spot to hitch from, which is essential for getting rides. You need a place with a long, open straightaway ahead of you so that the drivers have plenty of time to see you and react. And then you also need a fairly long, open area behind you, with enough side-road space for a car to easily pull over without blocking traffic. If we were in a bad location, our chances of getting a ride could be nil. We would sometimes have to walk an hour or more along a road to find a decent place to hitch from. What's important for successful hitchhiking is the same as for buying real estate; location, location, location.

Having found a real good place to hitch from along the main road with a lot of consistent traffic going by, I said to John, "I figure we outta make some good distance today."

"Yep. It'd be nice to get a good start and make some mileage."

"In this spot, with all these cars going by, we should be ok."

"Yep. It looks good."

"Yeah. Real good." I agreed.

TRAVELIN' MAN ACROSS THE SAHARA AND BEYOND

Man, were we wrong. That morning, that day, that night and the following morning turned out to be the worst stretch of hitchhiking I ever experienced in all my years of traveling. In fact, it's the worst stretch I've ever even heard of. We spent 22 hours on the road hitchhiking and we got one, that's right, one single fifteen minute ride. That's 22 hours out there standing next to the road in the sun, in the day, in the night, in the cold, in the rain.

We started to hitch on the outskirts of Paris with the early morning rush-hour traffic, and there was unending wall of cars, just one after the other zipping by. So we started with high hopes, expecting a ride any time. After a few hours, with the rush hour traffic flow slowing down and fewer cars, we started losing our optimism.

We then started walking along the road with the traffic while hitching, hoping to change our luck. It didn't change. John and I walked and hitched, walked and hitched for another 3-4 hours and few kilometers with still no ride. It was now mid afternoon and we were a little ways outside of Paris getting into the countryside. By now we had not only lost our optimism, we were getting downright frustrated.

As we were standing by the road with our thumbs out, John looked over at me, "I can't believe this. It must be about seven hours we've been out here and not a single ride. What's up with this?"

"I don't know." I grumbled, "I hitched out of Paris last summer with my buddy Tom from Birmingham. We had good luck. We traveled Europe together before I started the semester at Harlaxton. When we were in Paris, it took awhile but we got one great ride…For about 10 hours."

"A ten hour ride?"

"Yeah." I replied. "Took us all the way to southern France, almost to Italy. The guy even stopped and bought us dinner along the way."

"It would be nice to get one of those rides today, but it doesn't look good."

"Somebody's gotta stop sooner or later."

"I'll believe it when I see it." John said with disgust. "I don't know what the problem is."

Later on, with still no-one stopping to offer us a ride, I found a big scrap of paper, and out of frustration, we made a sign that said, *"Si vios plais"* (please) in French and held the sign while hitching. It didn't help.

We continued walking and hitching until late afternoon. Still with no luck. We were now further out of the city into the open countryside. We

TRAINS, TRACTORS AND HITCHING

had been over 10 hours out there on the road, tired and frustrated, without a single offer of a ride. While no one gave us a ride, many of the passing drivers continued making a lot of odd gestures at us from their cars all day long. It was a one-day thing. It never really happened again in France or anywhere else we hitched on the trip. Strange!

Then...suddenly...finally, after over 10 hours out on the road hitching a car stopped. A ride!

John and I happily ran up and hopped in the car, relieved to have our first ride of the long day. It was a newer car driven by a well dressed Frenchman.

John said to the driver, "Thanks for stopping. Where ya going?"

The Frenchman said something in French.

John and I both said, "Excuse me?"

The man said something in French again.

John and I looked at each other. We didn't know what he said. We assumed it was the name of the French town he was heading to. We had never heard the name before.

We both just smiled and said "*Tres bein.*"

We were very happy to just be off the road and in a car heading somewhere. At that point, it didn't really matter where, as long as we were moving, and not hitching. And after hopping in the car with this guy, we were now definitely moving. We were hoping the guy would be someone heading our direction a long ways, maybe a couple hundred kilometers or so - to make up for our lousy luck that day, but he wasn't.

He was just a guy heading home from his city job and he only drove us about 20 minutes; just enough to get us completely lost out into the countryside away from Paris, and onto some small country roads. (When hitching I never know where I would be let out – I always had to be prepared and aware.)

It was early evening when the Frenchman let us out of the car with a smile and a quick wave. The weather had now changed from the early morning sunshine to a cloudy and cold, early evening. We walked and hitched, without a single ride, for several more hours – walking through the rolling French countryside, passing thru a few small country towns along the way. In one quant, little town, we stopped briefly in a small shop to buy the usual daily meal of a loaf of fresh bread and Coca-Cola.

I ate a lot of bread and always drank a lot of Coca-Cola on the road traveling in my younger days. When I was on the road in those long ago days,

Coca-Cola was one of the few items from the US that I could buy almost anywhere.

Back then in many far off places, there were very, very few things available from the US, but I could almost always find good ol' Coca-Cola, in its same classic style bottle I drank from at home. I usually avoided drinking the local water, and back then there was no such thing as bottled water. Coca-Cola was almost as much a part of my travels as my trusty old backpack and chained wallet that I always had with me for years on the road.

Besides, I've always liked the taste of Coca-Cola, and when I was on the road in some far off place it always reminded me of America. I grew up drinking Coca-Cola and when I was way out in some distant land on some adventure, having a bottle of Coca-Cola always made me feel a little closer to home.

Later that evening after enjoying our Coke and bread, under the cloudy, starless night sky, John and I were still walking and hitching unsuccessfully as the traffic got less and less until there was barely a trickle of cars coming by. It was now evening, very dark and the wind had picked up. I was cold and frustrated.

Pointing to a street sign across the deserted country road, I picked up a small stone and challenged John, "I bet I can hit that sign more times than you can. Whattda ya think?"

"No way! Your on."

"Most hits out of 10 throws, wins."

"Wins what?" John asked.

"I don't know. I don't have anything to bet."

"Me neither. Were both broke."

"The winner gets bragging rights." I replied with a grin.

"OK." John agreed, "I'll throw first."

Bragging rights were a big thing for us. When we were kids, my brother and I would compete in almost anything; Mini-golf, swimming races, racquetball, pool, hitting golf balls at the driving range, go-cart racing, baseball, darts, pitching pennies, cards…anything.

We ended up having about a dozen throwing matches out there on the road during the cold, frustrating night. I'm not exactly sure who won the throwing contests that night, but it helped pass the hours on the long night.

After more walking and fruitless hitching, at about 10:00 PM way out on an empty country road, John and I came across a cute, brave, little French girl who was backpacking by herself. Her name was Ting Remy. She was short, pretty and petite, with a cute smile. Her backpack was almost bigger than she was. We were quite surprised to see her out there on the empty road.

Ting said she was traveling around France on her own. John and I walked along with her for a short while, and then she said she was cold and wanted to get a room for the night. She asked us to come along with her to find a hotel, but we couldn't afford a room. She left us at one of the small towns… We continued on.

John and I continued walking and hitching. Walking and hitching, stopping occasionally. There were very, very few cars coming by. At one point, we came across a small train station in one little country town. We hustled to the station door. It was a very small station and there was a dim light shining through the window.

"Dennis, check the door."

"It's open."

I opened the door and looked into the small station. "Looks deserted. I don't see anyone around. There's some benches against the wall we can sleep on."

"Sounds good."

As we got settled inside, I said, "This will definitely do. It'll be nice to get off the road for a while. It was getting cold out there."

"Yeah, I can use some sleep."

"Man, what a day." I said yawning.

"That was a bad stretch of hitching, wasn't it?"

"That's for sure."

"Almost 20 hours and only one ride." I said in frustration, "Can you believe our luck?"

"Man, we've had some kindda bad hitching luck. Our luck better change or were never gonna make it."

After getting my backpack set up as a pillow on the hard bench, I looked over at John and said, "Let's get some sleep." .

We quickly got settled on the little benches with our backpacks. We were just getting somewhat comfortable and starting to doze when we heard a loud, angry French voice from across the room. It was an older man with a full head of wavy, graying hair, dressed in a faded train uniform of some kind. The train master. We looked up, surprised. After the trainmaster saw we were just a couple of young travelers, his attitude lightened up a bit.

I said, "We're just trying to sleep here. The door was open."

The trainmaster then switched from French to English, speaking in a heavy accent, he said, *"I'm soo soree. Butt, ahh, you canntta sleep heere. The station it izza clozing now. I'm soo soree. You mustta leeve now."*

We had only been inside a few minutes and now we had to head back out into the night again. This long night just would not end. We reluctantly got up, grabbed our backpacks off the benches and headed back out into the cold, dark night.

After leaving the station, we wearily walked along the same lonely, country road out of town, and just kept going. The road seemed to meander aimlessly through the listless, French countryside. To pass the time along the way as we hitched and walked that night, I quietly sang old Beatles and Bob Seger songs.

"Travelin Man" by Bob Seger: "Up with the sun, gone with the wind… Leaving my home, leaving my friends…Out to the road, out neath the stars, feeling the breeze, passing the cars." My favorite traveling song. I must have sung it a thousand times to myself over the years when I was out on some empty road at night traveling somewhere.

As an American male who was born and raised in Michigan, Bob Seger was 'The Man'. For me and a lot of my peers he represents the best of Michigan and the Midwest…hardworking, humble, true to his roots and dreams, and an American original.

I still remember as a 12-13 year old kid, climbing on top of the roof of a local club called the Hideout near my hometown of Birmingham to sneak a peek at Seger playing his music. That was still a few years before he broke it big nationally when he was already something of local legend.

Over the years to keep my spirits up when I was tired and out on the road hitching someplace, I often quietly sang his traveling songs to pass the long hours..

As the night wore on, John and I continued walking. By the time it got to be a couple hours past midnight, we were dead tired, cold, lost and hungry. There were very, very few cars coming along but we had nowhere to go and nothing better to do, so we stayed on the road. Walking was warmer than standing, so we usually walked. About 4:00 AM when we were out in the middle of nowhere, the dark, dreary, night sky opened up and it began to pour.

That sudden downpour started a series of events that I now find incredibly funny, but I certainly didn't think so at the time.

TRAINS, TRACTORS AND HITCHING

When the gusting rain started, John and I quickly looked around for some kind of shelter. But there wasn't any. All we could see through the rain in the black night were muddy fields, the outline of a few trees and the road.

John quickly asked me, "Do you see anything? Anyplace we can go to?"

"The rains too heavy. I can't see a thing," I said.

"Man, it's dark out here."

"Where did all this mud come from? My shoes are already soaked through with mud. I can barely walk"

Standing out alongside the country road in the open field, as the torrents of rain and wind picked up, John and I were shouting at each other to be heard. Our voices were getting lost in the wind and rain.

John pointed out into a field up ahead of us and yelled something to me.

"What?" I shouted back through the downpour.

"I think I see something."

"I don't see anything," I shouted back.

"I do. Out there." He pointed again, holding his arm like a beacon in the dark night cutting through the gusting rain.

I looked again in the direction he was pointing. I could vaguely see the outline of something out in the distance, "OK. I see something. I don't know what it is."

"Come on. Let's find out."

We ran and slipped through the muddy field and drenching rain as best we could in the direction John had pointed. It was slow going. I slipped and fell face-first right into a big puddle, soaking my clothes and backpack as well. We were both quickly caked with mud.

"It looks like a truck or something," John said, shouting through the wind and rain.

"No, I think it's a tractor. What's it doing out here?" I asked.

"Who knows? Who cares? It's something."

"Boy, it's big. Let's check the door."

It was really a big tractor. John climbed up and pulled at the door. It was open. So we quickly climbed in and slammed the door, shutting out the howling wind and gusts of rain. We tried to get comfortable with little success. It was cramped in the dark tractor with all the gears and levers. Not to mention we were bloody cold from our wet, muddy clothes.

I looked over at John and said, "It's not much, but it beats sitting outside in that miserable rain."

"Huh? Man, it's too cold in here." John said with a shiver.

"You wanna look for something else?"

Before we could even begin to contemplate that thought, we both fell fast asleep. We had been out on the road for a frustrating 22 hours with no rest; we were muddy, wet and dead-tired. Just moments after we closed the door of the tractor, we were sound asleep...

It seemed like only minutes but it was actually a few hours later, when we were rudely awakened by a very loud, angry banging on the tractor door. Before we had time to even react, the door was thrown open and we were dragged out of the tractor into the early morning sun. Although the weather had cleared, we were still wet and muddy.

John and I were facing a tough-looking construction crew of about 8-9 guys. They were dressed in muddy work clothes, worn-out heavy boots and hard hats. They were not a friendly bunch. In fact they were quite angry.

We could now see what we couldn't see the night before. The field was a small construction site and there were a few other tractors and trucks further out in the muddy field. We were sleeping in one of their tractors.

After some angry shouts and taunts, the construction crew headed out into the field to begin work and we were left with the foreman. The foreman was a big, barrel-chested man with an unshaven, blunt face, wearing work clothes covered by a long, dirty coat.

He roughly pulled John and me over to his headquarters truck. He must have driven it up because it wasn't there the night before. As he stood by the truck glaring at us, he reached for some kind of truck CB to call from.

He then started angrily speaking and shouting at us in French. I know very little French. But I did understand "policio." He gestured toward his CB phone and started saying he was going to call the "policio."

Those were the magic words. As soon as the foreman said that, John and I looked at each other. We both knew what the other was thinking.

"Let's get out of here," John said.

He didn't have to say it twice.

We immediately took off with a dash and started running thru the muddy field back towards the road, away from the construction crew. We were clumsily trying to carry our backpacks with socks and things falling out, slipping in the mud.

The foreman was caught completely off guard, so we got a head start before he reacted. But soon he shouted to the construction crew, and within a few moments we had about half a dozen construction workers in hard hats chasing after us across the muddy field. (It was like something out of a Monty Python movie.)

We ran back to the two-lane road. Now the country road was filled with slow moving cars and heavy, morning traffic. When we got to the roadside, we started running alongside the road with our backpacks bumping up and down, and our thumbs out hitch hiking.

Meanwhile, the construction crew was running and slipping thru the muddy field getting closer, angrily shouting at us. It was quite the scene. We couldn't outrun the construction workers, while carrying our backpacks and hitch hiking at the same time. They were getting closer and closer…

John and I made another split-second decision and ran a zigzagging sprint across the road thru the slow, heavy traffic to the other side. Now we started hitch hiking the other direction. By now the crew caught up and was on the other side of the road across from us shouting and waving their fists over the passing cars. For a couple of minutes it was something of a Texas standoff.

The construction workers didn't try to run across the busy road after us, but they didn't leave and go back to their work site either. We were standing, hitching and watching them, and they were standing, angrily shouting and watching us.

Then a truly amazing thing happened…A car stopped. A professionally dressed businessman opened his door to offer John and me a ride. I couldn't believe it. We had gone 22 hours with only one ride the day before. And now this morning, when we were muddy and still wet, within five minutes after starting to hitch-hike this guy was stopping to give us a ride in his very new, clean, expensive car.

He had no idea of the drama that was taking place outside on the roadside. And he had no idea how much that ride meant to us at that time. He also didn't seem bothered at all by our muddy clothes in his new car. I couldn't believe it. We got in his car and he cheerfully drove us all of 5 kilometers to a small railway station, where he was taking a little shuttle train into Paris for his job.

Although the ride didn't really advance our cause much, it was one of the best rides I've ever had. It got us away from, and out of sight of the angry mini-mob of construction workers.

Now, John and I were outside some little train station, in some little French town, somewhere in the beautiful French countryside. With all the walking the night before, the rain and the change in direction hitching this morning, we weren't quite sure where we were.

John looked over at me and asked, "You have any idea where we are?"

"Beats me. But I don't think we're anywhere near that road we need for heading south towards Italy."

"Yep. There are no major highways anywhere around. With all the walking last night and the rain, I think we're a long way from any highway."

"We mustta walked through 3-4 little towns last night. That was a long night on the road." I said.

"You got that right."

"So now what? Where do we go from here?"

"I'm not sure." John shrugged, "After our luck yesterday, I'm not exactly thrilled about spending another day hitching."

"Me neither."

"Besides if we start hitching from here, it's gonna take us a day or two just to get to a major road heading our way. We're really out in the country here." John continued.

Glancing around at the gently rolling green hills, with stone farmhouses and majestic forests scattered about in the distance, I said, "It's really beautiful out here, though."

"It sure is. It's great the weather's cleared up, too."

The early morning sun was just rising in the sky over the distant green hills, with something of a red hue, glowing mist rising off the still wet fields. It was a beautiful sight.

"Yep." John said. "Maybe the sun will give our clothes a chance to dry out. All my stuff is still damp and muddy."

"Mine too."

After a short pause, I asked again. "So, whatta you think? Where do we go from here?"

"I think we should get out of the country…Off these small country roads."

"I agree with that…But how?"

After a moment's thought, John replied, "How about a train?"

"You mean here?" I asked, "From this little train station?"

"Why not?"

"That guy, who saved us with the ride, said this is only a shuttle service. It only goes into Paris."

"Yep, I know."

TRAINS, TRACTORS AND HITCHING

"You mean you wanna go back to Paris. After what we went through yesterday - trying to get away from there. You wanna go back?" I asked incredulously.

"What else can we do?" John said, "We take this shuttle back to Paris, get our bearings. Then we catch a train heading toward Italy."

"Huh?"

"There are no major roads around here, and who knows where there's a train station…It's our best move."

I hated the idea of backtracking. But it made sense. It could take us all day hitching out in the French countryside before we found a road or train station that could even take us in the direction we needed to go.

"OK. You got a point." I grudgingly admitted. "This shuttle train should get us back into Paris in about an hour."

"Yep."

"Then we take the first train leaving Paris. The first train going anywhere…south to Italy or east to Switzerland. It doesn't matter."

"OK." John agreed. "Let's get a ticket. How much is a shuttle ticket back to Paris going to cost us?"

"Ah, I think it's 12 Francs. About $2.90."

"That's a lot. It's only, what,…not even 8:00AM and we're already down three bucks today."

"Yeah. That's a big hit for us."

"No kidding"

"Hey, how are we gonna pay for a train ticket out of Paris?" John wondered, "It'll cost us a lot more than the three bucks this shuttle ride is costing us."

"Yeah. It will. We don't have the money to pay for a train."

"So whattda we do?" John asked.

"We sneak on the train. What else?" I said grinning.

"Of course. What else." John replied nodding and smiling.

We certainly didn't have any money to actually pay for the train rides, so it seemed only logical to us that we would sneak on them.

So that was our new plan of action. We would take the short shuttle to Paris, get our bearings, and start sneaking on trains to get across France as fast as possible. We would start using our wits and nerve to make some distance riding the rails. We certainly didn't have enough money to actually pay for the train rides, so it made perfect sense to us that we would sneak on them.

◄ TRAVELIN' MAN ACROSS THE SAHARA AND BEYOND

We paid the 12 Francs fare to take the shuttle train back into Paris. It wasn't much, but it used up a good chunk of our total traveling and living expenses for that day.

After arriving at the Gare Du Nord Train Station in Paris, we quickly looked around for a train departure board to find the first train that was leaving in our general direction. We had to jostle our way through the train station's early morning crowds of businesspeople and office workers, hurrying on their way to work.

As we were fighting our way though the morning masses, I said to John, "We gotta get out of here, man. It's been two days and we're back in Paris."

"Yep. Right where we started. I can't believe it."

"We've been jinxed in this country. We gotta change our luck and get out of here." I said.

When we finally found a train departure schedule board, I asked John, "Do you see anything leaving south out of Paris? Anything?"

After quickly looking at the train board, John found one.

"There's a train leaving right now. Track 7. We can make it if we move now."

"Where's it headed to?" I asked.

"Orleans."

"New Orleans? Your joking?"

"No…Orleans!"

"Orleans?" I asked.

"Yes! Orleans."

"Where's Orleans?"

"I don't know exactly." John answered impatiently. "But I'm pretty sure it's somewhere south of here."

"Quick. Take a look at the map."

"What map?" John asked.

"The one Mr. Eram's father-in-law gave us." I replied quickly.

"I thought you had it."

"I don't have it.' I said. "You got it."

"No, I don't…You do"

"No, I don't."

"Ahh…Forget the map. Let's go."

We quickly sprinted through the crowded train station to track 7 to catch the train. I didn't really care where the train was going, as long as it was leaving Paris soon and headed in the general direction of Italy, it would do.

TRAINS, TRACTORS AND HITCHING

We had already spent one, long, tough day and night on the road, only to end up exactly where we started the day before…back in Paris. I just wanted to get out as soon as possible.

Our plan for hiding on trains was to first quietly board the train and find a compartment. That was the easy part - since no one checked our tickets until the train was on its way.

Once we were on the train would come the hard part. We would then have to keep continual look out for the conductor for hours on end, and somehow avoid him each time he made his way up and down the train clipping the tickets. It's a tiring process. It doesn't allow for any real rest because I've always got to be on guard, and watching out for the conductor. For those of you who have ridden on trains, you've also probably noticed there aren't exactly a lot of places to hide on a train, either. That tends to add to the challenge.

With the train leaving Paris at that moment, we made our mad dash thru the crowded station, and boarded the train just as it was pulling out. We climbed up and hurriedly entered the train to go finish the easy part, which was to quietly and quickly find a compartment in one of the train cars. The hard part would be later when the conductor started his rounds and we would have to start hiding and avoiding him.

We never even made it to the hard part. The first person we bumped directly into upon quickly climbing on the train was the conductor. He was a heavy-set, middle-aged guy dressed in a crisp uniform, wearing a conductor's hat. We were rushing to climb on board and bumped smack into him.

And even worse, we made eye contact with him. (Rule number six for hiding on trains – never, ever make eye contact with the conductor.) We looked at him. He looked at us. We were both startled.

John and I started slowly at first and then more quickly backing away from him as nonchalantly as possible. We then turned and started walking away as quickly and nonchalantly as possible. The conductor hesitated a moment but, obviously, was not thrown off by our nonchalant demeanor.

He called after us. "*Ticket. Si vous plais. Ticket.*"

We pretended we didn't hear and kept walking nonchalantly to the end of the rail car. We opened the door, entered the next rail car and quickly closed the door behind. We then immediately gave up any pretenses. We took off at dead run thru the train car, but before we could get to the following train car, we heard the door behind us open and I caught a glimpse of the conductor pushing thru the door.

The race was on.

We continued running thru one train car after the other as fast as we could, with the conductor in hot pursuit. After passing thru a few more train cars we lost sight of the train conductor. He was older and slower, but no less determined. We had temporarily lost the conductor, but we were facing a serious problem – we were running out of train. There are only so many train cars on one train.

We had nowhere to go. But we did have a place to hide, one of the little bathrooms that were at the end of each train car. Not much of a choice really, but what could we do?

So after running thru a couple more train cars, we stopped abruptly and jumped into one of the bathrooms together and slammed the door. We were jammed in there with our backpacks, trying to be as quiet as possible with our hearts pounding, while listening for any movements outside the bathroom.

We nervously waited for what seemed like a couple of days but it was probably only a couple of minutes, without hearing anything.

"Do you think we lost him?" John whispered to me.

"How?" I whispered back. "We're on a train. The only way we could really lose him would be if he fell off the train."

"I know. But do you think he'll find us here?"

"I'd say there's a very good chance of that."

"Yep. I know." John agreed.

"We're dead in the water."

"Yep. I know."

And we were. Suddenly, seemingly out of nowhere, the bathroom door swung open and standing there facing us was the puffing, sweating conductor. We were caught red-handed. We were definitely not having much luck in our two day old attempt to leave Paris.

But actually this train adventure turned out in our favor. The train conductor pulled us out of the bathroom and started heatedly jabbering away in French, which as I said before I understand very, very little. I heard the word "ticket" and "money" and "train" and "Paris". But fortunately I did not hear the magic word of "Policio," so I thought maybe everything would be OK. And in fact it turned out that way.

After heatedly talking for a few minutes the conductor began to lose steam and began to lighten up, while we continued to listen politely and plead ignorance. By this time the train was well out of the station and down the tracks. The conductor wasn't about to throw us off the train going 70 miles an hour. He also wasn't about to stop the train to put us off, and disrupt the train's entire schedule. As the conductor started calming down, John and I pleaded with him that we didn't have much money. The result was that he charged us just a minimal fare for the long train ride for a couple of hours to the next stop on the line. We had finally made some mileage and it only cost us a little money.

John and I quietly found some seats as the conductor looked on. When the train reached the next stop, the conductor walked us to the door and saw us off with a wave and just a hint of a smile. Like a lot of the train conductors I came across during my younger travelin' days, he was a good hearted guy.

I actually have a soft spot in my heart for train conductors. While I was on the road in my younger days, I was the recipient of some incredible good will by train conductors on many different occasions, including later on in this trip.

CHAPTER 4

Ride and Hide

So after being caught red handed in the bathroom with no train ticket, John and I were required to leave the train at the first stop outside of Paris. The conductor personally saw to that. As we walked out of the country train station to start hitching again, we decided to put our great plan for sneaking on trains on hold for a while, although it wouldn't be long before we would attempt it again. Occasionally more successfully, I might add.

The next couple of days on the road were going to prove to be extremely frustrating and difficult for us. It was days with little rest, lots of mistakes and backtracking, and seemingly endless frustrations. Days of grinding it out on the road trying to make some mileage but having very little luck. Like the previous day, it was a tiring and wearing couple of days, with the luck continually going against us. We really paid the price for any gains we made.

We left the train station and began walking through the small French town to get the lay of the land. It was a mid-size, country town with a few charming shops and cafes along the tree-lined main street. The late morning was now cold and cloudy, and we were hoping for some better luck on the road today.

John commented, "Our luck's gotta change sometime. It can't get any worse."

"Yeah. But then again - it doesn't have to get much better either. Does it?"

"We'll see"

"So, which road do we take here?" I asked.

"Beats me. I think this way is south. What do you think?"

"They all look the same to me. That road looks like it might head out of town, though." I said pointing in the other direction.

"Ahh, but that's going north, isn't it?" John asked.

"Maybe. Let's walk that way to see what we find before we start hitching. It'll be tough to get a ride here."

"All right."

After walking quite awhile without ever getting to the outskirts of town, we decided to ask someone for help so I approached a middle-aged Frenchman strolling down the street.

"Excuse me…Pardon me." I said.

No reaction.

"Excuse me, sir. Can I ask you something?"

The guy kept walking past without even taking a look at me.

John then approached the next guy we came across, a younger, casually dressed guy wearing a cap, "Excuse me, sir. Excuse me."

The guy momentarily stopped, looked at John and said in perfect English, "I'm sorry but do you speak French? I only speak French."

John said, "No. I speak English."

The guy kept walking on.

It wasn't such a big town, but it was big enough that it took a while to get out of it. We eventually did get some directions from a friendly, older Frenchwoman but either she gave us bad directions or we misunderstood her.

We ended up walking over a couple of winding kilometers through town, only to find we would have to walk back the same way and start over before we could really start hitching. The town streets were mostly narrow, winding streets that made it difficult to hitch from so we needed to get to the outskirts of town before we could we really had any chance to start hitching.

One of the biggest difficulties with hitchhiking is getting to a location where you can actually begin hitching from and begin making some mileage, especially in bigger cities. It often requires a great deal of walking, cross city hitching, taking city buses, several turns and/or special directions to get to the location or main highway heading out of a city in the direction you need to go. Sometimes it can take hours.

In cities, I would often without any hesitation walk 3-4 kilometers to get across town instead of paying 70 cents for a city bus. There was many a time I walked several kilometers to save a buck. I didn't think much of it at the time. It was just a necessity of my situation and of being on the road. With this town it took us almost two hours of frustrating walking and a little hitching to find *the road* heading our way. It was not a highway but a big country road.

We hitched for most of the rest of the day. It was a tough day. We waited over an hour for the first ride, which took us only about 15 kilometers. The French countryside was beautiful, but for the rest of the day we got rides at a slow, frustrating pace. None of the rides were the big one that takes you a few hundred kilometers.

We hitched about 150 kilometers during the day, but we really only made about 90 kilometers in the right direction. We always seemed to be let out in some hopeless spot that made it difficult to get where we needed to go. A couple of times we got rides only to find we were heading the wrong direction and had to hitch back to where we started, or get back to some road we had already passed.

Hitching is definitely not an exact science. You take the rides as they come, stay alert and hope for the best and a little luck. Each ride is unique; you never know when you'll be picked up, who will pick you up, or where you'll end up.

Some rides were very helpful and made sure they dropped us at a good spot to hitch from in the correct direction. Others would sometimes inadvertently leave us in the middle of nowhere or on some road that made it very difficult to get to where we were going. Others only ended up getting us lost, making us backtrack and lose time. Obviously, I always hoped for the first type of ride, and I would say a majority of the rides I had over the years were that kind of ride.

I must say that, while hitching, I did meet a lot of interesting people from all walks of life. I was picked up by everyone from rich, suited businessman and famous musicians driving Mercedes, Rolls-Royces, and Jaguars to guys, women, smugglers and traders driving windowless old vans, tractors, motorcycles, and rusted old jeeps with no car floor for your feet.

Also, with hitching, that gut instinct I talked about earlier is extremely important. A car stops. It's often at night and in dark, isolated locations. I was often alone. I'd run up to the car and open the door. Now I only had a second or two to make an important decision. - Get in that car or not get in that car. Once I get in the car I had given up a great deal of control of the situation, so it's an important decision.

It didn't happen often but on a few rare occasions when I opened that car door, I had a strong gut instinct that told me this guy's not safe…danger. In those instances I always quickly gave an excuse and closed the door, always.

Also, as happened more often, after getting in a car my gut instinct was telling me it was not safe, something is not right here. In those cases, I also tried to never hesitate. I kept my hand close to the door handle, my backpack ready.

At the first possible chance when the driver had to stop at a light or to make a turn, I would abruptly open the door, jump out of the car, say a quick, "Thank you. Here's fine," move away from the car and keep going.

There were also many times during my college days in Europe when I would take female friends with me on a trip and we would hitch together. I always enjoyed it, but it was somewhat stressful. I felt a tremendous responsibility for protecting the woman I was with, and I was always on guard, even more so than usual. Often the woman hadn't traveled much and was just out enjoying the trip, without a care in the world. That was not the case for me. I never said anything to the woman I was with, but my instincts and security habits were working overtime.

For example when I hitched with a woman, I never let her get in the back seat of a car without me. She always sat in the front and I sat in the back, or we both sat in the back. The reason is I always wanted to be sure she was last in the car, and she was first out… I didn't want to ever have some car stop and the woman get in first, then the car quickly take off and leave me standing there like a helpless fool. Or vice-versa, after a ride I hop out of the car first, the car door closes behind me and speeds off with the woman still in the car. That happened to a friend of mine.

I think most people have a good gut instinct but don't pay attention to it so much, or most importantly, don't act on it. It's not always so important in day to day life. Traveling the way my brother and I did and the situations and decisions we had to make several times every single day, really helped to fine tune that instinct.

When I was on the road, it became second nature to me. And I always tried to act on it. Always. The bottom line to staying safe and avoiding danger was to always follow my gut instinct and to always act immediately - without hesitation. You have only a split second to make a decision and to act on your gut instinct, in order to remove yourself from possible danger.

Decisions such as; whether to get into a car or not, to sit down in a train compartment or not, to go with someone or not, to share a room with someone or not, to trust someone or not, to stay in a place or not, or to accept someone's offer of help or not - I made those decisions every day on the road. It became an ingrained habit that anytime I entered a bus, car, room, building, train compartment, anyplace - I always scanned the place and identified any threats or dangers and any means to exit or secure the room or place I was in. I would also in my mind remember any safety routes or alternatives actions I could take to eliminate any danger. It was as automatic as breathing.

Being on the road in far-off unknown places, at night and in isolated locations, often alone, in vulnerable situations with people I didn't know, thousands of miles from home, with no-one knowing where on earth I was – those basic habits were indeed crucial to my safety and well being.

Fortunately, like I said earlier, 9 out of 10 people I came across during my traveling days helped me out in so many ways and showed such incredible kindness. It was just that other one out of 10 that I always had to be aware of and prepared for.

After hitching most of that day and making about a net 90 kilometers in the direction of Italy, John and I found ourselves near some small town. It was late afternoon and we wanted to keep making mileage since we couldn't afford to pay for a place to sleep, so we slowly (mostly by walking and a little hitching) made our way to the town's train station with the intention of sneaking on a train heading toward Italy.

As we approached the station John said, "Hopefully we'll have better luck this time."

"Yeah, we could use some."

"It'd also be nice to catch a little sleep on the train during the night ride."

We were both really beat at this point. It had been a long, tough day on the road.

"I'm dead." I said, "Sleeping on the train would sure be better than sleeping outside somewhere in the town tonight."

So after finding the train station, John and I walked inside and looked over the train schedule on the wall to see what trains were departing soon and heading our direction.

"Hey, I found one. There's a train leaving in an about an hour." John said.

"It's heading our way?" I asked.

"I think so. It's going south. I'm not sure how far."

'Sound good."

The station was crowded with waves of people coming and going. So we blended in with the crowds and killed some time before the train was to leave. I wrote in my journal and John caught a little sleep. We boarded the train about 10 minutes before it was due to pull out; Just enough time to scope out the train, and to find a good place to begin the game of "ride and hide" to avoid the conductor. We were hoping to make a lot of miles, but this ride didn't turn out that way because a couple hours after getting on the train, after passing maybe 3 or 4 stops, we were nailed by the conductor for having no ticket. We were standing in the noisy, rocking little walkway between train cars when the conductor just suddenly swung open one train car door and was right on top of us.

He looked dead at us and said, "*Ticket. Si vous plais.*"

In unison, John and I both asked as innocently as possible, "Ticket??"

The conductor repeated, "*Oui. Ticket*"

We asked again, "Ticket??"

For a third time, he somewhat irritably repeated, "*Oui. Ticket!*"

Before we could ask again, the conductor signaled for us to take out our tickets. So we started slowly fumbling in our pockets looking for the non-existent tickets, with no luck, of course. We then started slowly fumbling with our backpacks looking for the same non-existent tickets. Again, with no luck…of course.

And then we started fumbling and looking through our wallets and money belts. I guess we were hoping maybe we could somehow filibuster the conductor into giving up on waiting for our ticket search to conclude. Our little plan didn't work…of course.

We were nailed for having no tickets. Fortunately, we had been watching the station names. So when we were caught, even though we had already been on the train quite a while and passed 3 or 4 stops, we said the name of the last stop was where we just boarded and that we needed to get out at the next stop. So the conductor good-naturally charged us a ticket for just the one stop. It cost us only about $4 each, but that was still expensive for us. That was most of our funds for the entire day.

As soon as we arrived at the next station, we were forced to get off the train. After we left the train, John and I walked out into the train station and took a look around to figure out our next move. It didn't take long. We soon decided to find another train to sneak on heading our way.

We were nothing if not persistent.

"Let's try our luck again with the trains." I said, "I really don't feel like going back out onto the road to hitch again."

"Me neither."

"It's going to get cold soon. The sun's going down. I don't wanna get stuck out, in the cold, on the road again tonight."

"OK." John said, "But we just got nailed on the last ride. You wanna try again already?"

"Yeah. Let's catch the first train heading our way and just take it as far as we can."

'The longer the ride the better…"

"You got it." I said, "Maybe we'll have better luck this time. You know… ridin and hidin…nothing ventured, nothing gained."

So we walked over to the departure board to take a look and see what trains were heading toward Italy. After some time trying to figure out the train schedule, John said, "It looks like there's a train leaving for Turin in about an hour and half."

"Turin, Italy?"

"Yeah. It'd be a long ride."

"That would be a really long haul if we could make it that far without getting caught."

So we sat out leaning against the station wall with our backpacks and waited for our train. Although this one did turn out to be a long ride, it didn't exactly turn out like we expected.

After making it on the train with no problem this time, we found an empty compartment near the middle of a train car so we would have a clear view of the conductor coming from both directions. (There were maybe 4-5 compartments on each train car and each compartment had a sliding door, which opened to a small room with two, tight bench like seats facing each other. Each bench held three or four people.)

We put our backpacks down on the bench next to the compartment window and started playing the game of 'ride and hide' with the conductor. It was a game that we played continually for hours on end. But if we were lucky and good, the conductor would never even know the game was on.

John and I would take turns working lookout while the other one rested and caught a little sleep. When the conductor was spotted coming into our train car heading down the train checking tickets, we basically had three options.

RIDE AND HIDE

One option was to carefully move forward in the direction of the conductor and inadvertently pass him when he was in a train compartment checking tickets. It took a little daring and some nerve. This could sometimes be done on crowded trains. Once we passed him we would quickly find another compartment to stay in, or wait and later return to our old compartment.

We would then often have a long break time because a conductor usually would work his way all the way down the train in one direction and then later he would work his way back up the train in the other direction. Depending on the time of night, how many stops and how crowded the train was, it might be as long as couple of hours between ticket checks.

The second option was to hide. As I mentioned earlier there are a limited number of choices of where to hide on a train. There is choice A – the bathroom. There's also choice B – the bathroom, or choice C – the bathroom. In other words the bathroom. In that case when the conductor entered our train car we would quietly leave our compartment and go into the bathroom at the end of the train car in the direction the conductor was heading.

We would then have a long, tight smelly wait crammed in the little bathroom with our backpacks. We would wait until the conductor passed the bathroom and headed out of our train car to the next one. Then we would sneak back to our old compartment.

Or on some occasions we would actually sit in the smelly, cramped bathroom for hours at a stint. This option was sometimes problematic. That would be when another passenger would come and want to use the bathroom while we were hiding. It was quite humiliating to have to clump out of the little bathroom together with my brother while some passenger looked on in surprise.

The third option was to keep heading down the train in front of the conductor – staying just a little ways ahead of him - as he made his way down the train checking tickets. And then bide our time until there was an opportune moment to walk pass him either when he was in the aisle or when he was in a compartment. This option also took some nerve and was usually when the train was crowded.

Actually, there was a fourth option. You could also try to hide under the bench in the train compartment, but it was very tight and difficult to squeeze under there. There was also a major problem with that option - there were almost always other passengers sharing the compartment with you, who you didn't know. So you would have to squeeze under the compartment bench while some guy or woman was sitting there above you. And then stay under the seat for quite some time, while the other people sat above you and the ticket check was finished. I never did that. But I did have a rather strange experience related to that...

The following year, on one of my return trips to Europe I had flown standby into Frankfurt, Germany. I had been home to work in the US after running out of money during the semester break. I was now returning to England to attend my next semester at Oxford University, where I attended an overseas study program for two years after my freshman year at Harlaxton. I played rugby league for Oxford University and I traveled all over England playing rugby for two seasons while I was studying at Oxford. I was now in a hurry to get back to England for an important match against an Australian team based in London.

I had been at the Frankfurt train station for quite some time, waiting for my train to pull in on my way back to England. (I actually had a ticket this time). So when the train pulled in and was ready for boarding, I went ahead and got on the nearly empty train. It would not be pulling out of the station for another 1 1/2 hours, but I preferred waiting on the train rather than in the station.

So I climbed on to one of the empty train cars and randomly chose a train compartment to sit in. I went in the compartment alone, closed the sliding door behind me, took off my backpack and pulled out a book I had with me to read and pass the time. It was early evening and fairly dark outside, but there was dim light in the compartment for me to read by. I was in the compartment room alone reading for a full hour before anyone else entered my compartment to sit in.

Finally, just before the train pulled out of the station, three other people came in to share the compartment with me. They were Europeans and they sat in the small bench-like seat directly across from me. The train then pulled out of the station, and started rolling on its way. We soon turned off the light in the compartment and the other three passengers started dozing, while I was looking out the window at the German countryside.

Then a very strange thing happened. As I was sitting in the relative darkness looking out the window, I felt something bump my ankle from under my seat. It startled me. What happened next downright shocked me. A man's head and body crawled out from under my seat. As the young, dirty, black-clothed man quietly rose up, he looked back over his shoulder at me and put his finger to his lips in the international gesture for "shhh, shhh, quiet".

He then very quickly and quietly left my train compartment without looking back. The other dozing passengers never saw him. It took me a moment myself to believe what I had just seen. It seemed almost like a mirage but it wasn't. He had made some noise when he opened and closed the sliding compartment door, and it stirred the other passengers.

I had never left the train compartment since the moment I had entered it three hours earlier. The guy had been lying quietly, directly under my bench seat for almost 3 hours without my knowledge. I had sat there alone in that compartment with him hiding under my seat bench for over an hour. It was very unnerving that I hadn't noticed or sensed something; so much for my instincts on that one.

He had lain there waiting until he thought we were all asleep before he got up and left the compartment. I saw him by chance.

Who knows how long he had been there, or why? Was he hiding from someone? Smuggling something? Was he a fugitive of some kind? Just trying to avoid the fare? He may have been there even long before the train pulled into the station. Who knows??

It was another one of the many mysteries I encountered on the road.

CHAPTER 5

Where Are We? ... And How Did We Get Here?

After getting on the train heading south to Turin, and without the conductor spotting us, John and I quickly got situated in our compartment. We were on our way...Yes, we really were on our way. But to where or what? Well, that was another question. It was a question that John and I were to get a shocking answer to.

As the old train rocked down the tracks, it got quite crowded and our compartment filled up with various travelers getting on and off the train during the late night ride. Although the crowds made the ride less comfortable, it made it much easier to avoid the conductor and blend in with all the other passengers. There was mix of backpackers, families, businessman and couples passing in and out during the tiring night.

Our luck on this ride held up and we avoided the conductor on four of his trips up and down the train checking tickets, but that was the only luck we did have. With our continual attempts and efforts to avoid the conductor, we didn't have much chance to pay attention to the names of the train stops.

By now it was very late, we were both dead tired and despite our best intentions we fell fast asleep. The slow rocking of the train, not to mention the snoring of the other travelers in our compartment didn't help. I slept for what seemed like minutes, but was actually a long time.

Sometime later John and I both awoke with a start when we heard a whistle blow somewhere outside our compartment. It took me a moment to realize where I was. I had a brief flashback of the tractor in the field outside Paris and half expected to see a gang of angry construction workers.

WHERE ARE WE? ... AND HOW DID WE GET HERE?

Instead I saw not a soul. The train was dark, silent and deserted. After a moment I also realized it was stopped. We were no longer moving. It took me a another moment to realize where I was. Even when I woke up and realized where I was - I still wasn't where I thought I was. (If you didn't catch what I just said, you will in a minute.)

Now that we were wide-awake, John and I looked out the train window at the empty train platform and saw it was a big platform inside a very large, cavernous train station. It was very still, dark and quiet; actually kind of eerie.

"Is this it? Where are we? Did we make it to the end of the line?" I asked.

"I don't know. I fell asleep somewhere awhile back." John answered as he stretched.

"Yeah. Me too."

"Man, it's quiet. Where did everyone go?" John wondered.

"I don't know. It's kinda spooky, though, isn't it."

"No kidding."

Looking around John continued, "This is a big station. It must be Turin, Italy, the end of the line. Why else would the train stop and everyone unload?"

"Yeah. This must be Turin." I responded, "That was a long haul. We finally made some distance. Huh?"

"Finally...Italy. We made it outta France. It's about time we had some luck. Let's get out of here before somebody asks for our ticket."

We grabbed our backpacks, opened the compartment door, hustled down the empty train car, and jumped off the train onto the quiet, train platform. We didn't know how long the train had been stopped or why nobody had woken us, but at this point we didn't really care since we had made it all the way to Italy.

We quickly hustled our way down the platform where we finally saw a few people milling about. We avoided any eye contact as we didn't want to get asked for our tickets, which of course we didn't have. After making it out the platform exit and into the main part of the train station, we both gave a sigh of relief and felt a little elated.

"Hey, do you believe it - we made it to Turin. That was a long ride. All the way to the end of the train line." I said.

"No kidding." John replied with a broad smile. "We covered a lotta miles. I wonder how long we were sleeping?"

"I don't know, but it's great to finally make it to Italy."

"I know what you mean. With all our bad luck and backtracking trying to leave Paris, I never thought we would make it."

"It was tough." I agreed. "But, man, we've made it to Italy."

Or did we?

We were soon stunned to find out that not only did we not make it to Turin; we had not even made it to Italy. Even more surprising was that we were no longer even in France. We were in Switzerland.

You might ask 'How did we ever manage to get on a train in France, which was going to Italy - but after falling asleep for a while, wake up in Switzerland?' You can believe we were certainly asking ourselves that question right about now.

It turned out that after we had fallen asleep, the train stopped and was divided into two. The front section of the train with several of the train cars attached then left and continued on its way to Turin, Italy - while the back section of the train with the rest of the train cars was then reattached to another locomotive engine, which changed direction and headed east to Switzerland. To Bern, Switzerland to be exact. Hard to believe!

Before then, I had never heard of something like that. Although I learned later it was not all that uncommon. It was our misfortune that we happened to be in the back section, and had slept thru the changing of the engines and somehow (I don't know how) had gotten thru the Swiss border crossing without being awakened and having our passports checked.

In those days in Western Europe, usually the train would stop and custom officials would enter the train and quickly check and sometimes stamp passports. Then the train would move off again. Border crossings in Western Europe were usually a fairly standard process. But not so in some other countries I traveled, such as behind the 'Iron Curtain' in Eastern Europe, where crossing borders was a very tense and dangerous event.

CHAPTER **6**

Rules of the Road

After in-advertently crossing by train into Switzerland from France on our way to Africa; with an unbridled sense of determination, we continued on our way. Determined, but also slightly confused…Two feelings I often had during our adventure.

Even though we had made an awful lot of kilometers on the overnight train ride; a good deal of them were in the wrong direction. Having finally learned we were in Switzerland, we left the quiet train station and walked out on the street.

Looking back at the train station with a dazed expression, I said, "Man, I've made some wrong turns before…But nothing like that. I've never ended up in the wrong country."

"Hard to believe." John said in disbelief, "Go to sleep for awhile and we wake up in the wrong country. Who ever heard of that?"

"It feels like were traveling in the twilight zone."

"Actually, much of this trip has felt like that, hasn't it?" John added with a grin.

"Yeah." I said, "It keeps it interesting though."

'That it does. All part of the adventure, right?"

"Right." I agreed. "No guts, no glory…Like dad says, most things worth achieving or having aren't easy. It's tough. It takes work and sacrifice. Heck, if it was easy to travel the world, everyone would do it."

"Dad got that right." John responded, "Especially the 'tough' part."

As we walked out on the streets, it was very early morning and the winding, hilly streets were pretty much empty. The weather was also noticeably different than several hours ago in France when we boarded the train. The air was thinner, chilling, crisp and cold and the scenery was also very different. We were in a quaint Swiss town up in the towering Alp Mountains. It was breathtakingly beautiful with far ranging mountains and valleys rolling across in the distance. There was also heaps of snow in the distant surrounding areas, glazing the rambling range of mountaintops.

We tried to gauge our location and the best way to hitch down to Italy. By chance, we finally found the map that Mr. Eram's father-in-law gave us way back in Paris. We had assumed it was lost right after we left Paris, but earlier in the day while scrounging through my backpack for some coins I came across the crumpled little map.

So we now had a map to use for some sense of direction, but even still from the limited map we now had, we weren't really sure of the direction for heading to Italy.

After looking at the tattered map, John said, "I think we need to head down this road. It should take us toward Italy."

"Are you sure? I think it heads west back to France. No way I'm going back to France and backtrack."

John was now pointing, 'No. Look. This is the road north and that's the road south."

"I don't think so, John. <u>This</u> is the road heading south." I said pointing in the other direction.

"No. That can't be it."

"Yeah, it is. I'm pretty sure."

"I don't think so."

"I think it is. It's gotta be it." I said.

"No, man. I don't think it is."

We had many a conversation like this during the trip. We were often slightly lost…on more occasions than I like to remember.

When traveling in my younger days, I basically had three strategies for when I was lost or trying to find some place, such as a certain road, a town or train station.

One strategy was to look at map if I had one. Sometimes it was helpful and just about as often it was not. On major roads or highways they were usually helpful, but at that time many maps did not have the smaller roads or city roads listed very well. Also, they were often confusing, and sometimes were unreadable because of the language used, or the condition of the map itself.

A second strategy was to ask someone for help and try to follow their directions. Often the directions were helpful. Sometimes they were not.

The third strategy was to head the same direction as the first pretty woman I saw. (If one was in the area or on the street.) When I didn't know where to go, I would just head the same direction as the first pretty woman I saw and go the same direction she was going. I figured it was at least as effective as making a guess - So why not head the same way as a pretty woman for awhile. I actually used that strategy quite often in my younger days. It made sense to me, and usually worked out pretty well.

In this particular case we finally decided to use option 2 and ask someone for directions. We spotted one of the few people on the street at this early hour, a tall, slim Swiss man.

We approached him and I asked, "Excuse me, sir. Which way is it to Italy?"

He looked surprised and responded in English, "Pardon me."

"Can you tell me which road goes to Italy?"

"You go to Italy?"

"Yes. Italy." I replied.

He seemed to think it was a pretty strange question. I didn't think it was at the time, but in hindsight I could see where it might have been. Italy is kind of a big target and we were nowhere near it. It would be kind of like standing in some small town in Colorado and asking someone, 'How do I get to Mexico?'

The Swiss man's answer was not very detailed, but was nevertheless actually helpful. He said, "Go south."

And he pointed to our right.

So we turned to our right and started heading that direction down the road. We walked quite a ways thru the rolling town with very little traffic until we came across a bakery that had just opened. We bought our usual food supply for the day, a couple of loaves of fresh Swiss bread. I still had some Coca-Cola left over from the day before, so we good to go.

We found a comfortable spot and sat on the curb of the road in this scenic, little Swiss village with the impressive Alp Mountains towering before us and all around us. It was quite cold sitting up in the mountains, but the view was spectacular.

"Check out that view. It's something, isn't it?" John said.

"That's for sure."

"It's a nice way to start the day."

◄ TRAVELIN' MAN ACROSS THE SAHARA AND BEYOND

We just relaxed a few minutes, looking out over the sweeping valley in the distance with the rolling, towering, snow covered mountains in the background seemingly breaking through the sky as the early morning clouds were just beginning to burn off. We sat and quietly ate our bread and drank our Coke-Cola, watching the sun rise in the morning sky. It was a beautiful start to the 5th day of our adventure.

When we finished our light meal, we continued resting a while, too tired to get up and face another day – At least not just yet. I leaned back against my backpack and just soaked in the magnificent scenery in front of me.

After resting, John and I slowly got up, and started wandering down the road to see what challenges and adventures we would face this day. As usual there would be plenty.

We soon found a decent place to hitch. The rides came slow but consistently as we made our way winding through the massive, Swiss Alps, following the narrow road as it rose and snaked its way up and over the ridges and edges of the snow covered mountains. We continued at a slow pace for the entire day passing a few, loosely connected, snowy Swiss towns until nightfall approached.

As the sun was setting on the grinding day, we found ourselves in a small, enchanting village near the top ridge of a mountain peak. It became much colder very quickly as soon as the sunset, in fact it was bone chilling. Having been born and raised with Michigan winters, I was used to cold weather and it rarely bothered me. John and I, on more than one occasion, went ice fishing bare-chested during the Tip-up-Town winter festival near our cabin at Houghton Lake, Michigan on sunny days during the dead of winter. We would smoke a cigar and get some sun out on the ice while fishing. However, the cold this night in Switzerland really got to me, and like I said I never traveled with a sleeping bag or much in the way of clothes. This was one of the nights I was paying for that decision.

John rummaged through his backpack and pulled out the map Mr. Eram's father-in-law gave us. John was now in charge of the map because I hadn't done such a good job keeping track of it since we left Paris – it had been lost for most of the time. Not that it made much difference. The map didn't last long as it was dropped in the snow and mud, crumpled and quickly became pretty much illegible and beyond use. It was soon lost and never seen again.

"Can you figure this map out?" John asked.

I stepped over next to John and looked over his shoulder at the map. "I don't know. I can't tell where we are on that thing. Can you?"

"Not really. It's in French, plus it's all smudged."

John and I kept studying the map, trying to figure it out.

"I think this might be the road we're on now." I said pointing at the map. "So it should take us up over this mountain range here…and then lead us down to the next town on the other side of the mountain."

"Uh-huh. You think so?" John said, not exactly buying what I was saying.

"Maybe. I'm not really sure."

"Well, let's follow this road and I guess we'll find out."

We continued hitching and walking for a couple hours with little luck. We had one short ride that took us up near the ridge of the mountain at the very outskirts of the town.

Despite the bitter cold, it was a beautiful night. Stretched out in the distance behind us were some very fashionable, Swiss-chalet type homes blanketed in fresh snow, standing in a line along the winding roadside leading down the mountain into town. With smoke curling out of many of their chimneys and the backdrop of the towering mountains with the crystal clear, star-filled sky; it looked like a painting.

The beautiful scenery was memorable, but even more memorable than anything from that night was the cold. I layered on almost all the clothes I had in my backpack, including my old high school letter jacket, which I had with me. I'm not sure why I had it with me, except that maybe it was the warmest jacket I owned at the time.

Even after putting on all the clothes that I had in my backpack (which wasn't much), I was just plain freezing. It was bitter cold and the slightest wind would just chill to the bone. There was almost no traffic on the road. After our last ride, the traffic just dried up and no cars came by. The road itself had some snow on it and we couldn't see where it led beyond the dark ridge up ahead of us.

We were out there in the bitter cold until about midnight, waiting for a ride. It was a long, cold, few hours. I was worried about how we would make it through the night since there was no shelter anywhere nearby.

While standing in the snowy roadside waiting in vain for a ride, I said to John, "Man, it's cold. This weather kind of reminds me of home, don't you think."

"Yea, Good ol' Michigan winters." John replied.

"How long you think we'll be out here?" I asked.

"Could be a while."

"I don't know about this road. It looks like a lot of snow on the road up ahead.," I said, "You wanna walk up and take a look over the ridge? See where were going...What's up ahead."

"Not really."

"Me neither."

"If we don't get a ride, it's going to be a long, cold night." John said as his breath fogged up the cold air.

"No way we're spending the night out here. It's too cold."

I started running in place and doing a little shadow boxing to keep my blood circulating and to keep from stiffening up.

While running in place I said to John, "I hate to say it but this is one time I wish I had brought a sleeping bag with me. It sure would be nice to have now."

"Yep, you say that now. But come morning, that sleeping bag would be in the ditch and you'd be heading down the road without it."

"Maybe so, but it'd still be nice to have now."

We talked, joked and did exercises and continued moving in place trying to keep warm. While we waited in the cold for our next ride, I remembered I had some dry cereal packets with me that I had saved from the breakfast meals at Harlaxton University before the trip had started. So I pulled out a few and passed a couple over to John to get us a little food and energy. We had much earlier in the day finished off the bread that we had bought at the bakery that morning.

Before I had left my university I had also saved several big jars of peanut butter and jam and taken them in my backpack. The jars had only lasted about a day and no, I didn't eat them all in the first day. I had thrown them out. I didn't like lugging around the extra weight all day. As I said I like to travel light.

Fortunately, the cereal packs were light and I had saved them. Actually, on most of my trips I would come back weighing about 10 pounds lighter - From the light meals and all the walking, mostly from all the walking. This trip was especially tough. It was going to be a 15-20 pounder.

John and I ripped open several of the dry cereal packs and ate them as we stood in the cold night along the roadside. Although we had no milk to add to them, they tasted real good and were a tasty change from the bread we had been eating for most of the trip.

RULES OF THE ROAD

After eating we waited until finally, around midnight a car stopped alongside the snow covered road and we happily hoped in. Driving the car was an older, hawk-nosed, balding Swiss man, who spoke pretty good English. As we got in the car, the heat from inside the car hit me like a blast furnace. It felt good. Real good.

Before starting to drive off, the driver turned toward us and asked in English, "Where are you going at such a late night."

"We're following this road over the mountain to the next town." I said, as we both pointed to the mountain ridge up ahead of us where the road led.

The thin Swiss man looked up quickly and said, "You can't do that."

We thought he meant he wouldn't take us there. We wondered why he even stopped.

John said, "No problem. We'll catch the next ride."

We weren't going to argue.

Then the Swiss man said, "No, you can't go there."

"What do you mean we can't go there?" John replied.

"You can't go there." The Swiss man repeated.

Now we beginning to think this guy didn't know the basics of hitchhiking 101.

For those you unfamiliar with the rules of the road...When hitching the driver wasn't obligated to take us where we wanted to go, and we aren't obligated to take the ride and go the way the driver's going. We would ride together for as long as our destinations matched, and under no circumstances did the driver tell us where we could or could not go.

However, having said that, there were a few times hitching when I did completely change the direction I was going and go the way the driver was headed. Often there was some special reason like an offer of a free place to stay, or to meet someone's family, or to see a special place or site. Usually, it turned out very well, was a great experience for me and added to my travels. A few times, however, it didn't turn out so well. There were a couple of times guys wanted me along to point the blame at or to share the blame for something illegal they were carrying or smuggling. They were looking for a fall guy.

It happened a few times, once with a fast-talking, bearded, Iranian guy who picked me up hitching in Germany and talked me into going with him down to Paris under the pretense of having a free place to stay at his girlfriend's hotel.

◂ TRAVELIN' MAN ACROSS THE SAHARA AND BEYOND

I was 20 years old at the time and hitching alone. After the guy picked me up, as we were crossing the border to enter France he was apprehended. I think for smuggling goods, but not after trying to pin the blame on me with the French police and custom officials. Luckily I had been alert, and had visa entry dates and papers to dispute his bogus story about me.

That was the first time I was faced with that situation but it was certainly not the last. I learned from it. That same or very similar scenario has played out several times during my travels in many other border crossings; several times in several different countries, including when I was entering Tunisia, Israel, Poland, America and The Philippines.

I learned to be very careful about who I was with or around when I crossed any border or when I went through customs. Very often when traveling I would meet different people on the road and travel with them for a few days. Then split up later, when we headed different directions. That happened all the time. So I was often around and with other travelers, who I only knew a few days or hours. Many of them became good friends and I later visited them at their home or they later visited me in the US. (During one summer, 13 different foreign friends I had met overseas traveling came to my home in Michigan to visit. My parents were always wonderful to them.) Others I wasn't so sure about.

In every situation though, I always made it a point to physically cross a border and go through customs on my own - Never together with someone else. I was also very careful about what I was carrying. I never carried anything for anyone. I never put my backpack or bags on the same cart with someone I was traveling with at an airport terminal or for customs. If I was traveling with someone, I was also very careful the night before and the entire day before I crossed a border - about what was in my backpack and who had access to my backpack.

Often travelers with bad intentions, before crossing a border, would plant their drugs, smuggled goods or other illegal items on the person they were with. Then shortly after they crossed the border, when the risk was gone, they would secretly take the illegal items back. Or just before going through customs or a border they would struggle with their bags and innocently ask if you could carry one of their bags. The bag would contain the illegal items. You would be the one carrying the bag, and if it was found at the border you were the one being taken away. It pays to be careful.

So after a little more discussion with the Swiss driver who said we couldn't go the way we were going, it finally became clear to us that the driver did know 'Hitchhiking 101', and was only being helpful. He was trying to tell us that we couldn't continue on the road over the mountain because the road was blocked.

The Swiss man said, "Nothing can go through here this time of the year. The road is snowed-over."

"I didn't know that." I said.

"Yes, well, if you went much further it could be dangerous to get out. You're snowed in. We have severe winter storms here."

"I didn't know that either." I said.

"Yes, it's not unusual for this road to be closed for parts of the winter. Nobody travels over that ridge this time of the year." The Swiss man said matter-of-factly.

He seemed surprised that we didn't know that. I'm not sure how I would ever had known that little fact considering I had only been in Switzerland once before, and had never been in this particular town, let alone on this individual road.

"I saw you from down the hill." The Swiss man said, "I was wondering what you were doing out on this road...at midnight...in the dead cold. So I drove up to find out."

"Thank you. We appreciate the lift. It was getting cold out there." John said.

"Yes, well, I can drive you back into town. I'll take you to the train station."

"Train station? This town has a train station?" John and I asked surprised.

"Yes, of course."

"That's news to us," I said.

He didn't have to offer twice. It was nice being in the warm car as we were driven down the winding, snowy mountain road into the town. After arriving at the train station, we thanked the Swiss man for his help and bid him goodnight before walking into the station to find the first train heading to Italy.

After some checking, we found out there was an early morning train leaving for Italy in about 5 hours so we found a warm place to sit on the floor out of the way in a corner of the station, where we slept the night until morning. When our train was finally ready, we boarded the train without a ticket to attempt some riding and hiding.

The train was fairly crowded and a little cold as it rocked along the winding tracks through the majestic, snow-covered mountains and valleys of the Alps. It was some beautiful scenery along the way, with the train cutting in and out between the wedges of the towering, mountains and the crystal clear sky overhead. We weren't able to enjoy it too much, though, as we were on constant lookout for the conductor. We traveled on the train for several stops, and successfully avoided the conductor for the ticket checks.

Later, as the train approached the last few stops before entering Italy, I said to John, "I'm worried about crossing the border with no train ticket. We shouldn't do it."

"Why?" John asked, "We've gone a long ways on this trip with no tickets."

"Yep, but we haven't crossed any borders without a ticket…at least intentionally."

"You think that's a problem?"

"Yeah." I answered, "It could be, if they stop us and check us. They'll do a passport check. What if they ask us for our ticket at the same time? If we don't have a ticket – we'd be entering Italy illegally."

"I got that."

"Maybe they can deport us, or deny us entry, or fine us or something?"

"Yeah." John said nodding. "You might be right. It's risky."

After a few moments thought, I continued, "So why don't we just jump off the train at the last stop in Switzerland. Then hurry and buy a ticket that's good just for the first stop into Italy – then get back on the same train before the train leaves the station."

"Huh?"

"We jump off the last stop in Switzerland, hurry and buy a ticket for just one stop into Italy, then get back on the same train before it leaves." I repeated.

"Just buy a cheap ticket for the one stop to cross the border?"

"Yeah. If we're fast we can get back on this same train before it leaves the station. We'll have about 4-5 minutes. We then cross the border with a ticket…We're legal."

"Sounds good. Let's try it." John agreed.

And that's just what we did. When the train pulled into the last station in Switzerland before getting to the border, we immediately jumped off the train, and quickly sprinted over to the nearest ticket booth to buy a ticket. It was quite a change for us to be making such a strenuous effort to *buy* a ticket. It was something we were usually doing everything possible to avoid.

At the ticket booth, we bought tickets to the first stop within Italy and made it back onto the same train, climbing back on just seconds before it pulled out. It was a cheap ticket for only the one stop, costing about $4. After quickly re-boarding the same train, we traveled awhile and then the train stopped at the Italian border where custom officials came on the train and checked our passports and tickets along with everyone else. We passed the customs check with no problem and then traveled on to the first stop, which is what we had bought our ticket for.

However, we didn't get off there.

Instead we decided to press our luck, and stay on the train and continue to ride-and-hide. We ended up staying on the train for a few more hours traveling further into Italy. Since we had a ticket we figured we would keep going and if the conductor caught us we would just show him the ticket we had, and say we over slept our stop. Fortunately, we didn't need to use that story because we successfully avoided the conductor until hours later when we finally got off the train.

If you haven't noticed, we're getting somewhat better at hiding on trains since our first few blunders in France.

After hopping out of the train onto the train platform, John and I quickly walked into and out of the station and started hitching. It was early afternoon and a cool sunny day in the beautiful Italian countryside. Now that we had made it into Italy, which had been our general destination for the past few days, we were now heading to the city of Florence.

John had the address of a shop in Florence owned by the sister of a guy he had traveled with previously. I asked John about the guy.

John said, "His name is Dave. We traveled together for a lot of days through Asia last year."

"Is he Italian?" I asked.

"No. Dave's American. He's a good guy. His sister's name is Dede. She's married to an Italian man, living in Florence."

"Do you know his sister, Dede?"

"No. Never met her. I just have her address from Dave."

"Well, hopefully, she'll put us up for a night or two."

Out in the afternoon sun in the gently rolling hills of northern Italy, John and I spent a few hours hitching with mixed luck. We were able to make some distance with a few rides and then after stopping to buy some bread and Coca-Cola in one town, we noticed a train station across the road. We couldn't resist it. So after eating our usual bread and Coca-Cola lunch along the roadside next to a church in the quaint little town, we walked over to the train station to see what the train possibilities were. We were in luck - There was a train leaving for Florence at 8:10PM. It was an over-night train scheduled to go all the way to Florence, which is where we needed to go. It was too good an opportunity, so we decided to wait and take it.

With our plan set, we rested in the train station and also did a little looking around the markets and town for a while until our train pulled into the station. Shortly after it pulled in, we climbed on the train with no ticket to play our usual game of ride-and-hide. We had a very close call right away, almost getting spotted by the conductor just as the train pulled out of the station.

We decided to not take any chances and immediately went to option 3 for hiding on trains. In other words, we went to hide in the cramped, smelly, disgusting bathroom at the end of one of the train cars. It was not my favorite place to be, but hey, you do what you gotta do.

We only planned to spend a little time in there to make sure the conductor was out of sight, but in actuality we never really left the bathroom. The few times we attempted to move out of the bathroom and find a place to sit, there always seemed to be a conductor passing through. It was as though the train was packed with conductors on the lookout for these two, young American stowaways. I know it wasn't, but that's what it seemed like to me.

We ended up hiding on the train all night, and actually made it all the way into Florence, pulling into the Stazione Santa Maria Novella early that morning at about 4:00AM. In all we were on the train for over eight hours since the previous night, without ever getting nailed by the conductor.

We spent at least seven of those hours sitting jammed together with our backpacks in the train's smelly, uncomfortable, and cold bathroom. It's the longest stint I ever did in a bathroom. But it was well worth it – the entire cost for the train we took from Spier, Switzerland all the way to Florence, Italy costs us only about $4. That was the price for the single, short ticket we bought to cross the border legally.

When our train got into the city at 4:00AM, John and I were exhausted. We never really had a chance to sleep, crammed in the smelly, dank bathroom with our backpacks. So after we got off the train, we slept sitting against a wall at the train station for a few hours until the sun rose, before getting enough energy to make our way through Florence to find Dede's Tulip Shop. John had the address of her shop but that was it. No phone number or directions.

With the help of three pretty, dark haired Italian women we met while wandering the streets, we made it to the shop fairly easily. We had asked the girls for directions, and they ended up good naturally walking us all the way to the shop through the charming but confusing city. After thanking the women for their help, they giggled cutely, while we grinned broadly and we all waved goodbye. John and I then walked unannounced into the shop of the sister, of the guy John had traveled with the previous year. We introduced ourselves to Dede, who was an attractive, petite, American woman in her early 30's, with brown, wavy, shoulder-length hair. She was very friendly and sincere.

She briefly showed us around her shop. It was a small but very exquisite boutique. Dede then asked us to follow her as she left her shop to her assistant and took us to a nearby coffee shop, where we talked for awhile. I think to kind of check us out…See if we were OK.

"So how long you guys been traveling?" Dede asked good-naturedly, as she sipped some coffee while John and I drank water.

"We started in London last week." John answered. "We've been on the road about a week or so. It sure seems longer, though."

"You've made it a long ways. How's the trip been so far?"

"It's been great." John replied." We've had a few tough days but it's been great. We've covered a lot of ground. We're traveling light."

"Yes, I can see that." Dede answered with a smile.

John and I were both in rough looking shape. We hadn't shaved or washed since we left Paris and we also hadn't eaten much the last few days. I had also worn basically the same unwashed clothes since we started the trip. We were tired and grimy.

"Where do you go from here?" Dede asked.

"We're heading to Africa.' John answered. "We're going to travel across northern Africa and then make our way back to England."

"Are you serious?" She asked surprised.

"Yes."

"Really? How are you going to do that?"

"That's a good question…Well…Ah…Ah" John stammered.

"We'll cross the sea to Sicily and travel across Sicily," I interjected. "And then cross the Mediterranean to Tunisia…and then travel across Algeria, Morocco and northern Africa…and then…Ahh…We will ahh…"

"We're kind of taking it day by day." John added.

"That sounds like quite a trip. You've got a long ways to go." Dede said. "How long do you think it'll take."

"About a month or so. Maybe." John replied.

"You guys look like you could use a little break, and a good meal."

John and I both smiled brightly at that idea.

"I'm sure my husband would be happy to meet you and to have you stay with us. His name is Mossi. We live not too far from here. You're welcome to stay with us for a few days."

"Really? We don't want to impose or cause problems for you." John said.

"It's no problem." Dede said with a warm smile, "We would be happy to have you. My brother Dave, mentioned you in one of his letters. Mossi and I would be happy to have you guys stay with us."

"That would be great. We really appreciate it." John replied.

Later Dede closed up the shop and took us to her and her husband's small but very fashionable flat, which they told John and I was over 500 years old. It was very enchanting and liberally furnished with a variety of stunning pieces of art, kind of like the city of Florence itself.

When we arrived at their home we met her husband Mossi. He was a stocky, dark haired, friendly guy. Dede and her husband were both very warm hearted and hard working. We ended up staying two nights with them. It was rejuvenating to have a break from the road, with a bed to sleep in and real food to eat. Each night we stayed with them, they prepared wonderful 4 course Italian meals for dinner. The food was absolutely delicious.

After dinner the first night, they took John and me on an evening tour through the narrow, hectic streets of Florence, with its beautiful architecture and limitless artwork. They told us Florence is the capitol and largest city in the region of Tuscany, and lies along the Arno River, which was facing Dede's shop.

Florence made a strong impact on me with its majestic architecture, and the series of bridges crossing though the city with the hazy, misty, reds-hue color reflecting off the low, classic buildings, bridges and works of art. I've only been to Florence two times, but visually it's one of my favorite cities. I love the artistic and historical feel to it, not to mention the many beautiful Italian woman.

Dede and Mossi lived near the Ponte Vecchio, which is in my favorite area of Florence. On our tour of the city that first night, our hosts drove us all around the city telling us about the history of the city, with its famous families from the past and its history during WWII. They showed us where the Italian resistors snuck across the bridge during the war. It was a fascinating night.

We ended up spending two great nights staying with Dede and Mossi taking in the many beautiful and historic sights of Florence and enjoying some filling Italian food. It was a needed break from the road.

CHAPTER 7

The Race Is On...

After our refreshing two-day stay with Dede and Mossi in Florence we hit the road again. It was great to spend two days sleeping in a bed and having some delicious home cooked meals. Dede and Mossi were wonderful to us. The 2 days we were there I spent only $2. We offered to pay for the gas for the car and to buy some of the food, but Dede and Mossi would never accept any money from us. Our stay with them was to be the last time on this trip that we would sleep in a bed and have a home cooked meal.

While in Florence we had gotten some information from Mossi that there was a ship to Tunisia, Africa leaving from Trapani, Sicily two days later at 1:30 PM. If we missed it, the next ship we could take would not be for three days after that. We couldn't afford to just wait around the extra days because of our lack of funds, so it was very important to make the ship.

We woke early that morning, said our goodbyes to Dede and Mossi, and walked through Florence to find a good place to hitch south out of the city. We were already on the roadside hitching by about 6:00AM.

As we were hitching, waiting for our first ride, I said to John, "Well, we've got our first deadline to make. We'll need some good luck to catch the ship in Sicily."

"I think we can make it." John replied, not so confidently, "If we don't have any big mistakes or bad luck. But we'll have to travel hard and fast."

"That's for sure...How far do you think we have to go?"

"First thing we gotta do is get to Reggio C. (Reggio di Calabria) at the southern tip of Italy. It's a long ways. Mossi said it's about 600 or 700 kilometers dead south from here."

THE RACE IS ON…

"Yeah." I said. "I remember he said just keep going south and we gotta hit it."

"Then we have to catch a ship and cross to Sicily. After the ship crossing - when we hit Sicily we then have to travel half way around the coast of Sicily to the city of Trapani by 1:30."

"That's a lot of ground to cover." John said shaking his head.

"No kidding. Almost 1,000 kilometers all told."

"In two and a half days…We gotta make good time."

By about 8AM, we had gotten a few quick rides. Although they didn't take us very far at all, it was a good start to the day. We felt we had the hitching luck with us and we did. We had consistent rides for all of the morning and into the early afternoon as we made our way down the Italian peninsula close to the small town of Spoleto. But it was later in mid-afternoon that we got the best ride of the day. Actually, the two best rides of the day. The two rides covered about 150 kilometers, getting us south of Rome.

We were hitching along the roadside when a car with three, pretty Italian girls drove by going the opposite direction that we were hitching. They waved and whistled at us as they passed by, going the other direction.

"John, did you see that?" I said, nudging him in the ribs.

"I sure did. They were cute, but they don't compare to Pieternel."

Pieternel was John's lovely Dutch girlfriend. He had recently met her in the US and then later visited her in The Netherlands. He was planning to see her again after the trip.

"Yeah, I get that." I replied. "There is a lot of nice scenery here in Italy, though; in more ways than one." I said with a grin.

After a few minutes, a familiar looking car pulled up to us. It was the same car with the three pretty girls. After driving past us, they had quickly turned around and came back to pick us up.

As a travel safety habit, if I was hitching and someone turned around going the opposite direction and came back to pick me up - I always refused the ride. If someone is that interested in getting me in their car and giving me a ride, it raises red flags and warnings for me. I had learned that if someone is too friendly or helpful there is often an ulterior motive.

In this case, though, when three, pretty, smiling, Italian girls pulled up to offer us a ride - we didn't hesitate. There was a smiling, curvaceous blond and brunette girl in each of the front seats, and another pretty brunette in the back seat. We jumped in the car in a heartbeat.

The girls immediately took off down the road, driving us down the highway for a long ways.

"Where are you headed?" I asked the pretty blond who was driving.

She turned, smiled and then giggled. The other two girls also giggled. They didn't say a word, just smiled and giggled.

They were three, wild girls and spoke none-to-little English and as we didn't speak any Italian, there was a lot of gesturing and body language for communication. There wasn't a lot of talking, but there sure was a lot of smiling. We had the windows down, with the wind blowing through the girl's hair and some kind of Italian pop music on the radio. It was a very enjoyable ride. After over an hour ride they stopped to let us out, smiled and waved goodbye. We waved back and when they took off, and John and I went back to the roadside to start hitching.

Only a few minutes later, our next ride pulled up for us.

It was the same car with the same three, pretty girls. They had turned around and came back to give us a ride again. We jumped back into the same car and they drove us for another hour or so down the highway. This was turning into a really enjoyable day on the road.

We found out that they lived right near where they originally picked us up. They were driving all this way just to give us a ride, and spend time with us. When they let us out they would have to drive over three hours back to where we first met them to get to their homes. This time when they stopped to let us out, we exchanged addresses, took their picture and they took ours. They then smiled, blew us kisses, waved and took off back down the road. Weeks later they sent me a postcard to my university in England with a kiss mark from each of them.

Now John and I were about 50 kilometers from Naples. It was early evening and we were getting hungry, also a little cold.

On the road I was always 'a little' something; a little cold, hungry, tired, thirsty, lost…or some combination. We hadn't really eaten much that day since an early breakfast, but what a breakfast it was at Dede and Mossi's home in Florence; delicious and filling.

We hitched a little further but after no ride picked us up for quite a while, John suggested, "It's getting dark. Why don't we get off this highway and try walking into the next town."

"Yeah." I agreed. "The hitching's getting tough and there are fewer cars."

THE RACE IS ON...

"Maybe there's a train station in town. We can try to catch a train or sleep in the station."

"All right. Let's take this exit…get off the main road"

"How far do you think the town is from the road?" I asked.

"It should be just over that next ridge." John said, pointing up ahead. "Should be close"

It wasn't. The town turned out to be about 5 kilometers from the big road. We hitched while walking along the country road, but we ended up walking the entire way. It was a long, tiring walk, but it was a beautiful, early twilight in the Italian countryside with the green, rolling hills and vineyards around us. When we finally made it into town, it turned out to be a quiet, little Italian town. We ate our dinner of bread, cheese and, of course good ol' Coca-Cola, while sitting on a bench in a beautiful little park with squirrels and lots of birds, looking over an ancient looking Italian Church and courtyard. We had been on the road over 14 hours by now and it was getting dark and cold.

"We've made some good mileage today. I'm getting worn out. Why don't we get off the road for while?" I suggested after we finished eating.

"Yeah. Let's check out the town." John agreed, "See if there's a train station around here."

It took a while but after a lot of weary walking through the town, we did find a small station. There was a train passing through in a couple of hours that was only going a little further along to just south of Naples, so this time we bought a ticket and waited for the train. The ticket wasn't very expensive since it was only a few stops down the line before the train would stop at the last station for the night.

After the wait, the train did pull in right on time and we rode it down the tracks to its last stop. The train wasn't crowded and we had our own compartment. By the time we arrived at the last station it was pretty late, after 11:00PM. It had been a long day.

"Well now what?" John asked.

"This is the end of the line for the train tonight." I said, "Why don't we see if we can find a place to sleep around the station here. It's better than going out onto the streets. We can't really afford a hotel room…Here's our best bet."

"OK. But I'm getting kind a tired of sleeping in train stations."

"That's the truth."

◂ TRAVELIN' MAN ACROSS THE SAHARA AND BEYOND

We walked down the platform towards the station to see what we could find as the few people getting off the train were hurrying home and the station was quickly emptying out. Off to the side of the main station we found a small enclosed, circular waiting room that was left open. There were seats along the wall of the round room. It was outside the train station on the platform near the tracks. The train station itself closed down shortly after our train arrived – the last train of the night.

We moved into the waiting room with a couple of other backpackers from the train. They stayed just a short time and then they left to find a hotel, so John and I had the round sitting room to ourselves.

"Well, we got a place to sleep tonight." I said, while making myself comfortable on the circular bench.

"Yeah. This is not so bad. It's quiet and not <u>too</u> cold. We've got the room to ourselves. See if you can close that door. Is there any lock on it?" John said.

I reached over to the door and tried to close it.

"It won't close all the way. And there's no lock."

So we closed the door as best we could, and set a little glass bottle next to the door as an alarm, but we didn't have much to work with and we were dead tired, so we didn't really bother with it too much. There was no light in the room, but it was dimly lit by a platform light outside near the tracks.

I got as comfortable as I could. I used my backpack as a pillow and wrapped it under my arm to make it more difficult to be taken from me while I was sleeping. It got quite cold during the night and I put on almost all the clothes I had in my backpack.

John soon fell asleep. Fortunately, I was dead tired and I fell asleep a little later. I say "fortunately" because if I wasn't dead tired, and I mean *dead tired* - There's no way I could have fallen asleep after my brother already went to sleep.

That may sound a little strange. But there's a very logical reason why I couldn't go to sleep after John fell a sleep…He snores really loud! I mean big-time loud. It's kind of like trying to sleep with a hurricane blowing a few feet from you. That's why I had to fall asleep first, if I ever wanted to get any sleep when I was traveling with my brother.

That night after falling asleep in the train waiting room, I slept very well until…Sometime very early in the morning I was awakened by a huge booming sound. I thought I could feel the seats vibrating from the sound. At first I thought it might be my brother's snoring - but this deep, thunderous sound far exceeded anything I had ever heard from John. It sounded kind of like the rumbling of a train going through a deep tunnel - Except that it was musical and carried a tune.

As I wakened, I looked up and glanced around the small sitting room. I saw a very, very large mountain of a man in his 40's wearing farmers clothes and a cap sitting a few seats over with a wide smile on his broad face, singing some kind of Italian opera or something. He was singing to his heart's content. His voice and face radiated happiness and good cheer. It was one of the loudest voices I had ever heard, and in the small, enclosed circular room the sound reverberated back and forth through the room. I didn't know who he was or where he came from. But he was certainly enjoying himself and he paid no attention to me.

By now John had woken up, and we sat and listened

The huge man continued singing some Italian opera with his booming voice and wide smile for quite some time. When he finally stopped, he looked over at us and acknowledged us for the first time. He smiled; tipped the cap he was wearing on his large round head, got up, lumbered to the door and opened it. He was indeed a mountain of a man. He then turned towards us one more time, smiled again, nodded and left the room. I had no idea who he was.

After the huge singer left I turned to John and said, "Quite a way to start the morning, huh? At first I thought a train was running over us or something."

"No kidding." John agreed. "But I enjoyed it, actually. It was kind of like our own private opera performance."

"Yeah." I agreed. "He really had an incredible voice, sounded like Pavarotti. Kindda looked like him, too."

"Well, it was certainly a much better way to start the day than, say...getting dragged out of a tractor by a mob of construction workers." John said..

I just chuckled and nodded.

After the rousing, musical start to the morning, we walked out to the train station platform and looked around. It was very early, right at the break of dawn. The sun had just broken over the distant horizon and the evening darkness and cold was still slowly being burned off by the rising sun.

"There's very little activity around here. I don't see any trains that might be heading south as far as I can tell." John said, yawning.

◄ TRAVELIN' MAN ACROSS THE SAHARA AND BEYOND

I walked across the empty train platform, over to a departure board and took a look. "Yeah, it's pretty dead around here. I can't really read this board well - But it doesn't seem to show any trains leaving for at least another few hours."

"A few hours?"

"Yeah." I replied. "I don't see anything departing until 7:50."

"The heck with that. Let's head out of town and start hitching."

"Sounds good."

There were no major roads near the station to hitch from so we ended up doing a lot of walking, some cross town hitching and took a city bus to find the way south out of the town. We got some bad directions at one point and got turned around and lost for a while.

It ended up taking us three hours and it was almost 8:00AM before we ever got to where we needed to be to hitch. We had roughly 300 kilometers still to go in order to make it to Reggio C. at the southern tip of Italy and catch the ship to Sicily. We then had to hitch around Sicily and catch the 1:30 o'clock ship from Trapani to Tunisia the next day. If we missed it, it would cost us 3 days wait for the next ship.

We definitely could not afford 3 days making no mileage. We had traveled extremely cheap so far, with a few days holed up in Paris and Florence where we spent virtually no money so we were doing well. We also hadn't had any of those money mistakes or big rip-offs yet that cost 3-4 days traveling money in one moment or one quick shot. They would almost always happen sooner or later no matter how careful you were, but so far we had been lucky. Even so, in the back recesses of my mind I was already beginning to wonder how we could make it to Africa and back. We hadn't even taken the ship to Sicily yet - let alone crossed the Mediterranean Sea to Tunisia for the trip across Africa. We still weren't even close to the halfway point, and our money was very low…

For the first part of the day we hitched and made our way slowly down the Italian Peninsula. It was mostly slow going and a frustrating day, with a lot of walking between rides, and times getting lost or ending on the wrong road. We also took a couple of short bus rides along the way.

After eight hours hitching and about half of the way covered, we found a little train station in one town that had a train going on for the last stretch to Reggio C., so we waited for the train to pull in and we got on it without a

THE RACE IS ON...

ticket. We were hoping our ride-and-hide luck would hold up. It didn't. But then again it did in another way.

John and I got on the train with no problem, but a while after the train pulled out, the conductor made kind of a quick surprise pass through the train from the opposite direction we were expecting him. We didn't see him coming and there were few people on the train to distract him or hold him up, so we weren't able to avoid him.

He asked us point blank, "*Ticket, porfervor.*"

We looked at him with a pained, guilty expression.

He was a older man with a kind, friendly face, wearing a clean, crisp train uniform and train conductor's hat.

He politely asked again, "*Ticket, porfervor.*"

John and I then just kind of opened up and started talking about our adventure and trip to Africa, trying to explain what we had gone through the past several days and how far we had traveled.

"I'm sorry we don't have a ticket. We've been traveling for many days." I blurted out. "We have no money. We need to get to Sicily."

"Yeah, we traveled from England and..." counting on his fingers John continued, "then we traveled across France, Switzerland, and Italy. Now we really need to get to Sicily. We're going to Africa."

"We have to get to Trapani, Sicily very soon or we'll miss our ship. We can't miss our ship. We need to get to Africa," I pleaded. "I have to get back for university in England."

"Yep." John continued. "We've got only a little money and we're running out of time. And I have to get back to England to use my plane ticket to America."

John and I just kept talking, and talking about our plight. I think we were both quite exhausted and frustrated, and everything just came out all at once. The train conductor didn't say much, but just listened and even though John and I were babbling on very quickly in English, he seemed to understand some of what we were saying.

When we finished, the conductor paused a moment to think, as though he was making an important decision. Then he smiled graciously and said in accented English, "No worry. Come."

He had a very gentlemanly manner.

He led us to the very front of the train and sat us in some comfortable seats near where he had a little kind of workstation. He then brought us some coffee and got some small train maps. He smiled and showed us that we were on the wrong train to get nearest to the harbor for the ship to Sicily. He made a gesture as if it's OK.

He again said, "No worry." And added, "Here. Wait here, please."

As I said before, I have a soft spot in my heart for train conductors and this good-hearted conductor was another example of why. After riding the train for a long time in our comfortable seats, the train dead-ended on its train line at Reggio C., where the conductor had us wait until he made his rounds and checked that the train was clear.

After he finished his rounds he came back for us, smiled and said, "Come. Follow please."

We did as he asked. He took us off the train and walked us through the busy station with passengers hurriedly coming and going past us until we reached another platform where he sat us down on a bench.

He then just smiled and said, "Please wait here. It's OK."

I wasn't sure what was going on. For all I knew, he could have been going to get the police or some authority because he caught us with no tickets. But I had a real good gut feeling and trusted the kindly conductor so John and I just sat and relaxed in our seats.

It sure was nice to just sit and relax, and not have to be worried about hiding from anyone. After a short wait, the conductor returned talking with another younger train conductor, who I believe was his friend. They came back over to us together, talking and smiling. He introduced us to his friend, and then handed John and me tickets to Villa San Giovanni, which is where we needed to catch the ship to Sicily. It was a short train ride from where we were. At first we assumed we needed to pay. After all, we had never paid for the first train ride that he had originally caught us on. But when John and I reached for our wallets to get out some money, the kindly conductor put his hand on my arm to stop me, smiled, and said, "You no pay. It's my pleasure."

When we understood that everything was taken care of, we were speechless for a moment. We shook his hand and thanked him for his kindness and his help. He just patted us on the back, smiled and wished us well on our trip as his train conductor friend led us over to the train for Villa San Giovanni.

'"Man. What a good-hearted guy." I said to John as we walked over to our train.

"Sure was."

"Thank God for all the good guy train conductors of the world."

"No kidding." John said nodding.

THE RACE IS ON...

"They sure make up for a lot of the difficulties and dangers of the road. It's sure nice to have a little help once in a while."

After getting on the correct train, we took the short ride to Villa San Giovanni. It was evening when we arrived. After leaving the train station it took us a while to make our way down to the shipyard after getting directions to where the ship was docked. We had to do a lot of walking and ask directions several times before we found the correct dock.

As we walked down to the shipyard with the evening sky slowly covering the harbor and the moon starting to shimmer off the sea ahead of us, we felt relieved, but I soon noticed something important was missing. What was missing was a ship. There was no ship.

We were too late. The last ship crossing the Strait of Messina for Sicily had already left the dock. The ship ride was quite short, but now we were stuck for the night. We had no way of crossing to Sicily until the next day, and the next day we had to get all the way across Sicily to the city of Trapani. We would have to make some serious time the next day if we were to catch our ship to Africa. It was do or die time.

Before we left the shipyard, we checked to find out when the first ship would be leaving the next morning. We found out a ship was leaving very early at day break, so we went to find a place to sleep close to the harbor. It took a while but we found an enclosed, secluded area behind some older buildings where we set up camp with our backpacks to spend the night sleeping outdoors under the stars. It was a cold, uncomfortable night, but we made the best of it.

Early the next morning, shortly before daybreak, we made our way down to the shipyard again and caught the first ship crossing the Straight of Messina to Sicily. We paid for a ticket and hustled on board the ship in the cool, early morning. During the ship ride across the Strait of Messina, I stood out by the rail feeling the breeze, watching the waves, taking in the fresh sea air. It was refreshing and a great start to the day.

CHAPTER 8

The Race Continues... With Mario at the Wheel

After taking the short ship ride across the Strait of Messina to Sicily we arrived at the port of Messina, de-boarded and made our way into the city. It was about 7:00AM. Despite still being quite early, Messina was very busy with lots of activity and even crazier drivers than Italy. Our ship to Tunisia, Africa was leaving from the city of Trapani on the other side of Sicily at 1:30PM that same day.

We had less than 6 hours to hitch about 200 kilometers around the coast of Sicily, find the shipyard, find the correct ship and somehow get on the ship. Even if we managed to make the long hitch and find the shipyard and ship in time, we still weren't sure about that last part...We didn't know the exact price of the ship fare at this point. But we assumed it wasn't going to be cheap since the ship would be crossing about 250 kilometers of the Mediterranean Sea.

First thing, we found a bakery and bought some fresh Sicilian bread and Coke-Cola. We then briefly sat in a little courtyard near some ancient looking buildings and ate our bread and drank our cola, while watching all the activity and people going by around us. There were several kids playing soccer in the courtyard. Like everywhere I traveled there were always kids playing soccer..

Even though I got ripped-off when the guy overcharged me for the Coca-cola, I liked the feel of Sicily; a little hectic, active and dusty with an old country kind of feel to it. After a very short respite it was now time to make some distance and get to our ship.

THE RACE CONTINUES... WITH MARIO AT THE WHEEL

I looked over at John in the early morning sun and said, "We don't really have any margins for error now or bad luck."

"No kidding. This is crunch time."

The first of many we would have on this trip.

"How far do you think it is to Trapani from here?" John asked.

"I don't know." I shrugged, "Maybe about 200 k's. A map would be handy right about now."

"Yeah, but any maps are long gone."

We got some good directions and fairly quickly made it through the sea-side town of Messina and found the coastal highway heading to Palermo and then on to Trapani. It was a clear sunny day, one of the nicest days we had had on the trip to this point. It was also the hottest day we'd had. After a short wait we got a couple of quick rides that took us out of the city a bit. The last of these rides left us about 40 kilometers out of Messina near a town called, Barcellona Pozzo di Gotto. (I thought I would mention that because I love that name – it sounds so…so…Sicilian)

We were overlooking the Tyrrhenian Sea, which that side of Sicily faces. There was some beautiful, majestic scenery with the roadway often winding along the sharp cliffs and sandy beaches at the seas edge. With the sunny day, the Tyrrhenian Sea had a brilliant, blue shine to it that was breathtaking at times. It was a gorgeous ride along the seashore.

After our early good luck, we then hit a fairly long stretch of almost two hours with no ride. It was now well after 9:00 o'clock, we still had over 150 kilometers to go and were down to about 4 hours to make it. We were getting very concerned. We didn't have much time to spare. A ride then stopped with an old, grizzled man in a farming truck, and even though it was a short one it broke the dry spell.

Only a short while later we got our next ride. It wasn't just a ride - It was the ride. It was a young, dark haired, Sicilian guy in a small type sports car. He was a good looking guy in his early 20's wearing fashionable clothes with his hair greased back. After he pulled over, John and I quickly ran to his car and crammed in it with our backpacks.

"Thanks for stopping," John said smiling. "We need to get to Trapani."

"Trapani?" asked the young guy driving the car.

"*Si*. Trapani. We need to take a ship to Tunisia." John said.

"Tunisia?"

"Yes. *Si.*" John answered. "From Tunisia we're going to travel across Africa."

"Africa?"

"Si. We're in a hurry." I added. "We have to make the ship in order to get back to England in time."

"England?" The young driver asked.

"Yes. Si."

At this point we weren't sure how much English the young sports car driver spoke or what he understood. The conversation so far had been kind of speak-and-repeat performance. It turned out he spoke pretty good English, though, with a lot of body language thrown in for good measure.

"Youaa go nowwa to Trapani?" The young driver asked, pointing animatingly in the apparent direction of Trapani.

"*Si.*" I said, "We need to get to Trapani to take a ship to Tunisia. The ship leaves soon?"

"Trapani is a little far. No? What time - your ship?"

"1:30." I said, holding up one finger.

"*Si…Si…*1:30 o'clock." He said. "Trapani. 1:30 o'clock…"

Then he thought for a moment, before adding confidently, "No problemo. I takka youaa all the way to Palermo. I takka you there very fast."

"Great." I said with a smile.

"Then from Palermo you make it to Trapani – 1:30 o'clock. No problem. We go to Palermo now - very fast."

I believed him. We sat back in his car and he took off. I think he said his name was Mario, Mario Andretti. I'm just joking but he sure drove like he was. He drove that curving roadway along the edge of the steep coastline, through the tunnels, over the hills and small mountains, and around all the bends in the seaside road like an expert.

"This road," He said, gesturing down the winding coastal road ahead of us. "I drive this road many times."

"Yeah?" I said

"Si. I drive this road every weekka to see my girlfriend. Her name Sophia. She very beautiful girl."

"Really?"

"Si. Very beautiful. I know this road very well."

He wasn't lying. He got us into Palermo like a bullet, with a couple hours to make it to our ship in Trapani.

THE RACE CONTINUES… WITH MARIO AT THE WHEEL

Palermo was an expansive, very busy, and chaotic city with many low laying buildings nestled along the seashore. There were lots of people moving about, unending rows of buildings, cars backfiring, noise and hustle and bustle. I liked the city, but it was the kind of city it can take hours to make your way around on foot or by hitching.

Having made it to the city in no time, we were now faced with the tough part, which was getting through the city, and finding a good place to hitch from to go to Trapani. Fortunately, Mario, the young Sicilian guy who gave us the ride (I never did get his real name), was very considerate. He went out of his way and quickly drove us around the winding, confusing city streets of Palermo to drop us off in a good spot for us to head directly down to Trapani. We thanked 'Mario' for the ride as he quickly sped off with a friendly wave.

Before John and I started hitching again, we walked over to a little market area next to the road to buy some bread and Coca-Cola.

"You notice all the stares we're getting," I said to John.

"Yeah. What's going on?"

"I don't know. Did we do something?"

"Beats me." John said puzzled, "But everyone seems to be looking at us right now."

"They sure are. We're getting a lot of stares."

" But at least they're smiling."

"Yeah. A lot of friendly smiles." I agreed.

"People seem really friendly around here."

And they were. Very friendly. And like Mario – very demonstrative and energetic. As we walked over to the market area, there was a lot of activity and commotion on the street. Men in dark, classic suits and formal hats were hawking goods, older women wearing shawls and doing a lot of gesturing were haggling over the prices of things, little kids were running around kicking soccer balls, while fashionably dressed women sashayed down the street.

As we were walking a man selling oranges tossed us each an orange, with a smile and a wave. When we went to take money out, he smiled again and waved us off. At the little bakery where we bought some fresh Sicilian bread, the shop owner smiled broadly, shook our hands and waved profusely as we walked out the door of his shop. Everyone was very friendly and kind, and seemed interested in looking at us. The stares and attention, it was a new experience for me. But it would only continue much more so, as we reached Africa.

◄ TRAVELIN' MAN ACROSS THE SAHARA AND BEYOND

After eating our bread, we walked back out to the coastal road to start hitching. Mario left us in a great place to hitch from. It was just one straight, clear shot to Palermo, and it didn't take us long to get our first ride heading to Trapani. It took only two rides to get us all the way there. The last ride, with an older, dark-haired Sicilian man driving a coughing and sputtering truck, took us into the bustling, chaotic city of Trapani, almost all the way to where we needed to catch our ship to Africa.

With a tip of his hat and a cheerful wave, the kindly old man let us out along the road heading out of town down to the port. John and I then walked a ways before hitching a ride down to within sight of the port. The port was in kind of an isolated, open area about half a kilometer away from the main road. We ran into the docking area to find the ship for Tunisia, where we got directions from a ship worker. He pointed to a cramped, one-room ticket building set up on a low hill about 100 meters from the dock and ship. In and around the building there were only a few people getting tickets or boarding the ship. Most had already boarded.

John and I ran into the ticket building to see about tickets and the ship schedule. There were a few shipyard officials standing about, and we approached a haggard, but friendly official in his 40's who looked at us with a weary expression.

"We need a ticket to Tunisia. When does the next ship leave to Tunisia?" I asked out of breath.

"Tunis. You want ticket – Tunis?" The Sicilian official asked.

"Oh, yes...for Tunis. When does the next ship leave for Tunis?"

"Ship to Tunis. Leaves now. Very soon."

"The ship is actually on time. We had the correct schedule. I don't believe it." I said looking over at John.

"That's great." John said, "How much is the ticket?"

"Ticket - 220 lire." Said the ship official.

We did a quick calculation in our heads.

"That's about 27 bucks" John said.

"27 bucks! That's a fortune. That's about four days travel money."

Before we could deal with the price of the ticket, the ship clerk interrupted us. "First you get passport check to leave Italy...First pass customs. Then ticket. No?"

"We need to clear customs? Where's an immigration office out here?" John asked.

THE RACE CONTINUES... WITH MARIO AT THE WHEEL

The ship clerk looked to his left and pointed. "Behind. There. It's near. Customs building is behind."

Without a look back, we quickly hustled out the door to find the customs building. Actually, it wasn't really a building…It wasn't even really an office…But it really was nearby. It was more like a shed with a table. It was within a few meters of the old ticket building, almost attached to it.

We hurried into the customs building (shed) to the table where one bored-looking, uniformed official was sitting in a chair behind it. He was about 30 years old, with dark, unshaven stubble covering his jaw and wearing a grimy, custom uniform. We hurriedly gave him our passports. He looked at them and then looked at us. He asked for our shot papers, which we luckily had. Before we left England my brother and I had checked and we both got our shots for Northern Africa prior to meeting up in London. He checked our papers. Then he asked how much money we were taking out of Italy. Our funds were embarrassingly limited. We had mostly American dollars with some British pounds that we had started with. We now also had a few French Francs and Italian Lire – Leftover from our travels through France and Italy. We also had a little Swiss money but most of it didn't count because it was coins.

The custom official checked through our funds. After finishing, with a look of surprise, he asked, "Is this all. You more money? More money? No?"

John answered, "No. That's it."

"You sure. How you travel - So little money?"

"Very cheaply. We travel very cheaply."

"Where you travel in Tunisia?"

"Uhh, we're not sure." John replied.

"When you come back to Sicily or Italy?"

"Uhh, we don't come back to Italy." John replied again.

"No! Then what you do?" The custom official was a very inquisitive guy. He didn't seem to believe we could be traveling with so little money.

"We will travel across northern Africa." I answered.

"Northern Africa! Where northern Africa?" Now he really didn't seem to believe us."

"We will cross Tunisia, Algeria and Morocco." I answered, "Then return to England after that."

"How? How you do that? I never hear anyone do that."

"We travel very cheap…Very cheap."

◂ TRAVELIN' MAN ACROSS THE SAHARA AND BEYOND

With a skeptical look, he asked to see our backpacks. He looked through them very intently at first, but quickly lost interest after finding that all we had was some smelly, dirty clothes. I think he believed we must have been involved in drug dealing, smuggling or some other illegal activity because of how little money we we're traveling with.

Finally, the custom official made another quick look through the funds we had, grunted wearily, stamped our passports and gave them back to us allowing us to exit Sicily (Italy). We could now try to get on the ship to Africa.

Before leaving on this trip John and I had converted most of our money into US dollars, and kept some British pounds so we would have some money to use when we arrived back in England. Managing my currency and currency exchanges was crucial on trips like this when I had such limited funds.

At that time it was very beneficial and important to travel with US dollars. US dollars could always be converted to the local currency at banks or currency exchange offices anywhere in the world. Other currencies were very difficult and often impossible to exchange, especially in remote areas. Secondly, with American dollars I could also almost always use them outright on the street if I didn't have the local currency.

Additionally, in some countries I also could trade them "black-market" on the street for much, much more than their official bank exchange value... As we shall see later on in this trip, that's exactly what my brother and I did with an Algerian soldier (of all people) one early morning outside a little Saharan desert town.

This was all long before cash machines, easy instant money transfers, etc. So the money I had for a trip was the money I started with on me. That was it. It was very, very difficult and often impossible to get funds from home or anywhere sent to me in out of the way places. Heck, at this time it was often very, very difficult just to contact home. On this trip we tried for several days to get an overseas call placed to the US around Christmas time – we <u>never</u> got one single call through.

Making special arrangements for money to be wired or sent to me was almost inconceivable. And if money somehow actually was sent and somehow received at some out-of-the-way location, there was always that little problem I mentioned earlier of being ripped-off. It was very unlikely I would receive the money under any circumstances....

THE RACE CONTINUES… WITH MARIO AT THE WHEEL

So for my travels, the money I had was the money in my pocket and that was it. Or I should say the money I had was the money in my money belt or in the wallet chained to my belt. I had to be very careful with my money. If it was lost or stolen, I was up a creek. There was usually no recourse or help. I was on my own. The same for my passport, papers, documents, etc. If they were lost, stolen or misplaced it could mean serious problems for me…and in some places it could leave me very vulnerable and in a dangerous situation.

I'm proud to say that in my travels to over 50 countries, to hundreds and hundreds of cities, on dozens and dozens of ship crossings, bus rides, train rides and international flights; I have never lost my passport or any papers or documents. That will be hard for most of my friends and family to believe since, nowadays, I lose umbrellas, sunglasses, keys etc. like there's no tomorrow…But when I traveled, I had that travel mind set and security focus that was as ingrained as breathing.

When I traveled, I also always took a lot of small denomination US bills, such as $1 and $5 bills. Small bills gave me flexibility. For example, if I was passing through some country like on this trip when I just bought bread and one cheap train ticket in Switzerland. I only needed to exchange a few dollars. If I only had large bills like $50, $100's, or even $20's, I would have had to buy a whole lot of Swiss Francs that I couldn't use.

Then when I left the country I would have to exchange again for the next currency at a lower rate. Then when I leave that country I may be exchanging a portion of that same money a third time. With each currency exchange I'm losing money to the bank. I'm also losing any extra coins that I don't use because they can never be exchanged at any bank. (This was long before a single Euro currency came into being).

I also needed small bills for emergencies. For example, when I would cross a border on a weekend or at night and no banks were open to get the local currency. This happened fairly often. The US dollars could be used to hold me over. When I had no local currency I could usually use US dollars directly on the street. In those cases, I only needed a couple of dollars to pay for food, a cheap hotel room or assistance.

If you had large bills once you used it, the entire bill was gone. The change you got back was all in the local currency, and I often didn't know the correct value of the local currency, i.e. rip-off. Or sometimes when I had been traveling in a country for a while and I was about to leave, I only needed money for one or two more days. Again, I didn't want to break and lose a large US bill.

Lastly, in some restricted countries I traveled to - the local currency was worthless outside the country and could <u>never</u> be exchanged at any bank or anywhere once you left. You could only use or exchange the currency inside that country. So you only wanted to exchange US bills for the exact amount of money you needed for while you were in that country. If I had to exchange a large US bill for local currency, and then I didn't need to use all the local currency while in the country – the extra local currency became worthless the moment I left the country. This was true of Algeria, East Germany, The Soviet Union, etc..

Oh, there was also one more reason I sometimes needed small US bills and that was for serious predicaments (bribes). There were some times when I kept US dollars for predicaments with authorities, custom official, soldiers etc. There were several times when I kept the money handy for that purpose – and on a few rare times I actually used it…

Back at the little customs building at the Trapani port, John and I promptly had our passports stamped letting us exit Italy, so now we needed to get on the ship. We hadn't bought our ticket yet and the ship was due to pull out shortly, but instead of walking back over to the ticket building we just started casually walking down the hill in the direction of the dock and ship. John and I didn't really discuss sneaking on the ship. We just made eye contact, shrugged and headed down toward the ship to see what we could do.

As we walked down to the ship there were some other late passengers hurrying along in front and behind us. They were mostly older Tunisian men and women carrying lots of bags, sacks and belongings; Traders and others looking for bargains. We blended in with their group.

As we reached the gangplank at the dock to cross on to the ship, the boat official stopped and started checking tickets and belongings. I was sure he was the same haggard, helpful guy I saw at the ticket office a short time earlier. While he was checking the other passenger's belongings, things became a little chaotic. An older woman wearing a shawl and other group members started arguing with the boat official about one of her bags, causing quite a commotion and distraction.

John and I saw our opportunity and we slowly moved around the group, and when a few other passengers who had been checked for tickets started walking over the gangplank onto the ship, we just joined in and walked along. During the short walk over the water onto the ship, I was holding my breath expecting to be called back to shore at any second. But we weren't

THE RACE CONTINUES… WITH MARIO AT THE WHEEL

called back. We walked onto the ship right pass the boat man standing next to the plank on the ship. We just maintained a strong, neutral attitude as we walked past. He didn't say a word and never asked for our ticket

"I think we made it." John whispered to me as we got on the ship.

"Yeah. We better keep moving, before somebody asks us for a ticket."

"Just keep walking and don't' make eye contact."

We quickly made our way through the big ship getting away from the dockside. Once on the ship, we walked through it trying to avoid any ship workers, and trying to mix in with the other passengers. It was quite a large ship with a few different decks and fortunately for us, it was crowded. There were a lot of people on the ship for us to get lost in; families with a lot of bags and goods, children, traders with their large sacks and just a few other backpackers. The large ship pulled out of the port soon after we boarded and started slashing through the heavy waves and wind, while we wandered through the ship getting the layout and trying to find an out-of–the-way place to sit and lay low.

A short while later as we were walking through the ship, we came across the same haggard ship worker who we talked to in the ticket building, and who we saw at the dock as we were pulling out. We couldn't seem to stay away from this guy. It was the third time I had seen him. He must have known we hadn't bought a ticket because he was in the ticket building, and directed us to the customs building "office" without us buying tickets, and then he saw us again at the dock.

When we came across him this third time on the ship, he was across the deck moving my way. I just looked up and there he was, and by mistake I made eye contact. When I caught his eye, he gave a quick flicker of recognition, but he just continued walking by. I could swear he flashed a hint of a smile as he moved past me.

To this day, I've always thought that he knew we had snuck on the ship, but let us go.

Who knows?

CHAPTER 9

Stowaways Across the Mediterranean Sea

The ship had now pulled out and was moving out to the rolling Mediterranean Sea. It was going to be a long journey. We had heard we would be arriving at the Tunis, Tunisia port in northern Africa at about midnight. It took a while, but we found a private place to sit on a lower deck and got settled in. I had a great sense of relief and a chance now to sit back and unwind. It was great relaxing without worrying about the next ride or where we were going to sleep. We were safely on the ship, and we would be moving for the next 10 hours or more to our destination of Africa.

Since leaving Florence two days earlier we had been under the pressure of making it to Trapani, Sicily in time for the ships departure deadline. In the past two days we had covered over 700 kilometers of Italy, with dozens of rides hitched, a train ride adventure, a few short bus rides, crossed the Straight of Messina, and then (with special thanks to "Mario") traveled the beautiful coastline of Sicily all the way to Trapani. It was a long, tough haul. But we had made it.

Several hours later we would be arriving at the Tunis port…In Tunisia…In Africa. Soon the real adventure would begin. We had experienced some adventurous, difficult and amazing times on the trip. But what we had experienced so far was nothing compared to what lay ahead of us. We had no idea what was in store for us…However, before we could set foot in Africa we had to make the long journey across the Mediterranean Sea. It proved to be an interesting and beneficial ship ride. After the ship had been at Sea for

STOWAWAYS ACROSS THE MEDITERRANEAN SEA

a few hours, no ship stewards had done any checking of tickets and John and I felt more comfortable moving about.

Also, we were hungry - very hungry…And dirty...And tired. We had slept very little the past two days, and had not eaten since having a little bread that morning in Messina. We also had not washed at all for over two days.

"Let's see what we can do to improve our situation." John said.

"Ok. Let's take a look around." I agreed.

"It's a big ship. There should be something around here."

We got up and started walking around the ship. It was now early evening. There were crowds of people scattered around the ship, filling the chairs and sitting in groups on the floor. There appeared to be very few, if any, other backpackers or fellow travelers. Many people were in traditional Arabic dress and seeme3d to be traders. After a lot of walking about, we made our way down to a lower deck to an area where there were some private berths for the 1st class passengers. We eventually came across a narrow corridor with small private rooms on both sides of the corridor. There were maybe a dozen rooms on that lower deck. The only thing is there didn't seem to be any passengers staying in the berths. It was very isolated, quiet and there was no one around.

"Dennis, check some of the doors. Go ahead. I'll be lookout."

After slowly opening a door, I looked inside and said, "This one's open. There's no-one here."

We checked several rooms and they were all empty. We decided to do something about that. After carefully looking around the corridor, we picked one room, opened the door, headed in, quickly shut the door behind us and made ourselves at home. It was small and a little cramped. There were two small beds, a little table, a chair, a small closet and a shower.

A shower! Not only a shower - but also towels. No soap and no hot water, but at the time we thought we were in paradise.

"This is great. It's been a long time." John said.

"Yeah. I've got a layer of dirt and dust I'd like to get rid of."

"I'll take the first shower. Lock the door and don't answer it if someone knocks."

"No problem." I replied. "You shower. I'll sleep. Don't use all the hot water"

"Huh? What hot water?"

◄ TRAVELIN' MAN ACROSS THE SAHARA AND BEYOND

After not showering or washing for about three days and after wearing basically the same clothes continually since the trip began, it was remarkably refreshing to have a shower. It was great to wash away if not all, at least some, of the dirt and grime. John and I took turns using the shower while the other rested and slept. I didn't know it at the time, but this was to be the last time on the trip that I would take a shower.

Actually, it would be the last time I even washed with water on the trip, except for once with cold water in a little washbasin. That was it for the rest of the trek across North Africa and back to England. The odd thing was that after I reached about the 5th day without showering or washing it didn't bother me at all. I didn't even notice it. If I didn't shower for 2-3 days I really felt it, but once I got past five days it was no big deal.

While using the ships private berth, John and I also took the opportunity to wash, as best we could, some of the clothes we weren't wearing. There wasn't much to wash. Like I said before, I didn't have a lot of clothes with me. Besides extra pairs of underwear and socks, I could wear all the clothes I had with me at one time. I wore a single pair of tan corduroy pants for the entire trip. (Later on during the trip my pants could stand on their own. Heck, they were so dirty and stiff they could probably have walked away on their own if they had a mind to).

I also had a couple of t-shirts, a single pair of shorts, one plaid shirt, a single sweater, a long, light windbreaker and my high school letter jacket. That was it. There were a couple of times on the trip, when I was cold, that I did wear all my clothes at once.

A couple of hours later, after taking a refreshing shower, sleeping and enjoying the benefits of the 1st class compartment's facilities, we decided to leave the birth and go back up with the 2nd and 3rd class passengers.

"We better not overstay our welcome and push our luck." I said.

"Yep, not only do we not have a 1st class compartment ticket, we don't have any ticket."

"You got that right."

"I guess were basically passing international waters as stowaways." John commented.

"We can't afford to get caught here."

"Let's head out while the going's good."

"Good idea."

STOWAWAYS ACROSS THE MEDITERRANEAN SEA

Now that we had taken care of our first two problems – being tired and dirty – we needed to take care of the third problem I mentioned. We were hungry, very hungry. Now that we had time to relax and were not on the road, the hunger really set in.

Usually on the trip there were many other things competing for my attention. Things such as being tired, or cold, or lost, or planning what to do next, or how to avoid some danger, or where to stay, or how to get somewhere, etc.. Being hungry was often way down on my lists of concerns. It didn't make it to the top very often. I usually didn't have much time to even notice it, let alone think about it. But now I had had plenty of time and I was noticing it and thinking about it. - Big time!

We walked through the ship and found a few little food counters that were selling some food. There wasn't really a restaurant on board that we came across. But even the little food stands were way out of our price range. We just couldn't afford it.

That was a tough part of traveling in my younger days – passing by all the different restaurants and markets with all kinds of delicious food and rarely being able to buy or eat any of it. Just looking into the restaurants and seeing all the people enjoying their food, but rarely actually tasting it myself. It took a great deal of discipline to not break down and buy some food I couldn't afford, but I never did.

However, there were some exceptions to that case, such as when I traveled behind the Iron Curtain and I traded my western currency (mostly good ol' US dollars) on the black market and made a small fortune. I did this in a few countries, particularly in Communist Poland and Czechoslovakia in 1984, prior to the fall of the 'Iron Curtain' in Eastern Europe.

Traveling behind the "Iron Curtain' at that time was like traveling in another world; a world of darkness, danger and intrigue. But by trading on the black-market, I had a small fortune to spend while I was there…and I mean spend. I had to spend the money in country before I left. Not only was the money worthless once I left the country, but it was also very dangerous for me to have it on me when I crossed the border, unless it was being kept for predicaments (bribes).

CHAPTER **10**

Out on the Open Sea with… the Fonz?

Back on the ship steaming to Tunisia - it was now about 7:00 PM. By now John had found and stopped off at a private area of the deck to catch a little sleep while I continued walking around the ship. A short while later while exploring the cavernous ship, I found a very big, open TV room on the second deck. It was a very wide room with one, small, beat-up, fuzzy, black-and-white TV up on a wall in the middle of the room. Everyone in the crowded room was intently watching the tiny screen.

As I walked into the room, I quickly glanced up at the screen. For a moment I thought I saw Fonzie speaking some kind of Arabic or maybe it was Italian. I wasn't sure. The TV was tiny, the screen was fuzzy, and the room was crowded, and I wasn't paying attention so I ignored it and kept moving to find a space to sit among the crowd.

When I finally did find a place to sit, I looked back up at the tiny screen again and I'll be darned, if I didn't think I saw Richie and Mr. Cunningham talking away in Arabic or maybe it was Italian. I still wasn't sure which. After a closer look, I was now sure that I was indeed seeing Fonzie and the Cunningham's talking away in Arabic or Italian - while a room full of mostly Tunisians and a few Italians were all listening intently between their loud bouts of laughter.

Amazed, I sat in the open TV room watching all these Arabs and Italians watching 'Happy Days" on the ship's TV while we slowly cut our way through the misty waters of the Mediterranean Sea on our way to Africa. I stayed a while, but the picture was fuzzy and they were speaking something I couldn't understand, so I soon left the crowded room to go and find John.

OUT ON THE OPEN SEA WITH... THE FONZ?

I found John in the same spot I had left him. He was sleeping, but I quickly woke him.

"Hey, John, you'll never believe who I just saw."

"Who?" John asked somewhat irritated after I abruptly woke him.

"I just saw the Fonz."

"The Fonz? What are you talking about? What would he be doing on this ship way out here?"

"No. I mean on TV. I just saw him on TV."

"TV. What TV? Your joking...Where's a TV out here in the middle of the Sea?"

"No, honest. There's an old black and white TV on the second deck. They were showing 'Happy Days' on it."

"You serious?" John asked, still thinking I was pulling his leg.

"Yeah. I swear it was the Fonz, Richie and everything. Just like at home...Only they were speaking Italian or Arabic. I'm not sure which."

"This I gotta see to believe." John said, still not believing me.

I led him through the ship to the big TV room where the antiquated TV was a still on. With the crowd, the fuzzy small screen and the odd language the Fonz and Cunningham's were speaking, it took a few moments for John to actually believe that it was 'Happy Days.'

But, finally, he nodded and said, "It's really the Fonz. Who wouldda believed it?"

It truly was an odd experience to see 'Happy Days', an iconic American TV show that I grew up watching in my home in Michigan, late one night on a remote ship out in the middle of the rolling Mediterranean Sea heading to Africa. The scene of this large room full of Tunisians out at sea on this rocking ship, listening and enjoying Fonzie was just so totally out of place then."

At that time there was very little communication or globalization. There was no internet, no videos, camcorders, cable TV, fax machines, no MP3's, cell phones, no ATM cash machines. Nothing of the kind. It was nothing like today where you have access to almost any media, information or communications from anywhere in the world at any time in one little phone.

Even in England when I was at Oxford University, it was a huge deal to see "The Muppets Show" from the US on Sunday nights. There were a very few other American shows, such as cop shows, but it was very limited and at special times.

◄ TRAVELIN' MAN ACROSS THE SAHARA AND BEYOND

I certainly never expected to see Fonzie out at sea on my ship to Africa. Nowadays you have access to more media, music, entertainment, communications and information from around the world in one little cell phone – Than we had access to in a year's time from any and all sources back then.

At that time, even in England some of my English friends had a distorted view of The States based on the limited number of American TV shows that were shown. At that time, the few American TV shows on British TV were mostly cop shows, such as "Banachek". Some of my British friends, on more than one occasion, asked me how many shoot-outs I had seen, and how many car chases I had been in. They assumed a shootout was a daily occurrence that happened on street corners all across towns in America on any given day. That's because on the American TV cop shows they saw - it was.

I know, myself, when I traveled to different countries I sometimes had a distorted view before visiting the country based on some limited information or media I had been exposed to.

After John finally believed me - that it was really the Fonz, we got up and left the crowded TV room.

"There's a beautiful night sky." I said, "Let's go up top and take a look and get some fresh sea breeze."

"OK, sounds good. I could use some fresh air."

We made our way to the top area, kind of above the upper deck. There were a few other backpackers already out there. They were the only other backpackers or travelers we had seen on the entire ship. All the other passengers looked like people heading home or some kind of traders with their many bags and sacks full of goods. We introduced ourselves to the small group. The other travelers were European and they were only going as far as Tunis, the port we would be landing at. They planned to stay for a few days in Tunis and then return on the same ship to Sicily later in the week.

John and I talked with them for a while and sat out under the beautiful night sky with the waves lapping at the hull of the ship. I really enjoyed that night on the ship out on the top deck, with the sea wind blowing and the clear, star-lit night sky; Knowing Africa was out over the distant horizon waiting to be explored.

It was a great feeling and I breathed deeply and took it all in. I was living my dreams and even though I was only 19 years old, I knew I was experiencing something special.

OUT ON THE OPEN SEA WITH... THE FONZ?

There were certain times on my travels or during my experiences overseas that I made a point to really bury deep in my memory some scene, or place, or person that was really special to me. Even at that young age, I had a very strong sense of my youth and a sense that some of the things I was seeing or experiencing were rare and unique, and that once this time passed they would be gone forever. That beautiful evening out in the rolling sea, on deck knowing that Africa was approaching over the distant water's edge was one of them.

That brings to mind another very special scene that is chiseled in my memory. It's a certain view at the university I was attending during the time of this trip. As I said I was attending Harlaxton University in Lincolnshire, England. I attended one year – my freshman year. Then the following two years I attended an overseas study course at Oxford University where I played rugby, so I lived and studied in England for 3 years.

Those 3 years were some of the most exceptional years of my life. I would go to university in England and just study, study and learn. I didn't like the idea of studying so much, but I loved learning and being challenged intellectually. Then as soon as the semester finished, I would take off on some rugged travel adventure somewhere across the globe until my money ran out. I would then catch a very cheap standby flight to the US, and return to my hometown of Birmingham to immediately go to work.

I would usually work 70-80 hours a week at Peabody's restaurant, where both John and I had worked during high school. I would be home maybe only 17 days or 22 days, but I would work every minute and save as much money as I could. While I was spending all those long hours working, in my mind I wasn't at work; I was visualizing the places I was going to travel, the people I was going to meet, the adventures I was going to have. I was completely focused on my dream.

Mr. Peabody and the Peabody family were very kind to me and my brother. They let me work as many hours as I wanted; busing tables, washing dishes, cooking, and cleaning the grills when the restaurant was closed.

My mom would always be there to pick me when I arrived back from overseas - no matter what the time or where I was flying in from - she would always be there for me. On many trips home my mom would pick me up at the airport after my long flight home from Europe, and I would go straight from the airport to Peabody's restaurant to start working to make money.

TRAVELIN' MAN ACROSS THE SAHARA AND BEYOND

I would then work and save money every moment I could while I was in Michigan.

I would then return to England for university and study and learn…then go on some travel adventure…then run out of money and fly home to work and save…then fly back to university to study and learn…then go on some travel adventure…then run out of money and fly home to work and save…then…

I did that for three years and traveled to over 30 countries before I was 21 years old. The money I made at Peabody's restaurant paid for every mile of my travels on all my trips. John and I worked, saved and paid for every dime of our travels. It was tough, but we were fortunate our parents paid for our university tuitions. It would have been really tough without that. I was blessed with wonderful parents who always backed me in pursuing my dreams. If I ever wanted to do something or travel somewhere, they would say 'Great. Work hard, save your money, plan it and do it. We're here to back you up and we'll be here if you need us.'

And Harlaxton was the most amazing place I've experienced in all of my travels. Even a little more so than studying at Oxford, or working for the US Congress on Capitol Hill, or any of the many sites and places I've seen on my travels throughout the world.

I had a wondrous year of study at Harlaxton, which is an overseas extension campus, previously affiliated with Stanford University and now affiliated with the University of Evansville.

When I was there, Harlaxton had about 150 students from all over the world. We all lived and studied together in the enchanting, mysterious, vast, ancient castle called Harlaxton Manor. The manor sets, majestically and mysteriously (especially at night), back on a hilltop a mile from a small country road near the small town of Grantham, England, out in the British countryside.

I have visited dozens and dozens of palaces, castles, towers, monuments and temples all over the world, but Harlaxton Manor is the most interesting and amazing building I've ever been to. It was built in 1842 by an eccentric (crazy?) earl named Gregory Gregory. In case you're wondering, I didn't just repeat myself. His name was Gregory Gregory.

I was told he built the Manor so that it had one more room and one more window than Beaver Castle. Gregory's archrival lived in 'Beaver Castle. On a clear day you could vaguely see Beaver Castle off in the great distance, as could Gregory in his day. I'm sure he took great pleasure in having his one extra room and window than his rival. Although I wonder how he could have known for sure, since the two buildings are massive and have hundreds of rooms and windows.

Gregory built Harlaxton Manor with hidden passageways, small parts of huge walls that moved and opened into little walkways between rooms, underground tunnels, secret ladders between the walls that led from one floor to another floor, hidden staircases, separate and sometimes secret servant quarters, and fake Roman ruins outside in the courtyard. That's to mention just a few of the wonders of the building.

Not only that but many of the vast rooms, hallways and stairways were of a totally different design, often strangely different. The architecture of the rooms were usually unrelated to the next, with all kinds of strange, beautiful, creative and startling artwork and designs using marble, wood, cedar, steel, etc..

Because of its mysterious, magnificent and sometimes intimidating appearance, it has been featured in several movies such as "The Ruling Class," starring Peter O'Toole about a nobleman who goes slowing insane. More recently "The Haunting" starring Owen Wilson and Catherine Zeta Jones was filmed there.

After living in that building for a year – I do believe it is haunted. I actually spent one night in the manor building entirely alone. I don't know of anyone else who has done that. I never heard of anyone staying there alone. I had a very scary, unsettling experience with the night porter earlier in that evening before he left at midnight.

When I attended Harlaxton about half the students were American and half were from various other countries all around the world. There were students from Turkey, Iran, Spain, England, Oman, Ghana, Morocco, South Africa, Jordan, and many more countries. We all lived together scattered in various rooms throughout the huge Manor. We also took our classes in the manor as well. Several of the students were from very prominent families in the Middle-East, Africa and elsewhere.

It was an incredible experience with all these students from so many different cultures mixed together, living in this enchanting castle out in the British countryside. I had so many remarkable and memorable experiences that year.

There was one view from the Manor that I've always remembered. As I said, I made a point of burning it in my memory. It's from a little balcony along the winding wooden staircase on the side of the manor from about the 3rd or 4th floor. It overlooks the side grounds and rolling hills in back of the manor. In the view are the fake Roman ruins that Gregory Gregory had built, with the green grass, water pond, statues and gently rolling British countryside in the background of the Manor grounds.

The balcony was off a winding wooden stairway next to my girlfriend's room, where I used to say good night. I spent countless nights looking out from that little balcony over the ruins and the enchanting grounds of Harlaxton Manor. I told myself then - that this was a special place and a special time and that I would always remembered that particular view…and I have.

Back on the ship as we made our way across the Mediterranean Sea, the water that night was a little rough. Rough enough for some rolling action of the ship, but not bad. It was just enough to let you know you were on a ship, and to add to the experience.

As the evening passed John and I stayed out on the open top deck for some time taking in the fresh sea breeze, the stars and sea water. It was a great feeling. After awhile, however, that old hunger I talked about earlier really came back. As I mentioned before, we were now clean and little rested, but, man, were we getting hungry. We still hadn't eaten since our light meal that morning and with nothing to be alert for or occupied with, the hunger really set in.

"Man, I'm hungry. Big time. We need to find something to eat." John said.

"You can say that again."

"I gotta get some food soon. You wanna take a look around? See what we can find."

"Yeah." I said, "There's gotta be something, somewhere on this ship. It's big enough. They've got to have food somewhere."

"We found the room and shower." John said. "Maybe we can find some food, too."

"Yeah. Our luck has been good on this ship. Let's see what we can find."

So we took off on another more detailed walk around the big ship to see what might turn up. After walking through the vast ship for some time, we came up through some deserted, back stairs on a lower deck, and came across a large kitchen gallery of some kind. I don't know if it was for the crew or for the passengers. We were walking up a small side stairway when

OUT ON THE OPEN SEA WITH... THE FONZ?

it just led us to the deserted kitchen gallery. There was a thinly barred door that appeared to be open leading into the large kitchen area.

"John, check the door. It looks open." I said nervously as he looked back and forth to see if anyone was around.

"Yeah. It's open." John said after pushing at the door and it swung open.

"Quick. Let's take a look around before anyone finds us here."

"OK. But we gotta hurry. We can't afford to get nailed here, especially with no ticket."

We hurried up the stairs and through the door and walked into the expansive kitchen. There were many rolls of bread in little plastic bowls sitting out on a table and there was no one around at all. It was as if the bread had been left out for us. (I know it wasn't but that's the impression we had, and it made it easier for what I was about to do.)

There was no other food out on the tables or in view, but across the room there were some huge refrigerators and food cabinets in the kitchen, that I'm sure were loaded with food. Even though we were starving, we didn't open or look in any of the cabinets or refrigerators. It didn't seem right. That might seem odd, considering on my travels I had snuck on trains and buses, traded "black market" for currency, slept in tractors and train stations, and was even a stowaway on the ship I was now traveling on.

But actually taking something that wasn't mine from a place I didn't belong didn't set well with me. It seemed different somehow from hiding on trains and using my wits and guts to get where I was going. Using my wits, and nerve, and doing what I had to do was part of the experience…Part of the challenge of traveling and making it on the road. It was a time-honored necessity of the road.

Taking food from a ship's kitchen gallery, however, seemed too much like plain old stealing – no matter what the circumstances. So I hesitated; something very unusual for me when I travel. As John walked around the kitchen, I stood there for few moments and looked around again. The bread was still just sitting there. Who was going to miss it? Right? It was just left out alone on the table?

While John looked around the kitchen, I picked up one of the small palm-size loaves. It was definitely fresh enough to eat. I finished hesitating. I grabbed about 6-7 little loaves and stuffed them under my shirt as John grabbed the remaining loaves, and we hustled out the kitchen gallery and back down the stairs to the main deck areas.

We now had some food and would be able to sleep the night without hunger problems. It filled my stomachache and tasted good. It made the remaining ship ride pass much more enjoyably, but it never set right with me. It was only a few dollars worth of bread. Really nothing. It was probably going to be thrown out - But I didn't know that. I've always kind of regretted that moment that I didn't stand taller.

I'm not sure why, but of all the things that happened on my travels, taking that bread is still something I look back on and feel like I didn't measure up. I've always remembered it. There were so many other extra-ordinary things that happened on my travels, and so many unusual, unique experiences I had, that I'm surprised I've even remembered that bread. It seemed like such a small thing. But although I never talked about it; I've always thought of it as a test of character that I failed.

I remember my father telling me when I was young, "Anyone can be honorable when people are watching…But the true test of a man's character is consistently doing what's right - including the small things - when no-one is watching."

My father lived by that and I've tried to live by that. What's always counted to me is what I see when I look in the mirror, not what everyone else thinks they see. I've always wanted to be able to look myself in the mirror and respect what I saw.

In this case I didn't…I thought I fell a little short.

CHAPTER 11

At Long Last Africa!

We spent a few hours sleeping on a lower deck and then later in the evening, went back up on to the top deck to watch for the African coast. It was late night when the Tunisian coastline vaguely came into view through the ocean mist. It was a moment of relief and anticipation.

I looked over at John and quietly said, "Hey, there it is. Africa. Do you believe it? We made it."

"Yeah, we did, didn't we?" John nodded.

"I can't believe it."

"It seems like it's been about a year since we left London, huh."

"Yeah. It's been, what, less than 10 days…but it sure seems like we've been on the road a lot longer."

"Now the <u>real</u> adventure begins." John said with anticipation.

"Absolutely. This is our time, man."

We had reached our goal. The objective we set back in London, when we took the walk in Piccadilly Circus, was finally before us. It had only been about 10 days since we made that fateful decision to go for it, but it seemed like a lifetime ago with all the difficult and extraordinary experiences we had had. But now, finally we had made it to Africa…

Well, almost…Before pulling into the Tunis harbor the ship stopped, however, and anchored off the coast. They were waiting for some reason before allowing everyone to depart from the ship, so we waited on the upper deck, dozing and chatting until the ship finally pulled anchor, lurched ahead and started moving again. It didn't take long for the ship to make its way into the harbor and dock.

◄ TRAVELIN' MAN ACROSS THE SAHARA AND BEYOND

After docking John and I, with the few other backpackers aboard, joined the masses of people climbing off the ship. We made our way into the large open customs building at the port. Most of the passengers were Tunisians returning home so there were not many people going through the foreigner's custom check line. A couple of the other backpackers went first and when one of them had his bag checked the custom official found something. He was immediately pulled from the line and urgently ushered with a grim soldier escort into a side room. I was glad I was not with him at the customs counter.

It was another one of those times I talked about where someone I was traveling with was taken away at a border crossing. I never found out why or what happened to him. I didn't see him again. When my turn came, my backpack was checked and cleared with no problem.

When John cleared through a few moments later, we headed out of the customs building with the other backpackers, minus the guy who was led away. The other backpackers were Europeans and didn't seem too bothered or concerned about one of their friends being detained or arrested. They had been traveling together for a while and a couple of them had started their trip together – Whereas John and I had just met them a few hours earlier on the ship.

Actually, they didn't seem to be too concerned about much of anything. They were reckless, lacking much judgment or respect for where they were or their situation.

When we walked out of the customs building they were laughing loudly, pushing and shoving their way through the crowds. There was a very small kind of open shuttle train outside the port building that led into the city of Tunis. The other backpackers we were with loudly jumped over the guardrail and noisily climbed on to the train. They were making loud, obnoxious comments about their surroundings and Tunisia, after only being in the country for a just a few minutes.

"Let's get away from these guys. They don't have much respect for anything." John said.

"Yeah, we should get some distance from these guys." I agreed. "Let's find some seats away from them."

I was always very careful who I traveled with, and who was around me. I met all kinds out on the road.

After taking the shuttle into Tunis, John and I moved away from the others and never saw them again. They didn't follow the same traveling code

John and I went by, and we made a point of putting some distance between them and us.

When the short train shuttle into Tunis, John and I spent some time walking about Tunis to check out the city. We felt somewhat cautious and very curious. Tunis had a very different look from anything I had experienced before. Gone was the majestic European architecture and ancient historic buildings. Tunis had a hot, dry, dusty feel to it with smaller, older buildings lining the streets with the unusual Arabic writing and styling. It was a big, busy city with several markets, shops and food stands with winding, narrow side streets full of lots of people out and about. The streets were dimly lit with street lights scattered about breaking up the darkness. Many of the people on the streets were in the traditional Arabic dress with the headdress, turbans and long robes. There was also a mixture of other Arab men wearing western style pants and shirts. I saw no other westerners on the streets, at least as far as I could recognize.

I immediately liked Tunis. It was uniquely different and a contrast to what we had seen crossing Europe. I loved the sense of experiencing something new and unknown. As John and I walked the streets, we stood out a great deal, particularly when we were carrying our backpacks. We got a lot of very intense stares.

After a little more walking down a crowded, dark Tunis city street, John said to me, "You notice we're getting a lot of attention around here."

"That's for sure. Everybody's staring at us…Are we doing something wrong?"

"I don't know." John answered.

"I hope not." I said, "We're pretty much outnumbered and isolated out here."

"No kidding. It's a little unnerving."

"Everybody seems friendly enough, though. A lot of smiles. I think they're just curious and surprised to see us."

There were, indeed, a lot of quizzical and friendly stares and looks. As we walked the streets, we were often approached in a friendly manner. We were quite an attraction for the local people. Later on in the trip when we got further into the Sahara, the reaction we got by the local people throughout the desert in Tunisia and Algeria was simply astounding. I've never experienced anything like it to such an extent…before or since.

It took some time making our way through the streets with all the Arabic writing but we eventually found a small money exchange shop that was open late and went in to change money. At the counter they asked for our passports and currency to change. When we put our US passports on the counter, there was quite a reaction from the bank teller and others in the shop. Everyone looked shocked, stayed frozen in place and just stared.

After John and I exchanged a few dollars for some Tunisian dinar, we walked back out onto the busy Tunis street and stopped at a little outdoor food stand for a bite to eat. It was good to eat something beside plain bread.

I liked the bread we had been eating – every country we had traveled to had delicious fresh bread. But it got old eating only bread every day. At the food stand we bought some kind of fried sandwich with several meats and many spices. It was very cheap and delicious. It cost about half a dollar for a meal's worth of food.

While we were in the little shop, Tunisian men kept coming in until there were about 8 or 9 of them crammed in the little shop, and they all crowded around us. They were very friendly and started talking to us and showing us things. They were laughing and seemed to really enjoy meeting us. The young guy making the sandwiches also gave us some free food - I think maybe because with the crowds we were attracting, we were good for business.

As soon as we finished eating our sandwiches, one of the Tunisian men named Keridin, who spoke a little English, asked John and me, "Please join us. We enjoy coffee together. Come."

After a quick look of agreement with me, John replied, "OK."

We walked with Keridin and some of his friends to a little outdoor coffee stand further down the road, where some small tables were set up out near the dusty street. Keridin was a slim, good-looking man of about 35, with a full beard covering his narrow face, bright eyes and a quick smile. Like some of his friends, he was wearing the long, traditional robes and a loose fitting turban.

We talked (as best we could) and laughed with Keridin and his friends for quite some time. I really enjoyed it. While we were sitting out by the road other men would come by smiling and greet us. Many would sit or stand, and stay and listen for a bit while Keridin roughly translated what was being said.

During the evening, I asked Keridin, "Is Christmas celebrated much in Tunisia?"

AT LONG LAST AFRICA!

He looked surprised by my question. It was actually quite a naive question considering Tunisia is an overwhelmingly Muslim country, which I didn't know. At this time I knew virtually nothing about Tunisia. Nothing at all, except that I thought it would be warm there.

"This will be my first Christmas away from home." I explained.

"Uhh…No. Christmas isn't much celebrated in Tunisia." Keridin politely answered, "But just the same, I wish you a pleasant day when Christmas day comes."

"Thank you." I replied.

Keridin was very polite and friendly as were his friends and the other men we met that evening.

Even though all the men were very friendly, being my first day in Tunisia I was on guard, as I usually was when I first arrived in an unfamiliar place and was meeting people on the road for the first time. It was that sharpened awareness and instinctive habit of evaluating my surroundings and the people around me to identify any potential danger or threats.

That night at that moment; John and I were very far from home, with very little money, with no way of contacting anyone for help, out late at night in a city we knew nothing about, with a group of about 10 men we had just met, and no family or anyone having a clue where we were. No-one even knew what continent we were in, let alone what city or country.

So it's a very vulnerable situation, as was much of the trip, and those safety instincts and habits kicked in big time. I was to find out, however, that the kindness, acceptance and friendship that we experienced that first night in Tunis was, for the most part, to continue and increase throughout the rest of our travels through the Muslim villages of the Sahara Desert across Tunisia and Algeria. Even though we were to encounter some extremely vulnerable and dangerous situations along the way, with a few notable exceptions, the people we met along our journey were incredibly kind to us.

Also, during that first night in Tunis and without really thinking about it, I started noticing something unusual about my surroundings. It was something that became much more distinctive to me later through the trip, as we got further into the Sahara Desert.

What I noticed was that there were just no women around. They were nowhere to be seen. That first evening in Tunis I thought maybe it was because we were out at night, or maybe because that area of the city was an area that women did not really go to, but I learned later that was not the reason. What I was just starting to experience was an entirely different culture...Muslim culture. I was soon to experience it at its most untouched, traditional and genuine form.

For the next couple of weeks and couple of thousand kilometers of desert travel through the unending Sahara I very rarely saw a woman and even then I only saw their eyes, as they were completely covered from the top of their head to the tips of their toes with the long white flowing gowns and head-dress.

I never spoke to a woman directly on the entire trek across the Sahara, with the exception of a single word I spoke to the mother of a Tunisian man we befriended, when I said 'hello' in the privacy of his home. She didn't speak back nor did she even look at me. On the entire trek there was also only one time I even made eye contact with a woman. It happened only once on a bumpy bus crossing the Sahara and even though it was only for a brief moment - it caused serious problems for us.

It was certainly a different and fascinating culture and the deeper into the Sahara I got, the more traditional the culture was. We met one man named Lahkdar, who told me his uncle had six wives; even though I had been told that by custom men were allowed to have 3 wives. I also met another man, who himself had 3 wives at his home.

It was like women didn't really exist in public, only in the privacy of a home. It was not until weeks later when we made it back up to the northern Algerian city of Oran along the Mediterranean Sea that I saw women in western clothes again and was able to speak to them. Being a red-blooded, 19 year-old American male, I can tell you after the desert, it was an incredible and enjoyable experience walking the streets that day with all the beautiful women in sight.

After spending time with Keridin and the other men at the little outdoor café, John and I bid them goodnight.

"We must go. Thank you for your company." John said.

"Yes. Thank you very much." I added.

"Yes. We must go now.' John repeated, "We need to leave early in the morning."

"Why?" Where you go in the morning?" Keridin asked, somewhat surprised.

"We are traveling on to Algeria." I answered.

"Algeria?" Keridin said, now very surprised. "Why do you go Algeria? Very few people go Algeria from here."

"We plan to cross Tunisia and travel through Algeria and then Morocco."

"Truly?" Keridin asked now startled. "How do you travel across Algeria and Morocco?"

"Ahh.. We don't know yet." I replied. "We're not really sure."

Actually, that was a major understatement. We didn't have the slightest clue how we were going to do it.

Keridin didn't respond, but gave us a very concerned look. He then spoke in Arabic to the Tunisian men grouped around us, explaining our plans. The men responded with murmurs and equally concerned looks, before politely bidding us goodnight. I wasn't sure what the reason was for their reaction.

John and I then went on our way and walked through the streets of Tunis to find a place to sleep. After quite a lot of tiring walking, on one of the side streets we eventually found a very cheap kind of hotel for the night. I say "kind of" hotel. It was a place to sleep but I wouldn't call it a hotel. It was a small two-floor building. The older, bearded Arab man inside seemed completely shocked to see two Americans arrive at his door, but like everyone else we had encountered that day, he was very friendly.

He led us to a small, box room with peeling paint. Inside the room were two sheets next to two mats on the floor. No beds. No chairs. Two broken, shutter windows that wouldn't close, and a single light bulb hanging by a loose wire from the ceiling with several other wires sticking out of it.

"Well, it's not exactly the Hilton, is it?" I whispered to John.

"Not even close. But it's a place to sleep."

"That's the truth. It sure beats sleeping out on the street or in some train station…It's not so bad."

"I've slept in many similar places in other countries."

"Me too." I replied. "You do what you gotta do."

We told the owner it would be fine and paid him for the room.

There was no sink or shower of any kind, so we couldn't wash at all. After taking a minute to get situated in the little room, there was nothing to do except sleep. However, as was my habit when I was on the road - before going to sleep I tried to make the room as secure as possible.

Anytime I stayed in hotels, pensions, hostels, boarding houses, etc, I always would check out the room and set up some kind of security system so that nobody could enter the room without waking me. It doesn't require much to do it. I never knew who else was staying in the hotel, who had keys to the room, or who was watching the room, etc. Staying in those kinds of very cheap rooms in out of the way places, you're often a target for getting ripped off, stolen from or worse. I've met many people it's happened to.

One of the easiest kinds of alarm systems I often set up; is to balance some kind of glass or glass ashtray on the door handle inside my room. Then place another glass, bottle, ashtray or something on the floor directly under the same inside door handle in the room... If anyone tries to enter your room, when they turn the door handle from outside the door - the bottle or glass will fall off the inside door handle, and smash into the glass or bottle on the floor inside your room. It makes a lot of noise. Nobody can even attempt to turn the outside door handle, let alone enter the room, without you knowing. It's a very simple but effective alarm.

Another thing I would sometimes do in an unsecured room is to just loosely crumple up a lot of newspaper and put it on the floor around the room, and around wherever I was sleeping. It's very difficult for someone to walk on it without making noise and warning you.

Also, as a habit when I first enter a hotel room I also always look under the bed, in the bathroom, closets, cabinets and in every part of the room before I close the room door behind me. I know a woman who was assaulted by a guy after she entered her hotel room in the US and went to use the bathroom. The guy had been hiding under her hotel room bed. (If you've been paying attention to this book, you'll remember the guy hiding under my seat in the train compartment in Frankfurt, Germany for three hours without my knowledge.)

I also always check any hotel room for any hidden compartments or sections of closets, walls that may move. A very crude scam that I came across more than once in out of the way places was the cabinet in my room contained a small, fake back wall. So when you put your wallet, passport, or valuables in the cabinet – the back wall could be pulled down from behind. A person in the next room can reach into the cabinet and take all your valuables without even entering your room. The back wall of the cabinet is then put back up, and you never know what happened to your stuff. I also came across that scam in a health club locker in Asia as well; the back of the locker had a fake wall and many people got ripped off and had no idea how it happened.

It only takes a couple of moments to set up an alarm system and to secure a room. It's a safety habit I always follow. It's just a simple necessity and one of the codes of the road.

AT LONG LAST AFRICA!

After taking a moment to secure the room, we tried to get as comfortable as possible. "It's cold and hard on this floor. Can you get that window shutter to close?" John asked me hopefully.

Trying to push it or jam it close, I frowned, "It's not closing. There's no way it's gonna close. Looks like we're gonna have some air conditioning all night - whether we want it or not. But I'll set up a temporary alarm for the window."

"That's a strong breeze blowing through. It's gonna be a cold night's sleep in here."

"Yeah and these sheets are pretty thin. They don't do much."

"Not much at all." John answered.

When I finished setting up a glass alarm for the window and with only the thin sheet for cover, I put on most of the clothes I had with me. The rest I threw over my sheet cover to try to keep warm. It wasn't much, but still it was better than sleeping outside or in some train station. At least we had a room. However, unfortunately for me, John fell asleep before I did, which meant once he fell asleep, not only was there a cold breeze blowing through the open window, but now it also sounded like a hurricane was blowing on the floor across from me.

As I mentioned before, my brother snores. Really snores…really loud. So I had a very uneasy sleep. It was also a cold sleep because all of the extra clothes I was using to cover myself ended up across the room scattered near my brother. Why is that you might ask?

Well, during the night as John was snoring and I couldn't sleep, I would throw something at him periodically during the night, such as a sock, a shoe, shirt, pen, jacket, etc. The reason? Each time I would throw something at him it would stir him and partially wake him up, and he would temporarily stop snoring. Then I would have to try and quickly fall asleep before he began snoring again. It was a race to see whether I would fall asleep first or he would begin snoring first. It was a race I almost always lost. It was a lot of pressure to try and fall asleep fast. Speed sleeping is not exactly something I ever trained for, but that didn't stop me from trying.

There were many a morning, over our different adventures traveling and also a summer when we lived together outside London in Southend-on-Sea when John would wake up with half of the room's furnishings and my items all over and around him. In most cases he would wake up totally refreshed with no memory of anything. Meanwhile, I would still be trying to get to sleep, feeling annoyed and very tired, with a sore throwing arm.

CHAPTER **12**

Into the Sahara …. Into the Unknown

The next morning we awoke early soon after the sun had risen…Or at least in John's case. In my case, there was nothing to wake up from since I never really went to sleep in the first place.

At any rate, we quickly made our way out to the quiet city street to get started on the road. It was shortly after sunrise and it looked to be a bright, sunny, clear morning. There were only a few people out and about at that early hour. We were looking to get an early start, and begin making our way into the Sahara and across Tunisia toward the Algerian border.

Our general plan (if you could call it that) was to head south into the Sahara, cross through Tunisia to the Algerian border, enter into Algeria and then head north out of the Sahara up through Algeria. We would then travel all the way across Algeria following the northern coastline along the Mediterranean Sea into Morocco. Then cross into Morocco and travel across Morocco. After that we would…we would…Well, we didn't really know. We had no plan.

We had never even discussed it, let alone planned for it. It may seem hard to believe, but we never once talked about our travel plans at all until we were already well across northern Africa, and then only vaguely.

When we actually finally did get around to talking about it, we vaguely thought maybe we could cross the Mediterranean Sea again (actually the Strait of Gibraltar), enter Spain and travel overland across Spain back up to France. Then travel all the way across France, and take a ship across the English Channel to England.

That would complete the roundtrip circle from England - through Europe to Africa - through northern Africa back to Europe - then through Europe

INTO THE SAHARA .... INTO THE UNKNOWN

back to England. That was the general idea. But then again, who knows? Maybe something else would turn up. We didn't plan anything for the trip at all. We just really didn't know.

To give you an idea of the extent of our planning and our situation, we didn't even have a map of northern Africa. Not a map of Tunisia. Not a map of Algeria. Not a map of Morocco. Nothing. When we had started the trip we had no maps at all. Later in Paris we were given maps of France and Italy, and also an old map of the northern tip of Africa. But I don't remember ever looking at the map of Africa.

The maps were now long gone. The maps of France and Italy had basically fallen apart from being crumpled up, held in the rain and snow, slept on, dropped in the mud, etc. They were lost or discarded somewhere early along the way in Europe.

The map of Northern Africa was never seen again after we left Paris. It was never used. We traveled almost 2000 kilometers through the Sahara and northern Africa all with no map...Actually that's not entirely true.

We did have something...The one thing we did have for directions or location was a very rough, hand-drawn map that I had made from looking at an old tattered map on the bathroom wall of a gas station in Italy. It was a map showing Italy in relation to northern Africa. Only the northern part of Tunisia, Algeria and Morocco were shown on the map.

While stopping to use a bathroom at a gas station as we were hitching across Italy, I had noticed the old map taped on the wall, so I took a minute and quickly tried to make a very rough copy of the tattered map. I drew it on the back of a torn piece of paper I found on the gas station floor. I tried to make a very rough outline, marking some of the roads, and towns running through the countries and Sahara by lines and X's. It was drawn by hand just by quickly eye-balling the map on the wall.

Also, the tattered map on the wall was in Italian so I couldn't write the names of the cities other than to mark their rough location with an X. There was no exact scale or measurements. I've picked up a lot of miscellaneous skills during my travels and over the years, unfortunately, map making by sight was not one of them.

My map was not very accurate at all, but actually, it later proved slightly helpful. Remember in the Sahara there were very few roads running through hundreds of kilometers of desert with only a few towns dotted along the desert landscape. We only came across a road for making a turn every few hundred kilometers or so, sometimes it was several hundred kilometers between turns.

It wasn't like there were a lot of different roads we had to be aware of. It was usually a choice of go straight ahead, or turn-around and go back the way we came or occasionally we would have the choice of turning north or going west. That was the extent of our road choices.

But even my hand drawn paper, with some lines for roads and pen marks designating towns, was of some limited help to us. At least, at times, it gave us some vague idea of our location and sense of direction.

My hand drawn map and my lack of accurate map drawing skills, however, later played a very important role in a fateful decision we made at the Tunisian-Algerian border. It was a decision that ended up dramatically changing the course and outcome of our trip, setting us off on an incredible adventure.

That morning, with our backpacks firmly on our backs as always, John and I headed out from the hotel through the streets of Tunis.

"Well, we gotta see what we can do to get out of Tunis and get on our way into the Sahara." John said. "Start making our way across Tunisia."

"Yeah." I answered. "Hopefully we can make some distance today."

"I wonder what were going to find out there - on our way." I said with a gleam of excitement.

"Who knows? We'll find out soon enough."

"Yes we will. We certainly will."

It was a bright, cool, early morning as we made our way across the city. I don't know what time it was, but the sun had barely risen over the horizon into the sky as we started making our way along the dusty, still streets. It was the first of several sunrises that I was to witness while crossing through northern Africa. It was truly a beautiful sunrise, even though this one was slightly obscured by the low buildings lining the streets.

Later, out in the middle of the Sahara Desert with nothing but endless desert sand surrounding me, I was to witness some starkly breathtaking sunrises as they broke over the morning horizon. As we continued along the street there was very little traffic and the streets were almost vacant, with only a few people out and about. They all pretty much stopped what they were doing and stared at us with curiosity as we walked past down the street. We walked and walked trying to find some kind of bus station or some form of transportation that could take us across Tunisia toward Algeria.

INTO THE SAHARA .... INTO THE UNKNOWN

After over an hour of walking through Tunis's winding streets, we finally came across what appeared to be a bus station of some sort. There were a few old buses parked out in a large, open area under a partial covering and a little station nearby, but there were no station workers or anyone around. It was still quite early in the morning, maybe about 6:00-7:00 AM.

With no-one around, we found a place in the sun near the small building, put down our backpacks, leaned back and waited.

"We might as well wait until they open up." I said.

"If they open up…"

"Yeah. Hopefully this is a bus station."

"Kinda hard to tell out here." I said looking around. "Do you have any idea where we need to head? The name of any city in the direction of Algeria?" I asked.

"Don't have a clue." John said, shaking his head. "How about you?"

"We gotta head west and south. That's all I know." I replied.

"Do you still have that map you drew in the gas station in Italy?" John asked me.

"I think it's in my backpack somewhere. I don't know how much good it will do, though."

"It's better than nothing."

"I'm not so sure about that," I said as I dug through my backpack looking for it. "It should be here somewhere I think."

The paper I had written the rough map on was wrinkled and dirty, with smudge marks on it. But I still had it.

"Yeah. Here it is. I got it." I said.

"Take a look."

Looking at the wrinkled paper, I said. "It's not much help. It's just some lines with X marks for towns. As best I can tell…There's several towns between here and the Algerian border. But no names."

"No names? That's not much help."

"The map I copied it from was in Italian, you know?"

"Yep, I know. How about the distance to the Algerian border from here?"

"I don't know. Maybe 400 or 500 kilometers…Maybe."

"Maybe?"

"Yeah. Maybe. Ya know, I drew this thing really fast just by eyeballing the map on the wall."

"I know…I was just wondering if you actually had your eyes open at the time." John said with a grin.

◄ TRAVELIN' MAN ACROSS THE SAHARA AND BEYOND

We waited and dozed awhile as the sun began to rise and the cool early morning warmed into daytime. Later a few men dressed in robes and turbans came by and started milling about, staring at us intensely. Then someone opened the little bus station office. We walked over and tried to ask for bus tickets south out of Tunis into the Sahara, but with little success. We didn't know the name of any city or town in that direction that we could use as a destination point, so it was very difficult explaining where we needed to go.

Actually to be completely honest; with the exception of Tunis, the city I was in, I didn't know the name of a single Tunisian city or town. I also didn't know the name of any Algerian city.

The only cities in northern Africa I had even heard of were two cities in Morocco. One was Casablanca, from one of my favorite movies. The other city was Tangiers, which is where one of the students from Harlaxton University was from. That was it. That was the total extent of my knowledge of northern Africa. As we prepared that morning to leave Tunis, it was totally unknown territory that we were heading into. We had no idea what lay ahead of us, how far we had to travel or what to expect.

I knew nothing of northern Africa. Nothing of Tunisia, or Algeria, or Morocco or of the Sahara Desert. No idea of the size, distances or culture. Nothing. Nothing, except I expected there would be a lot of sand. No idea of distance or where things laid or what came next. I didn't know what the people would be like, their religion (Muslim) or language (Arabic with some French also). I couldn't visualize the size or shape of the country, the landscape or countryside.

Nothing except for a few squiggly lines on a sheet of paper from the hand drawing I had made in Italy.

As I said, I loved that sense of discovery and exploration. Of getting lost out in the world and traveling into the unknown, and that's definitely where I was heading now... Into the unknown.

Soon several men, mostly wearing the long traditional robes, wandered over to see what was happening with the strangers. Eventually we had a big friendly crowd of men all trying to understand and help us. It took quite a while but eventually they understood what we needed.

We were told (not really told but via body language and drawings it was explained to us) that we could take a bus that would be leaving in about two

INTO THE SAHARA .... INTO THE UNKNOWN

or three hours. The time didn't seem to be to an exact sort of thing – more like a estimation.

Like in a lot of out-of-the-way places I traveled, schedules were not exactly a definite thing. They seem to depend on a lot of factors; such as someone's mood, the weather, the condition of the vehicle or the condition of the person driving the vehicle that particular day.

So we paid the equivalent of a few dollars and bought our tickets. We had our tickets - But we weren't exactly sure where the tickets would take us.

Looking at the ticket, John said, "As best I can tell, these tickets should take us where we need to go."

"Yeah. But where's that?" I asked.

"Where's what?"

"Where is it we need to go?"

After a pause, John shrugged, "That's a good question."

"Did you recognize any of the names or towns those guys said?" I asked.

"No. Not a one. How about you?"

"No. Nothing." I answered. "I didn't understand too much of anything that they were saying."

"I don't think they understood too much of what we said either."

"They sure were friendly and helpful though."

"That's for sure. A lot of very kind people here." John said.

"As long as the bus takes us south and west, or one or the other, we should be OK."

"I guess so." John agreed. "We'll find out when we get there."

"Hey, we've got some time to kill before our bus leaves in 'two or three hours', we might as well get some food." John continued, "Who knows when we'll have a chance to eat again."

"Sounds good."

So we headed out to find some food, walking around the area near the bus station through the narrow side streets, just as many shops were now beginning to open up and the city was coming to life. We walked quite a bit but didn't see any food shops, at least as best we could tell. We did, though, see a man with a large, wooden cart being pulled by a donkey. On the cart were stacks of fresh bread. We walked up to the rough-looking, robed, bearded man as he gave a quick look of surprise, and then broke into a wide smile at the sight of two young foreign travelers.

We made gestures about buying and eating the bread from his cart. He seemed to understand as he reached over and took out two big chunks (loaves) of the fresh bread and gave it to us. Before I could pay him, while I was reaching into my chained wallet, the man smiled and started on his way with the donkey pulling the cart. He never looked back.

He misunderstood that we were asking for him to give us some bread, and without a seconds hesitation he gave it to us. Not only did he give it to us, but he gave it to us with a smile.

Later on during this trip I was told by some Bedouin men we met out in the desert, that there is a strong tradition or custom among the Arab people who live in the desert – any request made cannot be denied. If another traveler or person makes a request for water, food, shelter or any kind of assistance, the request cannot be denied. I was told that because of the harsh and dangerous desert conditions that this custom was always adhered to since assistance was sometimes critical for survival in the desert. I don't know if what I was told was true, but based on my own limited experience, this certainly seemed to be the case.

I was also told to be careful about unintentionally making a request of someone because they would feel a great obligation to fulfill it…No matter what.

My brother John told me a story somewhat related to this in which he unintentionally made a request he didn't really intend. It was when he was traveling in Afghanistan a short time prior to this current trip. This is long before the newly elected Karzai government, before the Taliban, and even just prior to the Soviet invasion, which occurred on Christmas morning of 1979.

I was traveling in Turkey the day the Soviets invaded Afghanistan. The actual bus I ended up taking out of Turkey, the infamous 'Magic Bus', had previously passed through Afghanistan just 3 days before the invasion.

A year prior to the Soviet invasion when John was in the mountains of Afghanistan, he told me he met a tough Afghan man who had a very long, curved, beautiful dagger he was wearing in his belt robe. It was well over a foot long and very exquisite. John asked the man if he could see the dagger and hold it just for a minute.

The man said, "Sorry, no"

John asked again, "Please could I just take a look and hold it?"

The man again politely refused.

But John was somewhat persistent and asked again, "Can I please just take a look at it for a moment?"

INTO THE SAHARA .... INTO THE UNKNOWN

So the Afghan mountain man reluctantly complied.

But first before handing the long dagger to John, he pulled it out of his belt and held it in his right hand. He then pulled the robed sleeve up over his left arm, exposing his forearm. Next, he took the dagger and made a slice on his forearm, which caused bleeding. Then with no expression or explanation, he turned the blade around and carefully gave the dagger handle to a stunned John.

Later, John found out that the man was some kind of warrior and he could only draw his blade, if he was going to draw blood. To draw his blade, he <u>must</u> draw blood. His enemy's blood, of course. But in this case there was no enemy. So to comply with John's request while still honoring his own warrior code, he had to either draw John's blood or his own blood. Fortunately for John, he drew his own blood. As I said it's important to be careful about what requests you make on the road.

After eating our bread, John and I wandered back to the bus station to see about our bus. It wasn't leaving yet, so we waited. Nearby we saw some men sitting at a small table enthusiastically playing some kind of games on a board with small rocks. I didn't understand the game, but the men really enjoyed it. I was to see the men playing that same game often in the villages through the desert. I never did play that game with the local men I met, but John and I did have a lot fun playing cards along the way.

Finally, a man signaled that our bus was ready to board. We were directed to a dented bus that several Tunisian men were boarding.

"Well it's time to move. Let's go." John said.

"OK. Let's go." I said as he picked up his backpack.

"Hopefully, this bus will take us where we need to go."

"Yeah, hopefully…It would probably help, though, if we knew where we needed to go."

"It couldn't hurt." John said with a grin, "But we'll find out soon enough."

"One thing's for sure – the bus won't be heading north. It can't cross the Mediterranean. So as long as we head south or west ... and not east we should be OK."

"Two out of three chances aren't bad." John said.

We climbed on the bus and soon it pulled out. There were about a dozen others on the bus that morning, only men, mostly bearded men, with sun creased faces many wearing the long flowing gowns and turbans on their heads. Many of them were carrying sacks or bags.

TRAVELIN' MAN ACROSS THE SAHARA AND BEYOND

John and I found some seats near the center of the bus and set our backpacks next to our feet in front of us. All of the men on the bus stared at us, and seemed very surprised to see two young foreign travelers on their bus, but the stares were mostly the same friendly kind we had been experiencing since we arrived in Tunisia.

We rode the bus through the streets of Tunis for some time making a couple more stops to pick up a few more people before leaving the city and getting out into the open, endless desert. At first it was just partial desert with a few older buildings and remnants of the city in sight.

But after some time, we left any signs of civilization behind and we entered the northern tip of the Sahara. As we rode on the bus, the desert just opened up and totally enclosed us on all sides. The vast endless, rolling waves of sand became all-encompassing, surrounding us in all directions; nothing but vast, seemingly endless, rolling desert sand for as far as I could see. It was a majestic and intimidating sight.

We were following the single road which was nothing more than a thin, single strip of pavement winding endlessly through the desert. The pavement seemed to be just laid down in the middle of nowhere out in the desert sand with no other markings or signs of any kind on the road or alongside it. From a short distance away the road just disappeared and faded in with the sand. You wouldn't even know it was there unless you were almost right on top of it.

As we were riding on the bus through the desert that first day, and also on other days, the bus would very occasionally make an abrupt stop along the way. There were very few other cars and no people, nothing but desert... and vast emptiness.

That first day, the bus just unexpectedly stopped along the empty, desert road out in the middle of nowhere. The bus driver didn't pull over to the side of the road. There was no need. There were no cars to be seen anywhere.

An older bearded, robed man with a face darkly marked by the sun carrying a sack over his shoulder and holding a walking stick, stood up and slowly got off the bus. The bus then started up and pulled way as the man started slowly walking out into the desert sand.

"John, did you see that guy?" I said, looking back out the bus window at the man as he continued walking straight out into the desert away from the road.

"Yeah, where the heck is he going?"

INTO THE SAHARA .... INTO THE UNKNOWN

"I have no idea." I replied. "We're miles and miles from any civilization or town."

"Yeah, there's nothing out there."

We both stayed turned in our seat, looking back at the man, amazed, as he continued walking further and further straight out into the Sahara. His form becoming smaller and smaller until he just faded into the endless desert sand landscape and disappeared.

"Man, there's nothing out here. There's nothing but endless desert in every direction." I said astonished, "What's he doing? How's he going to survive?"

"I have no idea." John replied.

We never did find out…Another mystery of the road.

After over an hour on the bus in the desert, we came into a town. It was the first sign of civilization we had seen since entering the Sahara. It wasn't much, just a little speck of a town surrounded by the vast desert, really a little desert village oasis.

The village consisted of a few dusty, dirt streets, lined with narrow, single-level, white clay homes and little shops, and there was a little well in the town center. At the back of the little village a trickle of a stream snaked past, lined with a few bushes, trees and some sandy vegetation. The few bushes and trees near the stream provided the only color on the barren desert landscape. Most of the small villages dotted along the desert, seemed to be built along a little stream or oasis.

For the next several days in the Sahara, not only did we rarely see any women, but we almost never saw any bright colors. All we ever saw around us was the windswept brown and gray colors of the desert sand and flowing robes.

When we drove into the little village the bus pulled up and made a short stop. While a few of the men got off the bus, an older, grey bearded man with a woman accompanying him climbed up on the bus. The woman was wearing the full hajib gown and headdress, covering her face. Like usual she was completely covered and I couldn't tell if she was 16 years old or 60. She was the first woman to enter the bus. She sat next to the older, stern-looking, bearded man in the seat directly across the aisle from me in the same row of seats.

Just before the bus pulled out two other young men hopped on. One was a young, dark, good-looking guy with a bright friendly smile. He was wearing western style pants and a jacket. He sat in the seat directly in front of John and me. His friend, who was wearing a robe and turban sat with him.

Soon the bus pulled out and headed back out into the Sahara. Within a few minutes the bus left the small town far behind and we were back out into the endless rolling sand. As we rode along the single strip of road, the ride got a little bumpy, and the bus was really old and the seats did not have much cushion so it was quite rough.

During the bumpy ride, I noticed the woman sitting in the seat across the aisle from me shyly looking over at me a few times. After hitting one bump in the road her headdress fell from her face, and I could see her face for a moment. I was surprised to see that she was a beautiful, young woman with very refined features and black hair. A short time later she looked over at me again and I looked directly at her, smiled and gave a little wave. I was just being friendly…Big mistake.

After I did that, the mood on the bus suddenly changed quite dramatically. Gone were the friendly stares and curiosity. All the men stopped what they were doing, looked at the young woman and then looked at me. They continued glaring at me in a serious, offended manner. The mood on the bus had suddenly changed from one of friendliness to open hostility.

The men now began speaking in hushed conversations, as they occasionally glared over at me. I now felt very uncomfortable and vulnerable. We were out in the middle of the desert, on some bus, without a clue where we were, sitting with a group of about 20 Muslim men, who now appeared very hostile toward me.

After a few minutes of hushed conversations among the men, the bus suddenly stopped dead in its tracks in the middle of the road. All the men on the bus abruptly stood up and stormed off the bus. John and I, along with the young girl, were the only ones left on the bus as the men gathered outside in front of the bus on the road

"Man, whattda ya think is going on out there?" I asked John.

"I have no idea. But they seem pretty teed off about something."

"No kidding."

"From the looks of it. They seem to be angry at you." John said looking over at me with concern.

"Yeah. I kind a picked up on that. What did I do?"

"It mustta been because you waved at that girl." John said, as he discreetly pointed toward the girl in the seat down the isle from me.

"It was only a little wave."

"Doesn't take much with you."

"Whatta you mean?"

"Your whole life, there's always been a girl. Why should the Sahara be any different?" John said with a nervous grin.

From my seat, looking out the front window of the bus, I could see that several of the men were having a serious, agitated discussion. They talked for some time while glancing back at me. As they continued talking, I became more concerned about what they were discussing, and more importantly, what they might do.

The group of men heatedly talked for some time before they finally trudged back on the bus, took their seats and sat in silence. Several of the men looked at me sternly for a few tense minutes, and then eventually went back to their business and the tension slowly faded while the bus headed on its way through the Sahara. I didn't find out what had occurred out in the road among the men until later.

What I found out later from Muhammad, the young guy who sat in front of us, was that by smiling and waving at the girl directly, I had made a great offence against her father, who was with her. I had also indirectly offended every man on the bus, since I had violated their social customs.

I was told that in their culture men and women did not make contact or communicate with each other directly. If a man wanted to speak to a woman, he would only speak to her through the woman' husband or father or brother...Not directly, especially an unknown stranger such as myself.

When I had waved and smiled at the young girl sitting across from me, I had offended all the men on the bus. After a brief discussion they stopped the bus so all the men could get off the bus to decide as a group what should be done with me. Muhammad said that after some discussion, it was decided that I did not mean to offend and that my action was one of ignorance, not one of contempt. So it was decided to let it pass and not take any action... Lucky for me.

As we bumped along the desert road, the young guy who was seated in front of us turned around again and continued communicating with John and me. We found out his name was Muhammad Adi...a great guy. He was a good looking, slim, dark skinned guy with thick black hair, and stood a few inches shorter than myself. He had a bright, friendly smile and a gracious manner, and wore western style clothes. He continued talking to us.

Well, not really talking…but communicating with a combination of body language, gestures, French (Tunisia and Algeria are former French colonies and French was widely spoken), a little broken English and drawings. For most of the trip that was the combined method of communication.

Muhammad invited us to get off the bus at his village, which he explained was the next stop along the way.

I turned and asked John" Whatta you think? Should we get off with these guys?"

"Man, I don't know. The nearest town is miles and miles away. We're really out here in the middle of the desert. And we've already paid for the bus tickets to take us further on our way."

"It might be interesting though."

"Yep. True. And Muhammad seems like a good guy."

As John and I continued discussing what to do, Muhammad could see our indecision. He started explaining that he could arrange a place for us to sleep at a hotel, and that the people of his village would be very happy to have us stay. (That turned out to be an incredible understatement).

He then also communicated that John and I could stay at his village for free. Once we heard that, it closed the deal.

"OK. Let's do it." I said to John.

"Yep. Let's do it."

We looked at Muhammad and gestured 'Yes"

Muhammad smiled back brightly and nodded, as we made our way down the open road to his village, not quite sure what to expect. Stopping in the little village of Habjib, Tunisia turned out to be a great decision, and for me one of the highlights of the trip.

Dennis on the road in Southern France On the trip we traveled by hitching, walking, sneaking on trains; and by bus, jeep, tractor and as stowaways on a ship across the Mediterranean Sea.

Brothers Dennis and John on ship crossing Strait of Messina from Italy to Sicily.

*Habjib, Tunisia
Long lost brothers - Muhammad, Dennis, Slah, Mohsloh and 'village haircutter'
We were treated with great friendship & kindness in the Muslim villages of the Sahara*

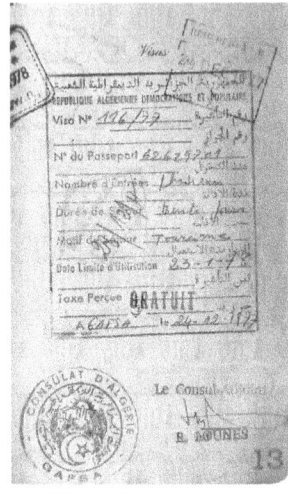

Tunis, Tunisia - Dennis holding daily meal of bread.

Dennis' passport visa for Algeria

Dennis at market in Gafsa, Tunisia.
The Muslim culture was very traditional in the Sahara. We never spoke a single word to any woman for over two weeks while traveling across the Sahara.

Boucherka, Tunisia
At remote town near Tunisia Algeria border. Soon to make first attempt to cross border.

"No Man's Land" - John walking to Algeria border post from Tunisia.
The desolate Tunisia-Algeria border crossing was out in the middle of the Sahara.
The nearest town on Algerian side turned out to be 80 kilometers away.

The Sahara
Dennis in Lahkdar's jeep that had no floor. Lahkdar was mechanic. His job was to follow a supply truck across the Sahara and fix it if it had problem. There was no emergency service... It was make it to the next town or abandon the vehicle.

CHAPTER **13**

Habjib, Tunisia: Long Lost Brothers

As our bus came over a ridge in the vast desert, a small but wide-spread village appeared as a blur out in the distance on the horizon. It was a little oasis that seemed to be out in the middle of nowhere. It was Habjib, Tunisia.

When we pulled up into the village along the single road connecting the village to the outside world, I could make out several single level, white, clay buildings along a distinctive white wall that surrounded the back part of the village with some trees and vegetation hugging the wall. All the solid, well-built buildings were one level. There were no two-floor buildings anywhere to be seen. The white wall running along a large area of the village, as well as many of the buildings, were very well maintained and had a distinct, white color that stood out against the mostly gray-brown of the desert sand and landscape.

Habjib had a few swirling, dirt streets leading into the dry, windswept but active village. I could also see up on a ridge at the rear of the village an oasis area with desert trees and sandy vegetation spreading out for several hundred meters down a ridge into a low laying valley. Cutting through the oasis was a narrow, trickle of a stream. At the end of the extended area of trees and vegetation, the Sahara desert once again harshly met up against the village, but not so much with desert sand. It was more of a hard, rocky desert surface - rather than the hills of endless sand I had mostly seen before.

During the course of my travels through the northern tip of the Sahara, I was to see all different types of desert. Some areas of the desert were like huge, endless rolling waves of fine brown sand that had an awe inspiring beauty to them. That was the image I had of the Sahara before I traveled there. It reminded me of being out in the middle of a sea of gigantic waves with no land in sight – but instead of being an ocean of moving waves of sea-water, it was an ocean of rolling waves of sand....

Other areas of the desert were of a barren, dead-flat, rocky surface that stretched out in an absolute flat line in every direction without the slightest change in elevation. It appeared like the entire earth's surface was one long, flat, rock surface with small, hard-edged stones carelessly scattered throughout it. The dead flat desert seemed to end at some point in the distant horizon with a complete drop-off, as though that's where the world ended. It reminded me of what I imagined areas of the moon's surface to be like.

The desert surrounding Habjib was mostly hard rock but not so flat. There were many red, rocky hills jutting up in the distance and scattered across the horizon. It gave off the impression of a harsh and dangerous beauty.

After the bus came to a stop on the outskirt of Habjib, Muhammad gestured to follow him and his friend Abassi off the bus. So we did. John and I followed Muhammad and Abassi into the village as the sand blew across on the wind. No-one else got off the bus besides us four.

John and I were out here on our own. We had just met Muhammad a couple of hours earlier on the bus, and now we were following him off into this isolated village somewhere in the Sahara. We had no idea what we were going to find.

What we did soon find was a fascinating, friendly village of people who treated us like we were their long-lost brothers returning home. I've never experienced such a welcome.

As we started walking with Muhammad into the village, at first a few people and soon a growing crowd of villagers started gathering around us, including several kids and some young men in western type clothes, as well as older men in the long traditional robes and headdresses. Their reaction was one of instant and total acceptance, kindness, curiosity, and friendship. There was not the slightest sense of hesitation or wariness. The crowd of villagers shook our hands, touched our sleeves, waved and smiled at us.

Muhammad made some introductions to various people and we smiled and said hello. By the time we made it across a portion of the village, I had shook hands and been welcomed to Habjib by a couple dozen people. They reacted to our every gesture and movement with incredible excitement.

I turned and looked at John through the crowds and said, "Do you believe this?"

"It's quite a reaction, isn't it?"

HABJIB, TUNISIA: LONG LOST BROTHERS

"Man, I feel like Elvis." I said smiling.

With the crowd following us, we walked across the dirt village square to a little outdoor place, a kind of restaurant, with several wooden tables set up by the street. The crowd followed our every move. When we sat down with Muhammad at a table, everyone who could manage it also scrambled to any open seat and sat down at the same time.

One of the guys we were introduced to at the table was a short, stocky guy named Slah. He looked to be in his early 20's, dark skinned, and was clean shaven, with a round, friendly face that was continually framed by a wide smile.

He spoke to John and me in English, "Hello. My name Slah. Nice to meet you."

Slah was the only person in the village who knew some English. He only spoke a little English, but at least we could communicate with him using some limited language. Not just gestures, body language, pictures and drawings, like we had been doing for most of the trip.

Slah was informally appointed our personal translator for our stay in Habjeb. Whenever we needed to know something or we couldn't get across what we wanted to know or say, Slah was called over. We became good friends with him. He was a really good guy.

We sat with Muhammad, Slah, Abassi and the on-looking crowd for a time and ate a meal of couscous, which I liked very much. It was very delicious and a tasty change from our usual meal of plain fresh bread. It was also very cheap, costing about $1. This was my first meal of many of couscous. It was a kind of stew with some kind of meat (I assumed), eaten with bread.

Couscous was widely available and it became our main meal during much of the rest of the trip, along with our usual meal of just fresh bread and Coca-Cola. I really liked the taste of couscous, but I soon learned that it had deadly effects on me. It gave me the runs…which I had for the next several days. That made for some difficult and awkward experiences for me, including a hilarious situation in a truck that gave John and me a ride a few days later. My problem with the runs was compounded by the fact that we hadn't had the use of a "real" toilet for the past several days, and we never would for the rest of the trip.

On top of that we also had had no access to a sink, let alone a bathtub or shower, for cleaning. And we also never would for the rest of the trip. For the entire length of the trip since leaving Florence, Italy - there was only one time I washed and that was with cold water and no soap. The only exception was the quick wash we stole on the ship across the Mediterranean Sea.

After our meal of couscous and a drink of Coca-Cola, Muhammad and his friend Abbassi told us they would take us to our hotel where we could stay, so John and I casually stood up getting ready to go. As soon as we did, everyone else around us stood up immediately as well. They all smiled and walked a short ways to say good bye.

We were then taken to our "hotel" room, which was a ways across the same swirling sand, village square. It was a small, single room attached to one of the long, low buildings kind of surrounding the central, dirt square in the middle of town. The single room was Spartan with a hard floor, some blankets and a very basic toilet with no seat. (a nice hole in the ground). There was no washbasin or water in the room. The door to the room opened right out onto the dusty street in the middle of the town square.

Muhammad called it a "hotel, but it certainly didn't seem to be a hotel in any way, shape or form. I think Muhammad called it a hotel to make us feel more comfortable about it. But I tend to believe it may have been one of the villager's small homes or rooms. I don't know for sure. We we're never charged for the room and when we later offered to pay for the room, no-one ever accepted any payment from us.

After thanking and saying farewell to Muhammad and Abassi, John and I spent some time getting set up in our little room.

"Well, it's not exactly the Ritz but it's a place to stay." John said.

"Yeah. It was nice of Muhammad to arrange the room for us. He was true to his word. I'm glad we got off the bus with him."

"Me, too. The people here are incredibly friendly. I can't believe how excited everyone seemed to see us."

"No kidding.' I said. "It was an amazing reaction out there wasn't it."

"I think we must be the first travelers who've passed through here in a long, long time."

"I bet you got that right. Based on their reactions, we're probably the first Americans to hit this town in years, if ever."

As we sat in the little room I wrote some in my journal, and we both wrote out some postcards. The postcards were sent the next day. I have the postcards yet today. My mother wisely saved them and gave them to me years later. The postcards were our first message home from Africa and our first message home since we were in Florence, Italy. What I mean is...

HABJIB, TUNISIA: LONG LOST BROTHERS

they would be our first message home when they reached America about 15 days later. The only other time we were able to send a message home was on Christmas day from Algeria, also only postcards.

Fifteen days was the quickest contact we could make with home. We tried at different points along the way to make a reservation at a phone bank and to place an international call home. We tried a few times. It was very difficult, time-consuming, and cost us money we couldn't afford. We <u>never</u> succeeded in getting a single call made.

Through much of this trip we were definitely "lost" and completely out of touch out in the world. Literally. It was a true travel adventure into the unknown. No family or friends had any idea where we were, and we had no way of telling them or contacting them. Things were different 30 years ago.

Sometime later in the early evening, Muhammad and Slah came to our room to get us. They took us a ways down the street to a large room in one of the single level clay buildings in the dirt town square - For some evening entertainment. It was some type of restaurant or meeting room where the men, always only men, played cards, dominoes and that other board game with rocks that I never did quite figure out. It was the only place open in the evening in the village. And even it closed down at 8:00PM.

As we walked across the dusty, dark, street to the café, we were warmly greeted by several men we had met earlier during the day. They all came hurriedly right up to us to say hello and wish us well, also to pay their respects to Muhammad. It had become obvious that Muhammad was very respected and well-liked in his village. The people of the village, even men much older, showed him a lot of respect.

After slowly making it across the village square, John and I walked in to the café- meeting room. It created quite a commotion. It was a large, open, well lit room with several older, bearded men playing cards, seated at various tables scattered about the room. As usual, there was not a woman in sight.

We were quickly given seats at a table and most of the other men in the room got up to come over and excitedly gathered around our table to watch. With Muhammad and Slah standing by, three Tunisian men sitting at the table showed us a card game to play and invited us to play with them. The other men at the table and many of the other men in the room were older; bearded, with rugged, sun streaked skin and were wearing the flowing gowns and turbans – In striking contrast to the appearance of Muhammad and Slah, who were younger, basically clean shaven and wearing western style clothes.

After learning by example and with a few helpful hints from Slah, we got the basic gist of the game and we started to play a game with them. We ended up playing several games with them. It was quite the event.

As we were playing, the crowds around the table grew until the entire room, as well as out front on the street, were filled with men jostling and trying to catch a glimpse of what was going on with the two American strangers who had wandered into their way-off the beaten track village. Every time we played a card the crowd reacted with either hoots and friendly jeering, or pats on the backs and cheers depending on how well the play was perceived to be. As John was sitting with his back to the open room with the crowd of men around him, several of them excitedly tried to coach and give advice to John as he was making card plays. It was a great time.

When we finished playing a few games, which my brother and I lost, John then began showing the crowd some card tricks. The crowd of men got the biggest kick out of it.

At 8:00PM the room was closing and we were ushered out. When John and I stood to leave almost all the men in the room did likewise and as we walked outside into the dark, empty, street, we were followed by everyone else. The entire village shut down at 8:00 PM and everything was dead quiet, with just a few limited lights here and there casting shadows breaking up the darkness.

When we were outside, many of the men waved goodnight or quickly shook our hands and headed to their homes. Muhammad and Slah also said *'shocurum Saheb'* (goodnight friend) and left us to go to their homes. A group of about 9-10 mostly younger guys, however, stayed behind gathered around us in the shadowy street. A tall, solid, young guy with a dark beard, named Mohsloh, was trying to show us things and ask us things using gestures and drawings. The others would say something to Mohsloh in Arabic and he would try to communicate the questions to us. They asked us about our family and home, and we did likewise to them. They also all proudly told us each of their names, as we spent about 40 minutes standing out in the empty, dirt street with them.

As I looked around the dark, deserted streets of the village and into the vast desert night out in the middle of nowhere, it seemed odd how totally safe it seemed...Here we were in the middle of the desert on a dark street, at night, in a village we had just arrived in hours earlier, with a group of men

HABJIB, TUNISIA: LONG LOST BROTHERS

we had just met, with no police or security of any kind within hundreds of miles and yet it seemed there could be no safer place for us to be.

After talking with the group of young men, we were walked back to our little room by Mohsloh and another friendly young guy, who Slah had earlier introduced to us as the "village haircutter" and was thereafter always referred to that way. I never did get his name.

That night the sky above was dotted with a kind of magical display of stars, and lights, and both the night sky and open desert land gave a sense of such utter vastness. It was my first night out in the Sahara, and the night sky and surroundings gave me an incredible feeling. Such vastness and emptiness spread out so far and wide, with the desert horizon barely visible where it met the night sky seemingly at the end of the earth.

Back in our small room John and I got ready for an early sleep, as we would every night in Habjib. There was no choice but to make it an early night

"8:00PM and everything in the village is dark and closed." John said. "It's a bit different than London on a Saturday night, isn't it?"

"No TV, no radio, no phones, no music." I replied. "Nothing of the sort. It's definitely lights out at 8:00 around here."

"No kidding. Did you see how dark it was out there?"

"For sure."

"Our first night in the Sahara. I love it. That's an incredible night sky out there. I can't believe it. I can't believe we're here."

"Yeah." I said, "Making it here was one thing…Making it back will be another."

"You got that right."

We woke up early the next day with no specific travel plans for the day. We had enjoyed the previous day so much and felt so welcome that we thought we would not be concerned about making mileage that day. We would just see what the day brought us. The only goal we had as we left our room onto the street - was to mail our postcards and change a few more dollars at a bank. We hadn't seen anything resembling a post office or bank the previous day, so we planned to venture out to see if we could find them.

As soon as we walked out the door of our room onto the windy street, we bumped into Mohsloh. I think he may have been waiting around for us to come out. He would have been too polite to just knock on our door. Each morning we were in Habjib there always seemed to be someone we knew, who just happened to be outside our room as we came out. Whoever was waiting that particular morning offered us assistance.

We showed Mohsloh our postcards and money and with a few gestures he understood where we wanted to go, so he became our guide for the morning and we headed out with him. He took us through the village streets to a place that was the post office.

When we arrived at the post office, I looked over at John and said, "Man, I never would have guessed this was a post office."

"No kidding. We never would have found it ourselves."

"Yeah. It was nice of Mosloh to help us out."

"The villagers here are incredible, aren't they?" John said

"That's for sure." I agreed. "Everyone here treats us like a long-lost brother."

"It's amazing."

After we mailed our postcards, Mosloh then he took us to the lone, village bank and we changed a little money.

As we walked through the sand covered streets with Mohsloh, we were continually approached by men on the street coming up to greet us, smile, shake our hand, or to show us something. Most of them we had met the previous day or evening. If we hadn't met them before, Mohloh formally introduced us. The manner of all of the men who approached us was very friendly and respectful, not at all aggressive or intrusive. The people of Habjeb were nothing but warmly gracious and friendly. Anyone on the street who did not approach us, just plain stared at us in friendly astonishment, or gave a little wave or friendly smile.

After we had taken care of our business at the bank and post office, Mohsloh offered to give us a tour of Habjeb, so we spent the morning walking through the village with Mohsloh.

The streets were all dust and dirt, nothing paved and not very wide. Lining many of the street were these long, white, low, clay buildings that were usually connected. They seemed fairly crude but quite sturdy and were nicely designed and painted white. Inside the long, low buildings were usually small, single room shops that opened up to about the size of a nice living room. There would then be some shelves lining the walls inside the shop with various items for sale, or sometimes out on the street in front of the building a small stand would be set up.

As I was walking through the small village, there was a lot of activity and commotion in the sandy streets. Many people, most always men, were moving about the streets. Bearded, rugged, leathered-face men wearing traditional Arabic robes and turbans were leading donkeys through the streets with sacks of olives or other items on their backs. Others were riding the donkeys as well. Occasionally tall, long camels would also be led or ridden pass me with their loping strides, carrying sacks of goods slung over their backs.

Bearded, robed men were hunched against the walls of the buildings playing cards or that board game with rocks that I never figured out. Little smiling kids and sometimes teenagers were running around playing soccer or trying to catch each other. They often followed us closely as we walked the streets, clinging to our sleeves, smiling and waving to get our attention.

A few of the older kids or young men wore the gray robed garbs like the older men, while many wore western style shirts and pants. There were also a few ancient model cars or trucks noisily rocking by on the street…Very, very few…and very, very old. The main means of transport seemed to be donkeys, with camels a close second.

The sand of the Sahara was ever present. I never got away from it. Not anywhere. It usually seemed to be slightly swirling or floating on the air, as it was continually kicked up by the activity of the village or by the wind. My clothes and hair were continually layered with it.

While walking with Mohsloh through the narrow active streets, Slah saw us and came running out of a shop to greet us. He invited us to come in and sit with him in his shop for a while. It was a shoe shop. So Mohsloh, John and I, along with a large group of young kids who had gathered around us, all entered Slah's small shoe shop.

We sat on a big long wood box that Slah pulled out for us. Slah then good naturedly shooed most of the kids out of the shop. Some of them left the shop, but none of them went away. They stood outside and continued to peer at us with eager curiosity.

We then sat for quite awhile talking as best we could with Slah, while watching the activity out on the street in front of us.

Later Slah told some of the kids to run and get us some tea and bread. So we ate some food for the first time that day. It was good. Slah and Mohsloh then suggested we take a walk around. So we did. We went down a small hill to a soccer field on the outskirts of town, where about 20 kids were playing soccer on a desert sand soccer field. Even out in the Sahara, the village had its own regulation size soccer field, complete with net goals.

It must have been about the 25th soccer field we had seen since starting this trip. Almost every town in every country we passed through there were soccer fields with kids playing on them. And if there weren't any soccer fields around, there were kids with soccer balls playing out in the dirt or on the streets or in the grass fields. Hajib was no exception.

John and I continued our tour around the village with Slah and Mohsloh and later we were taken to an area away from the soccer field with a little stream, where the village ladies washed clothes using pans and their hands. It was interesting to see. We didn't go close and only saw the ladies from a distance. Many of the women were wearing loose fitting western style skirts or clothes as they crouched in the stream washing the laundry. Seeing the women at that moment felt like something we shouldn't be privy to. Before getting too close Slah and Mohsloh led us away.

When we got back from the stream, Muhammad and a friend of his, along with about a dozen little kids were waiting by for us. Muhammad and his friend greeted us warmly, and the kids excitedly gathered around us. After the kids had a chance to look at John and me, with some of them shaking our hands or touching our sleeve Muhammad sent them away.

The six of us, minus the kids, went back to Slah's shoe shop, which Slah re-opened. He had closed the shop when we took our walk. We sat together, talked and ate some oranges to pass the time. As we sat in the shop, men and kids came up to shake John's and my hands or to meet us. As always during our stay in Hajib, the people, we were continually being introduced to and meeting, were extremely polite and gracious. They all seemed so pleased and happy to meet us. I really felt like the long-lost brother who had finally returned and was being welcomed home.

That afternoon John and I went with Muhammad and Slah to the town's little café and played dominoes and cards again. And again we attracted a big crowd. It was a lot of fun.

Earlier in the day Slah had found out for us that there was a bus coming to Habjib at about 3:00 that afternoon, which could take us to a little town called Fierena near the Tunisian-Algerian border. From Fierena John and I would try to find a way to make it to the border. We intended to cross into Algeria that same day. We said our goodbyes (a lot of them) and left the card game and the little café to head back to our "hotel" room to collect our backpacks and belongings. We had offered several times to pay for the room, but we were never charged and they never accepted any money from us.

Carrying our backpacks and everything we had, we headed down to the bus station…Well not really bus station. It was more like a little carrousel with a single small table and a few chairs out on the dirt street.

Shortly after arriving at the "bus station" out along the deserted little road, Muhammad and some of the other friends we had made during our short stay came out to see us off. But while we were waiting for the bus, Slah came running up very excited.

He said worriedly, "Dennis, John…The bus now very late. Time changed. Bus here maybe at 5:00PM."

I said, "5:00 PM? Why? What happened?"

"I don't know. Often very late. Today again late." Slah answered.

"Well, we've got a long wait, then"

"No, no. Bus schedule also changed." Slah replied urgently.

"What do you mean?" John asked.

"No bus to Fierena today."

"Huh?"

"Now bus go only to Kasserine." Slah said. "Not to Fierena. Kasserine you must sleep night and take bus again tomorrow."

"Where's Kasserine?" I asked. "Can't we get to the border and get to Algeria today?"

"No. No. Kasserine too far from border. No border today." Slah said earnestly, "Why not stay here in Habjib tonight. Sleep in Habjib. Take early bus to Fierena tomorrow morning."

I looked at John. John shrugged. I shrugged back. John then looked at Slah and said "Ok."

As I said before, many travel arrangements, such as bus schedules, were not really a fixed thing in the out of the way places I traveled in those days. So instead of taking the bus out of town that afternoon, John and I went back to the little café with Slah for some more cards and dominoes. We played for a couple of hours, again, with a big crowd in attendance. We were getting to be a regular attraction there.

Later we ran into Muhammad again and he took us down the sandy, windy streets to his home, which was very interesting for me. It had a large open area in the middle under the open sky, with several entrances leading off of the open area. Each of the doorways had a thick large rug hanging over the opening leading into the various compact rooms. The rooms were painted white, very neat and clean. Muhammad shared a room with three of his brothers. In all, Muhammad told us 7 brothers and a sister lived together in his home.

When we first entered his home and walked into the open area of his house, his mother was standing there. Her face was not covered and she was wearing loose fitting, semi-western style clothes. She was an attractive, middle-aged, dark featured woman with black hair and distinctive features. I think she was as surprised to see us, as we were to see her.

She shyly smiled and made brief, fleeting eye contact with me as Muhammad introduced her. She did not speak and did not offer her hand. I was careful not to make physical contact with her or look directly at her.

To be honest, I was shocked to see her. It caught me by complete surprise. She was the only woman I met the entire time I was in the Sahara. Though ever so briefly, she was also the only woman I even made eye contact with while in the Sahara. (With the exception of the young woman on the bus across Tunisia.) I also never spoke to a single woman during the entire trip. After the brief introduction, Muhammad's mother quickly disappeared into the shadows and I didn't see her again. Even though it was a very brief meeting, she left a big impression. Later we returned to our 'hotel'. That night it sprinkled a little bit, the first and only rain on our trip.

The next morning we repeated our vigil at the "bus station" and again Slah, Muhammad, Mohsloh, the village haircutter and several others came out to see us off. This time the bus did arrive, only an hour or so late. We shook hands and said our goodbyes to the friendly villagers of Habjib, before leaving this magical place and heading out into the Sahara on our way to the border.

CHAPTER **14**

The Long Border Walk

John and I slowly rumbled along on the old bus through the rugged Sahara for several hours all the way to the town of Fierena, which was the end of the line for the bus. Fierena was small, windy, sleepy, little town not much bigger than Habjeb. After getting off the bus in Fierena, we checked around for a way to get to the Tunisian-Algerian border, which was still a ways from here.

It took a while, but we finally found a kind of transportation service, actually an old guy with an old jeep, that could take us to the town of Boucherka, which was the closest point to the actual border. Now when I say the "town" of Boucherka, I'm using the word "town" very liberally. I should say the few, dust-covered, windswept, decaying buildings that comprised Boucherka.

So after negotiating with the gray bearded driver, we hired him to take us to the border, paid him and climbed into his beat-up but very sturdy customized jeep. There was nobody else heading to the border, so we had the jeep to ourselves. I doubt if there was more than half a dozen people passing through that border in a month's time…Maybe in a few month's time. I had read one time that certain points crossing between Tunisia and Algeria were some of the most isolated border crossings in the world. I tend to agree.

Once we left the town of Fierena, it became tough going. The single, unmarked strip of pavement that we had been traveling on since leaving Tunis, had now turned into a rocky, chunky piece of concrete.

"Man, this is pretty rugged travel out here." I said.

"Yep. This road is really slow-going and bumpy." John agreed..

"This road is not doing much for my 'runs'." I said, "I gotta go to the bathroom again."

"Huh?"

"I really gotta go again. I think that couscous we had earlier is getting to me."

"Yep. I can smell it. You're passing a lot of gas. You got any TP left?"

"No I ran out of toilet paper yesterday."

"Well, good luck finding any out here." John said amused.

"How far is the border from here, do ya think?" I asked un-amused.

"I think not far." John said, "But with this rough terrain it might take a while."

"Yeah. These desert hills are pretty rocky and rough to navigate. I hope this driver knows what he's doing."

"He seems all right. I think he knows what he's doing."

"I hope we get there soon."

When we finally arrived, we found out the border was completely out in the middle of nowhere. After a long rough ride through the Sahara, we crossed over a rocky, slight, desert hill and there appeared out in the desert in front of us a few, decaying single story buildings which comprised the tiny border town of Boucherka. Only 2 or 3 people were visible around the isolated town. It had the look a ghost town.

As I was getting out of the jeep in Boucherka, I gazed over at the border crossing out in the distance in the Sahara. There was nothing out there but a single building, in the middle of just desert and empty, vast nothingness. It was a dark overcast day, and as we approached the border, the gloomy weather just added to the feeling of isolation. The paved, sand covered road headed out into the desert for less than a kilometer to the Tunisian border customs building. The Tunisian border post was a single, two-story, white building.

After winding past the Tunisian border building, the lone road led a few hundred meters through the desert to the Algerian Border building. One building was the Tunisian side of the border - the other building was the Algerian border crossing point.

That was it. Just two wind-scarred buildings, jutting out of the barren desert landscape in the middle of nowhere. As the single sandy road passed by the Algerian border building, it appeared to continue in a fairly straight line forever until it faded and disappeared in the distance desert.

THE LONG BORDER WALK

For every direction as far I could see there was nothing; nothing but barren, hard rock desert, with little rocky hills sticking out of the horizon at various points. I could see for miles and miles - to what seemed to be the very end of the earth…and there was just vast emptiness. I've never seen a border crossing like it before or since.

John and I started walking along the narrow, hard road toward the single Tunisian border post that sat isolated out in the desert in front of us.

"Man, there's nothing out here to show this is a border. No markings. No gate. Not even a sign. You ever see anything like this?" John asked.

"No. Never. It's really isolated out here. It's kind of a strange place."

Looking around, John commented, "There's nothing but empty desert for as far I can see."

As we walked up closer to the Tunisian border post, I said, "It's as though two buildings were just randomly dropped from the sky out in the middle of nowhere in the desert…and one building is one country and the other building is another country. I wonder how they distinguish where one country ends and the other begins?"

"I don't know. It's probably not so important. There's nothing but miles and miles of rocks and sand. Who's gonna care about who's sand it is?"

"You never know." I replied, "Countries have fought over less important things."

"Yep. You got a point there."

We needed to first clear customs and get our passport stamped at the Tunisian custom post to let us exit Tunisia…Then we would have to walk about 300 meters across the empty desert to the Algerian border post to get stamped and be allowed to enter Algeria. Only then could we continue our travels across the Sahara.

When we approached the Tunisian border building there was an unshaven Tunisian soldier wearing a torn, dust-covered uniform lazily stretched out on the stairs outside. The bearded soldier had a rifle leaning against the wall next to him. He looked up at us with a shocked, wary expression.

As we walked past the soldier into the building, I whispered to John, "I've got a bad feeling about this."

"Yeah. I know what you mean. Let's just try to get through it as fast as we can, and get out of here."

Once inside the building, we entered an open, sparsely furnished room with a single counter and a few tables scattered around. There were about 5 soldiers in the room, including the soldier from the steps who followed us inside.

The soldiers were a rather ragged-looking bunch. They were unshaven, with sweaty, dirty uniforms and bored, cold expressions. All of them were armed with large pistols, and a couple of them had rifles slung over their shoulders.

They seemed for a moment completely shocked to see two young Westerners coming through their border. For a brief moment they just stopped what they were doing, and froze while they stared at us. But they quickly hid their surprise and the cold expressions returned. Gone were the friendly, warm stares I had gotten used to since entering the Sahara.

The room itself was covered with dust and sand, and in some disrepair. As we walked into the room, it became quickly apparent to us who the man in charge was. One bearded, stocky soldier walked around behind the wood counter in the room and waved us over to him. He took on an air of authority as he commanded us to show him our backpacks, with the other soldiers looking on. While John and I stood in front of the counter, he opened our backpacks and rifled through the limited dirty clothes and few things we were carrying with us. He didn't seem too impressed. (I can't say I blame him).

He then spoke in Arabic and then French, and gestured for our shot papers, which I still had wrinkled up with my money. My money was incredibly limited, but I turned away from the soldier so as to not show any US dollars. I feared he would demand a bribe. He didn't. He just looked at our papers and seemed satisfied.

Speaking again in French he then asked for our passports. When John and I pulled out our American passports and put them on the counter, we were treated to the same shocked expression we had witnessed a few minutes earlier when we first walked into the room.

Each of the soldiers gathered around us first looked down at the passports on the counter, and then looked up at us. They held their surprised stare for a moment until the soldier behind the counter grabbed the passports off the table.

He started looking through them to find the Tunisian visa stamps for when we entered his country. He had difficulty finding the stamp in my passport

THE LONG BORDER WALK

because I had extra pages added to it since I had so many visas from previous travels. He didn't seem pleased about that, but he didn't say anything

Once the soldier in charge found the visa stamps, without saying a word he abruptly took our passports with him and went into another room with a couple of the soldiers following him. John and I were directed to sit on a little bench with the remaining soldiers looking on. They made no attempt to communicate with us.

I whispered to John, "This group is not exactly a friendly or talkative bunch, are they?"

"That's for sure."

"Man, out here, we're literally in the middle of nowhere."

"Yeah. I can't believe how isolated it is out here."

"Do you believe this border crossing?" I said, "There's nothing here. It's just empty. I hope there's no problem with our passports. I had no idea it would be like this."

I sat on the bench a while longer, feeling uneasy and isolated…Very isolated. After a short but nervous wait, the soldier with our passports returned. We stood up and he put our passports back on the counter. He then wrote some information on some forms. Then in front of us he stamped our passports, with exit stamps allowing us to leave Tunisia. He checked the exit stamps, handed us our passports and gestured toward the door, saying harshly in English, "OK. Go."

And that's what we did. We hurriedly left the building and walked down the steps out into the cloudy day and onto the windswept road. We were relieved to have gotten the exit stamps, letting us leave Tunisia. Now all we needed was to walk about a kilometer across the desert to the Algerian border post and get stamped, allowing us entry into Algeria. Then we could get away from the border and the soldiers, and be on our way.

With a sense of unease, John and I started walking along the single, unmarked paved road through the desert to the lone Algerian border post up ahead. The building was set up on a slight hill from where we were and with the dark, dreary sky and endless desert in the background - the weather beaten, isolated border post up on the hill reminded me of an image of the Bates house from Alfred Hitchcock's movie "Psycho." It just gave off an eerie feeling of total isolation and danger.

As we walked along the road in no man's land leading to the Algerian custom building, John said, "Man, I still can't believe we're walking between two countries."

"Yeah, it's definitely an empty border out here."

"Did you see the looks of those guys when we walked in." I continued. "They looked like they saw a ghost."

"I can't imagine they get many people coming through."

"Especially a couple of Americans, I thought they were going to drop when we put the passports down."

Looking around, John said again, "There's just nothing here. Who would ever know this is a border."

With a shrug, I said, "Heck, who would know it's even planet earth."

When we reached the Algerian customs building, there was nobody in sight. The building looked very old and tired, like it had been standing out in the desert sun for a long, long time and was in need of a break. We entered the old building and walked into a small room. There were several doors leading off the room.

There were about half a dozen soldiers scattered lazily around the various rooms. They were all wearing grimy, sweaty uniforms, and some also had big official looking military hats. Also, like the Tunisian soldiers, they all had pistols as side arms. There were rifles visible in the corners and placed haphazardly against the walls.

Some soldiers were dozing, playing cards or talking. They all seemed rather bored and distracted. It didn't appear that they were use to much border activity at their post.

When John and I walked in, there was another moment of stunned silence and then cold, frozen stares, like at the Tunisian border. No-one averted their eyes from us, they just continued coldly staring as we walked into the room.

We were then quickly directed into another smaller room, where one bulky, unshaven soldier gestured for us to show him our backpacks. Two or three other soldiers crowded into the small room behind us. The soldiers behind us roughly pulled the backpacks off of our backs and handed them to the soldier in charge. He placed the backpacks on a table and started pulling our things out of the backpacks, and carelessly tossing our items all over the floor with a look of disdain.

THE LONG BORDER WALK

When he finished with our backpacks, the big soldier roughly handed them back to us and signaled for us to pick up our stuff off the table and floor. So we did. The soldier then demanded our passports. When he saw the American passports, he gave a look of surprise and then took them from us and started carefully going through them, spending a lot of time studying each page.

He seemed irritated about my passport having extra pages attached to it, pointing to the passport pages and demanding, "Why? Why?"

I tried to answer that I had too many visas, and had to get extra pages added. But before I could, he cut me off with a quick hand gesture.

He then spent some more time looking through our passports before holding up our passports and angrily gesturing where's the visa?

This border crossing was obviously not going so good - and it wasn't going to get any better…We didn't have a visa. We didn't know a visa was required for US passport holders entering Algeria. Actually, I recently heard that not long after John and I took this trip in 1977, that the Algerian government did not issue any visas or allow any Westerners entry into Algeria for over 20 years.

Now, suddenly, John and I were in a very precarious position. The soldier had us go back to the outer room and made us stand along a wall with an armed soldier looking on. He then took our passports along with our backpacks, and marched into another room and slammed the door. We didn't know what he intended to do. We just knew we were in a vulnerable situation, since we had technically attempted to enter Algeria illegally.

As I said before, I've never liked border crossings and this one was no exception. Whenever I crossed a border and entered a customs building, I was putting myself in a vulnerable position because that custom official or soldier often had a great deal of control over me.

Sometimes total control…Such as in this situation, we were completely and totally isolated from any other controlling authority or assistance. At this moment, out here in the middle of the empty Sahara that individual soldier in the other room had complete and total control over us, and we had absolutely no recourse. He could do anything he wanted with us and no-one would ever know…He knew it, and we knew it.

It wasn't a good feeling. We worriedly waited wondering what our fate might be.

"What do you think he's going to do?" I asked.

"No idea." John said. "He can do anything he wants to do out here."

"This has never happened to me before. I've had problems at borders but not this. How about you?"

"No, not like this. There's no place to hold us out here, is there? What can they do with us?"

"Who knows? They could shoot us." I replied half-jokingly. "They can do anything they want to."

"You got that right. Who knows what he will do."

We waited nervously and after a while, the soldier came back out and brusquely signaled for us to follow him into the same small room we were in before. Once in the room, a couple of other soldiers came in. They seemed as anxious as we were to find out what he was going to do. I think it must have been a very rare case to have two Americans passing though, and then with no visas. I doubt it happened much - maybe never.

The soldier in charge then spoke in a commanding voice and said something to us in Arabic. John and I reacted with blank expressions. He repeated what he said this time in Arabic with a little French added for good measure. Again, we looked on with blank expressions. We didn't understand a word. We just smiled grimly and shrugged our shoulders.

Finally, he held up our passports and irritably said in English, "No visa – No enter. Go back."

He handed us our passports and pointed to the door. We still just looked at him.

He repeated firmly, "Go back."

This time he gestured and looked impatiently in the direction of the Tunisian border. We took our passports from him, picked up our backpacks and hurriedly walked out the building without looking back.

After we were outside, we walked just a short ways from the Algerian border building, stopped and set our backpacks down. It was still very cloudy and gloomy. The Tunisian border building was off in the distance in front of us and all around us was just vast barren desert with a strong wind blowing sand over us. Suddenly a truly foreboding feeling starting washing over me. It was just dawning on me – what our situation was.

I looked at John with a "Now what?" kind of expression.

John just shrugged and said, "I don't know...What can we do?"

We had just been denied entry into Algeria. We had nowhere to go. Really the only thing we could do was to walk back through the desert, across no man's land, to the Tunisia border post…And hope and pray they would allow us in.

The more we thought about that - the more we realized our predicament…We had just had a difficult time exiting Tunisia about an hour earlier and now we were going to go back to the same border post - to ask the same soldiers to allow us to re-enter their country when we had just left it… and after we had just been denied entry into Algeria.

We started getting very anxious. I was seriously concerned that we would be denied entry back into Tunisia. Actually, "concerned" does not really cover how I felt at that moment. We had no idea what the Tunisian visa requirements were for re-entry, especially for someone leaving and re-entering the same day…Actually, almost the same hour…And after being denied entry into a neighboring country.

But in reality, out here in the middle of the Sahara, any laws or visa requirements didn't really matter. What mattered was the soldier in charge. He was the only thing that mattered. He would be the sole and final authority of our fate. He could do anything he wanted with us…It didn't look good.

"What if they don't let us back into Tunisia. What are we gonna do?" I asked.

"I don't know – What can we do? We're out here in no man's land."

"Those soldiers at the Tunisian border weren't exactly the friendliest guys."

"I know…but what else can we do?" John asked.

"Go back to the Algerian border?"

"Go back and do what?" John said, "They barely let us out of the building when we had no visa. No way they'll let us enter."

"Yeah, I know…They'd probably shoot us, just for being stupid enough to come back with no visa. But what can we do."

"I don't know, but there must be something." John said.

"Like what?"

"Something...anything."

John pointed to the Tunisian border building in the distance, "Those guys got a lot of rifles in there. Did you see that one big soldier with the beard in the back room. Man, he looked like he'd rather shoot us than look at us."

"Yeah, I'm glad he's not in charge." I said.

"I don't really want to face them again. It was tough enough getting out."

"No kidding," I said, "They'll think were crazy for trying to get back into Tunisia after we just left."

"What'll we do if they don't let us in? We were just denied getting in Algeria. We've got nowhere to go." John wondered.

Looking around at the vast emptiness, I added, "Man, it's desolate out here…So what are we gonna do?"

We stood there in silence for another few moments with the wind and desert sand howling past us, avoiding the walk across the empty border, across no man's land. Avoiding what we knew we had to do. Finally, with a sense of trepidation, we started heading toward the Tunisian border post off in the distance…You do what you gotta do.

It wasn't far, but it seemed like one of the longest walks I've ever taken in my life. A dozen different scenarios raced through my mind. None of them ended well. After we slowly made our way to the Tunisian building, we took a deep breath, and walked into the same room to confront the same soldiers we had just left earlier.

When we walked back in, the soldiers stopped what they were doing and looked at us, not so much with shock. More like they thought we were just plain crazy. None of the soldiers moved or gestured for us to do anything. Nobody said a word. They just stayed frozen in place and glared, so we just stood there, while they continued looking at us.

Finally, the same soldier in charge walked over to the same counter and signaled for us to approach him, while all the other soldiers continued staring. John and I tried to explain with some gestures and body language what had just happened at the Algerian border. He watched us quizzically and then when we finished, without speaking, he gestured for our passports. He looked through our passports intently for several moments, I assume, looking for any Algerian markings or stamps. There were none.

He then paused and looked intensely at John and me – Like he was searching for some kind of answer in our faces. It was a tense moment.

He then paused again, before he decisively grabbed a pen, opened each of our passports and quickly scribbled something in them. He then directly looked at each of us for a second time, before handing our passports back to us. We were stunned. We didn't know what had just happened. So we just stood there holding our passports looking at him.

He then pointed to the door and said something in Arabic.

We didn't understand, so we still stood there

THE LONG BORDER WALK

He spoke again, a little impatiently, this time in English, "Go Gafsa. Visa."

We still weren't really sure what had just happened. We expected a long process. So we still stood there, probably looking like fools in his eyes. He had just given us a huge break and we didn't even know it.

He pointed again and, with what seemed to be a gleam of amusement in his eyes, he repeated, "Go Gafsa. Gafsa visa. OK."

It all happened very quickly. I expected a long, tense drawn-out proceeding but it was over in minutes. The soldier just crossed out our original exit stamp, and we were let back into Tunisia. Just like that.

So, John and I said "*Shocaran saheb,*" took our passports and we left the building.

CHAPTER **15**

Back Tracking

After spending hours going back and forth across the desert border between the two countries, we now found ourselves back in Tunisia. The same place we had started from, and now we would have to backtrack. We weren't sure how far. This was getting to be a bad habit. (I had flashbacks of our repeated attempts to get out of Paris.)

As we walked along the same single, sand-swept road back into the tiny, ghost-like town of Boucherka, I looked over at John and asked puzzled, "What's a Gafsa?"

"Huh."

"Did you hear him say visa – Gafsa?"

"Yep, he did say something about a Gafsa." John replied.

"Maybe it's the name of the Algerian immigration office or something."

"Who knows? I have no idea where we can get a visa." John shrugged, "It might take us days to backtrack and get one."

"Yeah, I don't think there are many places that can issue us an Algerian visa…anywhere out here."

"That's *if* we can even get a visa with an American passport." John added.

"That's a big if."

"I hope we don't have to go all the way back to Tunis."

"We can't afford the travel days and the money - going backward." John said glumly.

"Yeah. It's bad enough spinning our wheels and not making time or miles," I sighed, "But burning up our money going backwards. Man, that's tough to take."

John and I continued walking through the desert down to the empty, single street and few decaying, clay buildings that comprised the town of Boucherka. As we wandered along the lone, short road, we could see the entire town before us. It was only three or four single-floor buildings with a single street less than 100 meters long, so we could see everything in town in one glance.

Looking around, I said, "Whattda we do now? How do we get out of here?"

"The truck we took here is long gone."

"Yeah. And that town we came from to get to the border would be a long, long walk from here. Too long."

"It's getting cold out here, too." John said. "The sun's gonna be setting soon."

"We need to get out of here. There's no place to sleep. I don't want to get stuck out here in the desert for the night." I said. "I'd also like to get away from those border posts and all those soldiers."

"I agree…but how?"

We stood out in the deserted street under the darkening, cloudy sky with the Sahara sand sweeping past on the wind, considering what to do. As we stood there, a tall, older bearded man walked out of one of the few buildings in the town. He had leathery, rough skin and wore loose robes and a turban that was blowing around his face in the wind. He was the first person we had seen in the town.

He approached us and motioned like what did we need.

While gesturing like I was driving a car, I said slowly, "We need…to go…to next town. We need car…and driver."

John pointed down the road out of the town in the direction we needed to go. There was only one road and one way out of town. The same way we came into town earlier.

The helpful bearded man didn't seem to understand.

John asked me, "What was the name of that town we came here from."

"I think it was Fer… Fer….something."

"Ah,..Fierena.. It was Feriana."

John then turned and said to the man, "We go Fierena. To Fierena. We need ride to Feriana."

The man nodded his head happily like he understood. He then smiled and motioned for us to wait before leaving us and going into the same dark building he came out of. John and I sat outside against the wall of the clay building for a while, until the man came back out and signaled that it was OK. He then gestured again for us to wait and went back into the building.

"Apparently we have a ride," I said as we continued waiting, sitting with our backs against the wall.

As we waited, I asked John, "Where do we go from Fierena? What then?"

"We need to get the Algerian visa. Hopefully they issue visas to American passport holders."

"Yep. We have to find out."

"That soldier at the border kept saying 'Go Gasfa.'" I said. "That must be a place to get a visa."

It was a long wait on the barren street of Boucherka, but finally an ancient, worn-out truck came bumping into town, driven by a smiling young Tunisian guy wearing old, western style clothes. It was our ride. When the truck came into town, the older bearded man came back out onto the street to see us off.

We thanked the helpful man and asked him about getting a visa. Trying to explain what we needed, we showed him our passports and other visa's, but he seemed perplexed.

When I said, "Gafsa", he immediately recognized the word. He shook his head 'yes, yes' and drew something in the sand, like a map. It took a while but we figured out that Gafsa was a town in Tunisia. According to the rough drawn map in the sand, it looked to be quite a ways south of where we were. It's where we needed to go to get a visa.

After negotiating with the jeep driver, we paid him a few dinero for the ride and we rode the jeep through the bumpy, winding roads over the same hard rock hills back to the town of Fierena.

We arrived in Fierena at about 7:00PM, at dusk, and after some checking we found out there was a bus going to Gafsa at 8:00 AM the next morning. We weren't exactly sure how far Gafsa was or how long the trip would take, but regardless, we would be spending the night in Fierena and we needed to find a place to sleep.

As we walked the narrow, winding streets of Fierena looking for a hotel there were a few robed men standing along the streets along with some camels and wooden carts scattered here and there, and we were treated once again to the same friendly, kindhearted stares we had experienced before our failed border-crossing attempt.

We found an ancient hotel quite quickly at the end of one of the many low, clay single floor buildings lining the sandy street, and it seemed to be an actual hotel this time, with a small sign and everything. The room also had a sink with cold water. So for the first time in several days I was able to brush my teeth and do a basic wash - but with only cold water; no soap and no towel. Brushing my teeth was great, but the cold water wash didn't do much.

John and I then left our backpacks in the room and headed out to find something to eat.

Although I would sometimes leave my backpack behind, my money, passport and papers I always kept on me in my chained wallet. I was never without them, never…Which meant if I ever got pick-pocketed, mugged or lost my wallet I was dead in the water. It was crucial to my safety that they not be lost or stolen. It's something I couldn't allow to happen. As always, I had to be very careful and aware.

After walking a short ways, we spotted a little café a few blocks from our hotel, and when we walked in to buy some bread and Coca-Cola, there was just the middle-aged café owner and his young worker inside. After we got our bread, the balding, bearded owner gestured that he wanted us to play cards with him.

We sat down at one of the few tables in the café and the owner showed us a card game to play. Before long the café filled up with about a dozen young Tunisian men and boys, wearing a mix of traditional Arab garments and western clothes. They eagerly crowded around our table watching the card game and soon were spilling out in to the street. They were as friendly as could be, and were laughing, cheering and occasionally jeering good-naturedly as they watched us play. It was a repeat of our experience in Habjib.

We played their card game for about an hour and then we showed the café owner and a few other men who sat down, how to play 'rummy.' They loved the game and got the biggest kick out of it. While we were playing cards they kept bringing us Cokes and coffee free of charge.

When we finally left the café after a couple of hours; everyone stood up as we were leaving and shook our hands, with each person introducing themselves and saying their names. They were very polite and kind, not at all aggressive.

As soon as we left the café to start walking down the dark street to our hotel, one clean shaven young guy named Mahmood and soon several of his friends joined with up with us. When we got outside of our hotel they all gathered around us out on the street smiling and wished us goodnight as we went into the little hotel.

The next morning, which happened to be the day before Christmas Eve, John and I arose early and after quickly brushing our teeth, and headed out onto the streets to catch our bus to Gafsa. As we walked the narrow, winding streets, the sun slowly rose over the distant desert with a cool breeze blowing past under the cloudy early morning sky. It took a while as we had to walk quite a ways through town to the little bus station.

"If the bus actually leaves on time, maybe we can make it to Gafsa, get our visa, and get back to the border today." I said.

"Yeah, well that would be a first." John retorted.

"What do you mean?"

"We don't even know how far Gafsa is, or if there's a bus coming back here later today."

"Uh huh."

"Plus, who knows if the Algerian embassy or visa office is open today." John explained, "Or how long we'll have to wait to get a visa issued. It could be days."

"Yeah, I know what you mean. Getting a same day visa is pretty rare. Also, who knows what it will cost."

"Also, what if they won't issue us a visa?" I continued, "We don't even know if Americans can get visas for Algeria."

"I've never met anyone who traveled Algeria. In fact I've never even heard of anyone who traveled Algeria before. Have you?"

"No, never." I answered. "Based on the reaction of those soldiers at the border – I doubt many people ever do."

At a little after 8:00 we boarded our bus and started the trip to Gafsa, surprisingly leaving almost on time. We were backtracking further south into Tunisia into the tip of the Sahara. The bus ride took a few hours, following the lone paved road through the open desert. It was a long ride through the mostly vacant desert, following the single unmarked strip of pavement passing a few small desert villages along the way.

At each of the villages, the bus driver would briefly stop and a few men would get on or off the bus. It was always men. After a short stop the bus would just ramble along through the vast open desert until reaching the next little village. There were very few other cars or vehicles on the road. The bus ride was fairly uneventful – there wasn't any beautiful young girl on the bus for me to wave at and cause a commotion. The bus contained mostly only friendly bearded Tunisian men, never any other foreigners or Westerners.

BACK TRACKING

John and I arrived in Gafsa early in the afternoon. Gafsa was the biggest town we had seen in Tunisia since we left the capitol city of Tunis. It had several bigger, semi-paved streets winding through the hilly, town of Gafsa.

After we left the bus, we walked through the staring crowds at the bus station to a nearby market to try and find where we could get a visa. The market was crowded with many people moving about the narrow paths and stalls. There were also a few, small outdoor food stands with wood tables along the way where several men were playing cards and drinking coffee. Several donkeys and a few camels were standing or being led among the crowds.

We approached some robed, bearded men and asked, "Hello. Excuse me. Where is visa office for Algeria? Visa for Algeria?"

They didn't understand. They looked blankly back at us.

I took out my passport and pointed to other visa's on the pages and said, "We need visa – Algeria. Visa."

When they saw the American passport they seemed more surprised and interested in that fact, than what we were asking about. We weren't getting very far. We were about to head on. But then a younger, thinly-bearded guy approached us and asked in halting English, "You need .. what?"

Surprised, John looked at him and said, "You speak English?"

It was one of the few times we had heard anyone speak any English since arriving in Africa.

The young guy didn't answer. He just smiled and put his thumb and forefinger together in a gesture meaning 'a little'.

John said, "We need to get visa – Algeria. We need visa."

He looked quizzically at John. So I held up my passport again and showed him other visas in my passport.

He finally seemed to understand. "Ahha. You visa? Visa. Yes?"

"Yes, a visa for Algeria." I said pointing in the direction of the Algerian border. At least what I thought was the general direction of Algeria.

"Ok. Algeria? No one go Algeria? Why you go?" The young Arab asked surprised.

John and I just kind of looked back at him blankly and shrugged our shoulders. It was tough to explain. We weren't really sure why we were going other than because it's there, it's on the way and we're travelers. It's what we do.

Finally he said, "Visa? Yes. OK, I show you."

"Great. *Shocerum*. Thank you." John and I said.

We followed the helpful young guy through the hilly streets of Gafsa for quite a while until we came to small, single floor building set along the roadside on a sandy, narrow side street.

The young Tunisian said, "Here. Visa. Good luck."

Before we even had a chance to really thank him, he disappeared down the street, so John and I turned and walked into the little Algerian consulate building. The building was quite small and didn't seem to have any real official markings signifying that it was an official consulate of Algeria. We weren't sure what to expect.

When we walked in the building there was only a single room, with a desk and some older wooden cabinets behind a small wooden counter and one middle-aged Algerian man was sitting at the desk, leaning back in his chair looking out the window. He was wearing western clothes and glasses.

He quickly looked up at us as we entered the room. When he saw it was two young Westerners he smiled, quickly stood up, and walked over to us. He seemed surprised and pleased to have some customers come into his office. I don't think had he had much business issuing visas out of his office.

He greeted us with a smile, speaking in French.

"We need a visa for Algeria," John answered.

"Ah. English. No English. Sorry."

From there on we communicated with a series of body language, gestures, some French, and drawings. We were able to explain that we needed a visa to travel through Algeria, and that we were trying to get back to the border as soon as possible.

The consulate official understood what we wanted. He was very helpful and friendly.

He checked our shot papers and then asked to see all of the money we were taking into Algeria. It wasn't much. Not much at all. When we put all our currencies and money on the table in front of him, he seemed stunned and very concerned. He gestured like 'Is that all?' We nodded our heads 'yes.'

He asked again, not believing us. We nodded yes again, and pulled out our pockets in a gesture showing we had no more money. He hesitated and gave us another look of concerned disbelief before he dutifully documented all our foreign currency on a form and stamped it with an official Algerian seal.

Algerian currency was not traded internationally at that time. It could not be bought or sold outside of its borders, so all the foreign currency brought

BACK TRACKING

into the country was carefully recorded before entering. And every penny of foreign currency we exchanged and spent after entering the country - had to be officially documented and recorded.

When we left Algeria we would then have to show the documentation for all our financial transactions before we could leave the country. The documentation would have to match with the foreign currency we had left on us when we exited the country. It was how the government restricted and controlled the selling of foreign currencies on the black market.

It made it very dangerous to sell money 'black'...which, by the way, just happens to be exactly what John and I later did, within hours of entering the country.

It took about an hour to get through all the visa paperwork with the helpful consulate official, and everything was going smoothly until he asked us for passport photo's...We didn't have any.

We didn't know where or when we could get the photo's made. We were worried it might cost us a lot of time and money to get the photo's we needed, but it didn't. The consulate official closed down his consulate office and personally took us around the corner to a little shop where we got photos taken in a matter of minutes.

Back at the Algerian consulate office the helpful official then took our passport and stamped visas for Algeria in them. We were issued one-month, single entry tourist visas. As the consulate official was finishing our visa documentation, photos and paperwork, John and I were getting worried about the fee.

"He still hasn't told us the fee, yet." I whispered to John.

"Yeah. I'm worried about that.' John replied, "Now that he's finished everything, he can charge us anything he wants."

We stood at the counter, as the consulate official finished all the documentation and passed our passports back over to us. After getting our passports, we both stood looking at the guy with apprehension, wondering how much he might nail us for.

So how much did he charge for the photos, documentation work and processing our visas?...Nothing. Not a penny. He wouldn't take any of our money when we offered to pay him at least something. He said it was all free of charge. John and I were stunned. He just shook our hands, and wished us well. It was a tremendous act of kindness. Not only did he process and issue us visas in a matter of an hour, but he didn't charge us anything for it.

I think when he was doing our documentation he saw how little funds we had, and knew we needed every cent we had for the trip ahead, so he wouldn't take any of our money. He was a good hearted guy.

Having successfully secured our visas, John and I hustled it back to the bus station to see if we could get a bus back to Feriana. As we had discussed earlier in the day, we were hoping to make it back to the border and cross into Algeria that same day. When we had talked about it earlier, we never really thought it would be possible, but right about now it was looking pretty good. We were making really good time with no problems. It was a good day on the road.

After getting to the station and making our way through the crowds of onlookers, camels, wooden carts and donkeys, we found out there was a bus returning to Fierena in a couple hours, so we bought tickets and then headed out to find some food. Sitting under a small shop covered by a tent, we ended up having another meal of couscous, which meant I later had another case of the 'runs'. For the past few days now, I had been getting the runs most every time I ate some couscous. I really loved the taste of it, but for a while it made me feel sick.

After the meal, we came back to the station and took our bus back to Fierena. It was another long ride through the seemingly endless desert following the same single, unmarked strip of pavement. After passing through the same few desert villages, we arrived back into town at dusk just as it was turning dark.

Having made it all the way to Gafsa and back, we weren't sure if we should attempt a border crossing at night.

"Well, we got the visa…made it back. What now?" I asked.

"It's getting late but maybe we can still get a ride out to the border and cross tonight." John said hopefully.

"Yep, we could get some miles behind us and keep on the move."

"You got that right. If we stay here we'll just have to cross tomorrow, anyways."

"And we'll lose a day." I added.

"Let's go for it. Let's cross now."

"OK. Let's do it."

CHAPTER **16**

Crossing into Algeria…Finally! The Long(er) Border Walk

So that was it. After a short discussion, John and I decided to attempt to cross the border that night rather than wait for morning. But what we didn't talk about was what we would do after we got through the isolated border out in the middle of the Sahara, in the middle of the night. Actually, we never even thought about it.

With our decision made, we walked through the open, windswept streets of Feriana to find and hire a driver to take us to the border again. We found one fairly quickly this time. It was our second time, so we knew where to go.

After a little negotiating, we hired a slim, wiry looking guy in his 30's with a face weathered by the sun. He was wearing faded, flowing brown robes and a turban that was wrapped around his dark face. He led us to the back of one of the small, white, clay buildings lining the dusty street, and showed us a dented, rusting vehicle that he said he could take us to the border with.

Although it didn't look like much, John and I quickly climbed in and the driver took off to the border over the same rocky, rough road we had already been over two times before. While we were bumping along toward the border we witnessed a beautiful sunset, with the sun dramatically breaking out from the heavy clouds, before falling below the distant desert horizon in a searing blaze of orange and red.

By the time we got into the tiny, ghost-like border town of Boucherka, it was pretty dark. We thanked the driver, saying "*Shocerum Sahab*" (thank you friend) and he immediately turned around in a cloud of flying sand and dirt, and headed back down the isolated road we had come in on, disappearing out into the desert.

As we stood out alone in the empty, single street that comprised the entire speck of a town, the wind blew the desert sand in our face in billowing waves and I could make out the Tunisian border post a short ways across the desert out in front of us. The isolated border building looked like a darkened, desert lighthouse casting out a single, tiny beam of light that cut through the vast blackness of the surrounding Sahara.

It was really dark and eerie out there. Aside from the lone lights at the border posts, there were no other lights at all along the single paved road that snaked out to the two border posts and beyond. In all other directions, there was nothing but the vast emptiness and darkness of the Sahara for as far as I could see.

"Man, it's a dark, desolate place out here." John said looking around in the growing blackness.

"No kidding. There's just nothing out here."

"I can't believe how empty it is."

"Yeah. It's eerie out here at night. Last time we were here we at least had a little daylight." I said.

As we walked toward the border building, John continued, "They better let us through the border this time. I'd hate to get stuck out here for the night."

"That's for sure." I said pointing at the border posts up ahead. "Some of those soldiers were not the friendliest guys."

We walked the short route through the empty desert to the lone Tunisian border building and entered the same single, open room we had been in only a day earlier. The ramshackle room was in the same state of disrepair as when we were there the day before. There were also several, ragged soldiers again in the room, some with rifles slung casually over their shoulders and all of them wearing side arms on their belts. They seemed to be the same soldiers that were there the day before. I recognized some of them, but I wasn't' sure if they were all the same.

As we entered the border post they all stopped what they were doing and looked over at us, but without the same sense of utter surprise as the day before. I think the shock value of our appearance had worn off with our previous visit. Although still quite wary, the soldiers took our arrival this time more in stride.

CROSSING INTO ALGERIA...FINALLY! THE LONG(ER) BORDER WALK

The same grim soldier with the same sweat-stained, frayed uniform took our passports, and looked through them intently while a single, rifle-carrying soldier walked over and took up a position next to us. Most of the other soldiers continued with their conversations, only occasionally peering over at us.

The soldier in charge didn't bother with our backpacks this time. Apparently after looking through them the day before, he didn't have any interest in seeing our dirty socks and limited dirty clothes again. I can't say I blame him.

He seemed a little less tense about everything this time through. After completing his inspections, he stamped our passport for the second time letting us exit Tunisia. Hopefully, we would not need a third time.

After we got our passports stamped, John and I quickly left the building and started the short, black walk through 'no mans land' to the Algerian border post standing a distance ahead of us. Well, I should say 'barely standing'. The weathered border post looked like it was in the last round of a tough, twelve round fight and needed a standing 8 count, before it went down for the count. The old desert building had seen better days. It had obviously been beaten up over the years by the unforgiving desert surroundings.

As we walked over to the old border post, I looked over at John and said, "OK. One down, one to go."

"Yep. Now we got the tough one. To get into Algeria."

"We got our visa this time." I said, "What are they going to do – say we can't enter - after we backtracked to get the visa."

"We should be OK."

"Man, its dark out here. Where are the lights?"

"Yeah," John said, pointing past the lone Algerian post building to where the road continued on into Algeria, into complete darkness and the endless Sahara. "I can't believe they don't have any lights out here."

"But if you think about it, why would they have lights on the road out here." I said, "They would just be wasted. There's nobody out here to use them. I mean nobody."

"Yeah. Good point."

After passing the few hazy lights connected to the Algerian border building that lay in wait in front of us, the lone road continued into the shadows, and just disappeared into the total blackness of the Sahara.

It was kind of strange to have such blackness all around. With the exception of the little light ray of light being cast off by the two border buildings there was nothing but pitch blackness. The two border buildings were almost like two, tiny stars in an empty, vast, black sky. It was a cloudy night and there were nothing visible in the sky, so it was dark...Really dark.

After completing the trek to the Algerian border post we walked up to the door, took a deep breath and entered the building to find out our fate. As we walked into the building there were about 6-7 unshaven soldiers, many carrying rifles over their shoulders, standing and sitting haphazardly around in the various rooms.

Unlike the Tunisian border soldiers, the soldiers here reacted to our entrance with the same sense of intense apprehension and tension as our previous visit the day before. As we entered the border post, they immediately stopped what they were doing and intensely stared at us...I was getting that uneasy feeling again.

The same big, bearded soldier, wearing the same sweaty, stained uniform, stood up and walked over to the same small room and stood behind the same counter as the day before. With a grunt and blunt gesture he commanded us over to the small, side room. A few soldiers quickly crowded in behind us.

This time the soldier in charge passed over the backpack check and went right for our passports. I don't think he believed we could have backtracked, and gotten our visas so quickly.

The big soldier intensely looked at our passports and found our new visas. After checking the visas, with a grunt of approval, he set our passports on the counter. He then demanded to see our currency documents and all our foreign currency. We pulled out our currency papers, and put all our foreign currency on the counter for the soldier's inspection.

He carefully looked through our funds and diligently matched our funds with our currency documents. He made some notations and then stamped our papers. He seemed surprised at how little funds we had with us, gesturing like 'Is this it? Is this all you got?'

I was relieved when he pushed our papers and money back across the counter to us. I quickly took my cash and papers and returned them to my wallet chained to my belt. He then roughly motioned for us to show him our shot papers. Since he had already seen the papers on our previous attempt to enter Algeria, he just gave the papers a quick glance and shoved them right back over to us.

CROSSING INTO ALGERIA...FINALLY! THE LONG(ER) BORDER WALK

Without expression, the soldier then opened our passports to the page with the Algerian visa and stamped them, allowing us entry into Algeria.

He gruffly handed us our passports, as he pointed to the door and said sternly in English, "OK. Now enter."

When we took our passports, John and I both gave a sigh of relief. Finally, we were being allowed to enter Algeria and we could continue on our way. It had been a tough, difficult challenge, but after a lot of perseverance and two attempts we had made it through the border.

Now that we were allowed to enter Algeria, the question started dawning on me...How? How were we going to travel from the border post into the nearest town?

From our previous visit, I knew we were out in the middle of the Sahara with nothing but endless sand in every direction. I had no idea how far the nearest Algerian town was from the border. We had been so determined and focused on getting thru the border, we never really thought about what we would do after that.

After returning our passports, the soldiers went back to their business and left us alone. John and I stepped to a corner of the room to arrange our backpacks and I asked, "Hey, John, what do we do now?"

"Whattda you mean? We're all set. We got stamped. We're in."

"OK...But what do we do now?" I asked again, nodding in the direction of the empty, deserted road leading into Algeria.

After a moment, John replied, "Oh, yeah. What do we do now?"

We thought over our options for just a minute and then walked back over to the soldier in charge and tried to ask about transportation into Algeria. He didn't understand. So we drew pictures of a jeep and bus, and with a lot of body language he understood.

After some writings and body language of his own, the soldier explained to us that there was no transportation from the border that night or the next day. In fact, there was no transportation of any kind for at least two nights. Actually, as best we understood, there might be nothing from the border for the next three or four days. It depended if there was any vehicle coming out to the border from the Algerian side to drop travelers off to cross over to Tunisia. This was definitely an abandoned, empty border.

We were stunned. With our intense focus on just getting though the border check, we hadn't considered the possibility that there was no transportation into Algeria.

In hindsight, it's definitely something we should have considered and planned for. But, as you've probably noticed, for most of this travel adventure John and I were just intensely focused on getting through the next obstacle directly in front of us, trying to keep moving forward, and carry on.

During our entire trip we had an unwavering do or die attitude of no retreat…Just grit it out…Use our wits and nerve…Do whatever we had to do each day to keep moving and keep making time…I also just had an underlying belief and confidence that somehow we would find a way.

Having been raised a Christian with a belief in God, and although it's always been a very private matter for me; I must say that spiritual foundation and belief system gave me something to rely on when times were tough on the road. I knew there is always hope and always a way. It definitely gave me something to count on, and strength to draw from.

That belief system and traveling code served me well through many a trip and many difficult situations on the road. It never would have been possible to complete the various travel adventures I did to over 30 countries by the tender age of 21 without it.

But, on the other hand, there was still no way of avoiding the tough travel, extreme difficulties and danger, the occasional backtracking and mistakes; especially all the mistakes. We had already made a truckload of mistakes on this travel adventure and there were still more to come.

We moved away from the soldiers to the other side of the small room near the door and John whispered, "I can't believe it. No way outta here tonight."

"Not just that. There might be no way out of here for days."

"Unbelievable!" John exclaimed. "This is some isolated border." .

"I'm not spending the night out here.' I said in a low voice, "With all these armed soldiers…In this little border post. No way."

"OK, but then what? There's nothing out here. No place to go."

"We gotta walk it." I said, after a moment's consideration.

"Walk it?"

"That's right. We gotta walk it to the next town."

"Are you crazy! Take a look out there."

John then pointed out the door into the empty night and the isolated road leading into the pitch-black Sahara desert. It was dark and eerie out that door. It was not exactly a place I wanted to be going.

CROSSING INTO ALGERIA...FINALLY! THE LONG(ER) BORDER WALK

"But what can we do?" I said. "We got no choice. We gotta walk."

"How far is the next town?" John asked. "Do you still have that hand-drawn map you made back in Italy?"

"Man, I don't know. I haven't seen that scrap of paper with the map for a long time. Let me take a look for it."

After rummaging through my backpack, I found it.

"Yeah. I got it." Looking at the crumpled, hand-drawn map, I said, "Uhh…I think it's maybe 35 or 40 kilometers to the nearest town. Best I can tell."

"40 kilometers!! Are you serious?" John asked with alarm.

"Yeah, I think so…And the next town after that is much further. The first town looks to be about 35-40 k's, and then the next town north from there…ahh, looks like about another 100 k's."

"You sure?"

"No. Not at all. You know I drew this map really quickly." I answered, "If we're lucky, maybe I drew the line too long and the first town is closer."

"Yep, but maybe you drew it too short. Maybe it's further." John retorted.

We both thought for a moment about our options. We took another look around the isolated border building with all the armed soldiers…and then out the door into the black, silent desert. Neither option was very appealing.

"So, 35-40 kilometers, Huh?" John said.

"Yeah, best I can tell."

"We walk at a slow, steady pace - it will be tough in the pitch-black night. But if we go with a few breaks and walk at night, we should make it to town in a couple nights."

"Maybe." I replied, not convinced.

"Yep, probably two nights of walking. It'll be slow going at night."

"It'll be a tough walk, but what else can we do?"

"We gotta do what we gotta do." John said.

"Let's get started, then." I said. "This border post's not a safe place for us to be hanging around."

With our decision made John and I picked up our backpacks, took a look back at the soldiers in the room, and signaled that we were leaving and that we were walking. They didn't move or say a word. They just stood there staring at us, expressionless. I didn't know what they were thinking… Possibly something along the lines of 'Man, those two Americans are crazy.'

Without another look back, John and I walked out of the Algerian border post onto the road under the lone light shining down from the border building with darkness all around. The single, narrow, paved road headed out into the shadows and then quickly disappeared into the darkness…into the Sahara…into the unknown.

With our backpacks set on our back, and our destination before us, John and I gamely started out on what would be about a 40 kilometer nighttime trek through the merciless desert to the nearest town…That's what we thought, anyways.

Little did we know as we passed out of the shadows of the border building lights and walked out into the black night - that what lay ahead of us was actually over <u>80</u> kilometers of empty desert and darkness.

As it turned out, my hand drawn map was not very accurate. We didn't know it at the time, but the nearest town was actually an 80 kilometer walk away. We were heading into the heart of the Sahara on an 80 kilometer trek…at night, with no food, no water, compass nor real map. Quite a challenging adventure was before us.

John and I began our walk with a sense of quiet determination. We didn't talk about what was ahead of us after we made our decision. Like always on the road, it was just a matter of doing what we had to do.

As we started walking out into the desert it got very dark, very fast. Shortly after walking away from the border post, its light got hazy in the distance behind us, and eventually just faded into the black night, kind of like a match just slowly burning out, getting dimmer and dimmer. We became completely enveloped in the complete blackness of the early evening.

It was strange walking out there in the middle of nowhere, with no reference points in the distance or in the sky. Nothing but blackness. The dreary, cloudy day had been followed by a very black, cloudy, starless night.

The road we were walking was a narrow, unmarked road with just enough pavement for cars to pass both ways. There were no markings, signs or any paint of any kind, anywhere on or along the road. It was the same all through the Sahara; Just a thin strip of unmarked pavement lain out, like a thin pen line drawn in the sand out in the middle of the enormous desert.

As we were walking, John and I would sometimes almost lose track of each other in the darkness. I would just get lost in my thoughts and focus on the rhythm of my walking pace and trying to see where I was going in the darkness.

CROSSING INTO ALGERIA…FINALLY! THE LONG(ER) BORDER WALK

"John, are you still there? I can't see you." I said in a loud voice.

'I'm here. I'm a little ways behind you." John replied.

Startled, I turned slightly and squinting into the night, I could vaguely make out his silhouette outlined against the black skyline, "OK. We gotta talk more often. That's the second time, we've almost lost track of each other."

"It's easy to do out here, it's pitch black."

"So, how much ground do you think we've covered so far?" I asked.

"It must have been over an hour since we started walking." John replied, "It's really slow going in this darkness. Maybe a couple kilometers…at most,"

"Still no lights out here anywhere. This is an eerie place."

"Uh-huh. Over an hour walking out here and nothing." John replied apprehensively. "Not a car, not a light, nothing."

"I thought maybe there would be some lights out in the distance somewhere." I said gazing around into the blackness around me. "We should be able to see any light that's out there for many miles."

"That's for sure. But there's nothing."

"I don't think we'll see anything until we hit the town. Who would be out here?" I said, looking out in the utter blackness that was surrounding me.

"I don't know - but that's a scary thought. Anything could be out there." John said with a bit of an edge to his voice.

"Whooo," I said, laughing after making a ghost sound.

"Anything could be out there." John continued seriously. "There might be some nomads living around here."

"Yeah, remember some of those men who got off the bus back in Tunisia. In the middle of nowhere, and just started walking out into the empty desert."

"Yep. Maybe they're out there." John said.

"Could be…Who knows? But the Sahara's a huge place. Not likely we'll come across anyone."

"Maybe not. We'll see."

After a few minutes thought and some more walking, John said, "But what about snakes? We've gotta be careful walking out here in the dark. There are a lot of poisonous snakes that live in the Sahara, ya know."

"Yeah, I've heard that." I replied, "Remember that one guy we met a few towns ago. He said to be careful walking once we left the towns. That there are a lot snakes around in the desert. That they strike with no warning."

After a few moments of more thought, John said, "Yep. I also saw on a TV show about the Sahara, that during the cool nights, the snakes like to stay on warm surfaces that retain the suns heat, like rocks or the pavement."

"Uh-huh."

"They'd sure be easy to stumble on out here."

"That's for sure." I replied. "Especially walking on this road. It's really dark out here. I can't even see the pavement. Who knows what's on the road?"

"It'd be easy enough to step on a snake out here tonight."

"Man, can't let that happen." I answered, "We get bit, we die. That's it. There's no help or medicine anywhere out here."

With that uneasy thought, we continued our nighttime trek in silence, lost in our thoughts, walking and walking endlessly into the empty desert. Walking a little more carefully, I might add. It was a strange walk that night. Unlike any I've ever taken. With the unrelenting black Sahara surrounding us, not only did we have to be careful not to lose each other and not to step on snakes - But we also had to be careful not to mistakenly walk off the road out into the desert and lose our way. It actually would have been fairly easy to do.

The pavement and the flat, hard rock surface of the desert was often almost the same. With no markings or signs of any kind and the almost complete darkness, it was sometimes difficult to differentiate between the road and the hard rock surface of the desert. Even in the daylight, once we got only a couple hundred meters out into the desert, the road could be completely un-seeable. It just faded into the desert landscape.

While we were walking that night we would occasionally bend down and feel the road to make sure we hadn't wandered off into the hard rock desert. I have to admit after our talk about snakes, when I reached down to check that we I was still on the road, I did it a little tentatively.

Later on that night during the long walk, one of the most peculiar and unnerving things to happen on any of my travels began to occur. From the distant darkness near us, cutting through the light desert wind I heard a strange, shrill 'kkhisssh, hisshing' sound. After a short pause, "Kkhissh, hhiss' again.

"There's that strange sound again. Did you hear it?" John asked nervously.

"Yeah, I heard it…Again. What could it be?" I said, looking intensely out into the deep black night that surrounded us. "What could be out there?"

"You got me. But what ever it is, it's tracking us. We must have walked 2-3 hours since we first heard it…And whatever it is it keeps following us."

"Yeah, you got that right." I agreed. "It's been out there for a few hours now. We've walked a long ways and it's still out there. Still stalking us."

"At least it doesn't seem to have gotten any closer to us."

"I guess it hasn't." I agreed hesitantly. "Kinda hard to tell in this darkness though. It's tough to judge sounds and distance out here, especially at night."

John then asked a question that put me further on edge, "We can't see a thing in this blackness. How can it see us - if we can't see it?"

The question stumped me and got me really thinking about what could possibly be out there in the shadows, in the darkness? For the first time I felt like the prey being stalked by some unseen, unknown predator.

I gave John the only answer I could think of, "Who knows? Whatever it is, though, it's sure to know this desert area a whole lot better than we do."

"Man, what could be out there?"

It was strange and unnerving. We couldn't see anything. There was just a thick blackness all around us. The night covered us like a dark, heavy blanket. I often couldn't even see my own hand stretched out in front of me. Occasionally, when the heavy clouds would slightly separate and let a few rays of starlight peek through, we would catch glimpses of the road ahead or dim outlines of desert hills shaded against the night skyline. That was it.

For the next couple hours of walking into the desert night, we continued to hear the same strange, shrill, hissing sound. At varying intervals, from somewhere out in the darkness came the unnerving 'kkhissh, hisshing…' sound. We heard it periodically for the rest of long night as we were walking. In the night air and complete darkness, it was almost impossible to pin point where the sound was coming from. It was just a very disturbing, shrill kind of sound…piercing the air from the surrounding desert. We could tell the sound was coming from our left - to the south, and it wasn't the wind. But that was it.

How close was it? What was making the sound? What did it mean? Was it human or animal? We didn't know.

It was distressing not knowing what it was. After what seemed like hours on end, it became almost unbearable as the strange sound continued its relentless pursuit of us through the pitch-black, unending desert.

In our isolated, eerie surroundings my mind started playing tricks on me imagining possible sources and locations for the sound. A lot of images came to mind. Very few of them were re-assuring, actually most of them were quite horrifying. The unknown sound added a sense of urgency to our tiring walk. But we were facing a long, long walk (even in our mistaken calculations). No matter how fast we moved, we would be walking along following this forsaken desert road all night. It was a daunting challenge.

With the strange sound continually piercing the silence and cutting over to us on the night wind, John and I just kept at it. We just kept walking.

We kept walking…And walking.

I wasn't sure for how long. Even at our slow pace, we must have walked close to 7-8 kilometers. As I said, it was tough to judge time, or distance for that matter, out in the open desert in the darkness especially with the shrill 'hissing' sound pursuing us.

It had been a long, tense walk through the endless Sahara, when John finally saw something. It was the first thing we had seen since we started our trek several hours earlier. .

"Dennis, do you see that." John said with excitement.

"What? Where?"

"Behind us. Way out there behind us. It looks like maybe a light?"

I stopped walking and looked behind me.

"Where?" I asked again, squinting into the total blackness.

"There. It looks like a speck of light." He said, moving over closer to me so I could see where his arm was pointing.

I looked again, "I don't see it. Where?"

I kept looking and focused on the spot where John was pointing.

"Now I see it." I said. "It's a little point of light. Looks like a distant star."

"It's not a star. It's too low." John replied.

"It's getting bigger." I said.

"Yep, now there're two of them."

"Two of them?" I asked.

"Yes, two of them." After a moment John said, "I know what they are?"

"What?" I asked. I was still clueless.

"They're car headlights. It's a car…coming from the border."

We were surprised. It was the first thing we had seen since leaving the border many hours and several kilometers earlier. The lights were getting bigger and closer.

"Who could it be way out here?" John wondered.

"Must be someone passing through the border from Tunisia."

"Do you wanna flag it down? Maybe catch a ride?"

CROSSING INTO ALGERIA...FINALLY! THE LONG(ER) BORDER WALK

"We're really vulnerable out here." I cautioned, "Could be dangerous."

"Possibly." John said. "But people have been very friendly since we got in the Sahara."

"You got that right. Also the code of the desert, you know; never refuse a request for assistance, right?"

The lights were getting bigger and closer still.

"We should flag it down." John said.

"Do we have any choice." I said, "There's no place to hide from whoever it is. Those lights cast a wide mark. He's gonna see us anyways."

"OK. Let's try our luck. Maybe get a ride into town."

"Sounds good." I agreed. "It'd be good to stop walking and start riding."

With nowhere to hide, John and I just moved off to the side of the road and stopped walking, waiting in nervous anticipation. As the car approached we didn't flag the car. There was no need. We just stood by the road and waited. I was wondering who it could possibly be.

After hours of walking in the pitch black night, the lights of the car became incredibly bright and seemed almost searing as it approached us. The car pulled up in front of us and stopped. With the lights in our eyes we were blinded and couldn't see who was in the car, so we walked around the car to look in to see who was driving. We got quite a surprise.

It was a soldier; One of the soldiers from the Algerian border post. He was in the border building when we passed through. He was a brawny, heavy-set, dark skinned guy. He had a fleshy, sweaty face with a few days stubble covering his chin. Even sitting in the car, I could tell he was much bigger than either John or I. He was still in his ragged, worn-out uniform, but he had his military hat off. It was sitting on the dashboard in front of him.

His large, round head was covered with short black hair, and a small but noticeable scar cut though his dark skin running down the top of his forehead. The big soldier had his pistol attached to his belt on his right hip and a rifle next to the front car seat, on his left side nearest his door.

He looked up at us without any expression and roughly signaled us to get in his car. It wasn't really a request. We got in the car.

I did so with mixed feelings; relieved to have gotten off the pitch-black, empty road and away from the disturbing sound that had been relentlessly stalking us - But also apprehensive about the big, armed soldier giving us the ride.

CHAPTER **17**

The All Night Ride

As we got in the car with the soldier, John and I both said, "*Shocaren Saheb, Shocaren shaheb.*"(Thank you friend) John got in the front seat next to the soldier and I climbed in the back seat.

"We're going to the first town. If you could give us a ride to the first town that would be great." John said looking over at the big soldier.

The soldier gave no answer and no reaction. He didn't even look at us. He kept his large head facing the road ahead and didn't even glance in our direction. He just took off down the lonely, dark road into the desert.

"Yeah. We go first town."

Still no reaction.

"OK?" I added, holding up one finger. "We go to town, yes? The first town."

"We go to the first town with you." I said again pointing ahead, "OK?"

Still no reaction.

"Thanks for the ride."

Again, the big soldier didn't even look at us. He didn't even acknowledge us. He just looked ahead at the desert road and kept driving. As he drove, he kept his gaze constantly fixed on the road ahead, as his dark skin glistened with sweat even though it was a cool night. He never made any attempt to communicate with us. He just drove...and drove through the black night down the single, empty road cutting across the vast Sahara.

After driving for quite a while, John turned around from the front seat of the car and said in a low voice. "We should have reached the first town by now. It's been a long time since he picked us up."

"Yeah, we've covered a lot of road with him," I replied.

THE ALL NIGHT RIDE

"He's not going real fast, but we must have gone way over 30 kilometers by now. Still no sign of a town."

"Man, it's dark out there." I said, as I looked out the car window at the endless dark desert. "I'm glad were not walking this."

"It would have been a long walk."

We drove down the isolated road following the small beacon from our headlights cutting through the black night. Aside from the small beam of our headlight, we were surrounded by nothing but blackness in every direction. It was a long, dark ride.

Little did we know at the time – How long of a walk it would have been without the ride. The silent soldier kept driving for another hour before we ever did reach a town. We covered a lot of desert ground. The first town was a long, long ways. As I said earlier, much farther than we ever thought.

Finally, after a lot of miles, John said, "Hey. Dennis, I see some lights out in the desert ahead. It looks like something."

I looked out the car's front window at what looked like a miniscule campfire blazing out in the remote distance. As we continued driving, the blaze seemed to get slightly bigger.

"It's a small town." John said. "I can make out a few lights. Not much."

"Man, that town was a long ways from the border. That would have been a killer walk."

'No kidding, but now we've made it. We can get out of the car in this town."

"Yeah." I nodded. "Maybe find a place to sleep for the night. Then in the morning we can take the road north out of town and get up near the Mediterranean. Keep making good time."

As we drove up to the town, there were only a few isolated sand roads in the tiny, sleepy village, and I could see only a few dim lights and clay shops visible along the empty streets. It was dark and quiet. I couldn't see much at all. I believe the town's name was Tebessa. (We never had a chance to see it) As we were approaching the outskirts of the town, John and I started thanking the soldier, saying that we would get out here. We grabbed our backpacks and gestured toward the car door, signaling that we would get out now.

As he had for the entire drive, the big soldier didn't react or pay much notice to us. He just kept driving. Before we knew it, in almost a blink of the eye, we had passed by the town and the soldier had turned left heading out into the Sahara again. He never stopped. He was heading south out of town.

TRAVELIN' MAN ACROSS THE SAHARA AND BEYOND

There were only two ways to go, north or south...And we weren't going north. There were no other road choices and this guy had headed south dead into the Sahara, without stopping to let us out of the car. He just kept his eyes on the road and kept driving.

Within moments, the town was quickly disappearing behind us. It happened so quickly. Before we really had time to think or do anything, we were already out of the town and in the desert darkness again.

Just like that...our travel plans and travel route had changed.

It was to have a huge impact on our trip. First, it put us on a course heading further into the Sahara, lengthening the distance we needed to cover. Instead of heading north up to the Mediterranean coast and traveling the relatively easy route along the coastline to Morocco, we were now heading somewhere deeper into the Sahara – we didn't know where.

Also, more importantly and completely unknown to us at the time, we were now on a course taking us in the direction of the Sub-Saharan desert guerrilla war zone area. It was a deadly war being fought between Morocco and the Policario guerillas. The Policerio were launching wide-ranging desert raids from their bases inside Algeria. .

At this time, more than half of Moroccan King Hassan's armed forces of 100,000 were locked in battle with the Policerio guerillas. The Policerio were based and had sanctuaries within Algeria from where they would attack Western sources of mineral supplies in the Western Saharan zone occupied by Morocco.

We were not near the major battles (I think) but from where we were in the desert and the road we were on - It was a matter of only two road turns that would take us there. Just two turns. Like I said, in that part of the Sahara our travel choices were extremely limited; usually go forward or go back the way we came. We were to find out later that much of the supplies for the guerillas were brought in from the road we were on.

This little fact was soon to lead us on some daring and dangerous travel.

After having finally completed our half-the-night trek and ride through the desert and making it into the first town - we were now heading right back out of town into the desert again. We didn't really know where this new route was taking us. The limited haphazard map I had drawn in Italy didn't go this far south. It only showed the top part of northern Africa. So we were traveling completely blind.

THE ALL NIGHT RIDE

I leaned over the front seat, looked over John's shoulder and whispered, "John, where do ya think this guy is going? What do we do?"

"We got no choice." He said, "He's not stopping. We just ride it out."

"I guess so. We can't jump out anywhere. The guy's got a rifle. There's no place to hide or to go."

"Not much we can do. He's going where he's going and we're along for the ride whether we like it or not."

'Yeah." I said. "Who knows what he wants. I guess we'll find out what's up when he reaches the end of the line."

"Where ever that is..."

"You have any idea where we're headed? Where this road goes?"

"No idea. I just know it must be south." John said in a low voice, "I don't know where it ends up."

"Me neither. I have no clue." I replied. "We'll just have to ride it and find out."

After a few more minutes riding through the darkness along the lone strip of pavement, John looked back at me and whispered, "Just stay alert. We'll take turns sleeping."

"Uh Huh."

"If you want to - go ahead and sleep first. I'll keep lookout. Tap me when you wake up and we'll switch."

"OK. Sounds good."

And that's what we did. Or at least that's what we tried to do. But I don't think either one of us ever slept for more than a few minutes at a stretch during the long night ride. We just anxiously rode out the night with the big soldier driving endlessly through the black, empty desert.

We ended up driving almost all night, for over six hours in the cramped, little old car going further and further south…dead into the Sahara, just watching the road and the guy driving. Six long hours. Meanwhile, I don't think the big soldier ever said a single word to us. The big guy just kept driving and driving. With no markings, signs or paint on the road to give guidance, the soldier drove at a fairly slow but steady pace. We just cut through the complete blackness watching the pavement roll by. The second town we came across was even further than the first. It took a long time to reach it.

When we did, it was a very small speck of a town, I later found out was called Bir El Ater. It appeared to consist of only a few low, weather-beaten, clay buildings and a couple of narrow sand covered streets, but there was actually something open – a gas station. It was the only light I could see coming out of the seemingly empty, desert town. The soldier drove into and stopped at the gas station. It was the first time he had stopped since we got in the car with him hours earlier. We tried to thank him and leave the car with our backpacks but he wasn't having it. Again, he wasn't threatening us, but it was plain we weren't going anywhere. And besides, where would we go? There was nowhere to go. With the exception of the little gas station, the entire town was dark and quiet.

John and I spoke (gesturing and a little drawing) briefly to the young bearded Algerian guy putting in the gas. He seemed absolutely shocked to see two young foreigners in the car with the soldier. But he seemed to understand what we wanted to find out.

From the limited information we gleaned from him we learned three things; we were way out in the middle of nowhere…we needed to turn back…and there was no way through the way we were going.

"Did you understand him? Did he mean there's no way through the desert following this road were on?" John asked me in a low voice.

"That's what I got." I replied. "He seemed pretty strong that we should head back the way we came. He kept gesturing that this way is blocked. Go back. Go back."

"Why would that be?"

"Beats me. I have no idea where we're going."

"We're really heading deep into the desert."

Motioning toward the soldier driving the car, John whispered, "Yeah, where is this guy taking us?"

"I don't know. But if there's no way through on this road the way we're going - we'll have a lot of backtracking to do."

"You got that right."

As soon as the car was filled up with gas, the big, silent soldier just quickly took off and continued south back into the Sahara following the same single road. Since making the turn south out of the first town, we never came across another road on that long night ride.

We found out much later the road we were on - was the only road connecting the few, isolated towns along the desert landscape for hundreds and hundreds of miles. Once we passed that first town in Algeria, we had absolutely no choices other than to go deeper into the Sahara or go back the way we came. And with the soldier at the wheel, we were going further into the Sahara whether we wanted to or not.

THE ALL NIGHT RIDE

As I said, he drove for a good six hours that night heading mostly south cutting into the heart of the desert. During the entire ride we only passed through about three extremely isolated desert towns, and the soldier only made the one brief stop for gas. Otherwise it was nothing but endless desert.

The entire ride, I was thinking what's his deal? What's going to be the play? What does he want? There's usually something and I wanted to be prepared for it. I had a lot of different ideas but couldn't figure it out.

Like I said to John earlier in the car, we would probably find out when we reached the end of the line…And we did.

Finally, after the long hours and hundreds of kilometers of travel, we were coming up to outskirts of another little, desert village. John and I had no idea where we were. It was very late night, almost early morning – right at the flick of time between the darkness of night and the break of dawn. Our vision of sight was just starting to expand as the deep dark night was finally being burned off by the approaching sunrise.

This village was very small, even by the standards of the Sahara. From what we could see, there was just the road leading into the center of a little sand town square, with what looked like an old, dry thirsty well in the middle. There were a few frail trees and vegetation valiantly attempting, but not really succeeding, to grow around it.

Scattered around the town square were several single level, wind burned, white clay buildings mostly attached together in kind of a long row around each side of the town square. The lone road we had been traveling on for half the night just ran around the town square, around the old well, and then past the other side of town, and continued on its way into the desert again. There were only a couple of little sand side streets (alleys) that cut between the buildings, with a few more, smaller clay buildings alongside them. That was about it.

As we were reaching the very outskirts of the little town, the big soldier began to slow the car. He didn't pull over - there was no need. There never really was any need out in the Sahara. There were no other cars anywhere. During the entire night-long ride through the desert, not a single car ever came up to us from behind nor did I ever see car lights from behind us. I only saw about three cars go pass us coming from the opposite direction; three cars in 6 hours. It was an isolated, desolate road.

As we came to a stop, John and I immediately came alert and ready. It was now crunch time. The soldier had a pistol on his belt and a rifle next to him near the door. I was acutely aware of that and paying close attention to his movements.

He didn't seem overtly threatening; but being cramped in a little car, with a big armed soldier on the side of some empty desert road, in the early morning darkness, out in the Sahara, in the middle of who-knows-where; You can believe, in my mind I was evaluating any potential threats and options I had.

We were in the same positions as when we first got in the car with the soldier, John was still in the front seat next to the soldier and I was in the back. After stopping the car, the soldier turned his bulk toward us and acknowledged us for really the first time. He started gesturing with his heavy right hand, and speaking in Arabic.

Out of the side of my mouth, I said thickly, "What does he want? Do you understand?"

"No. Not at all." John replied.

"He seems to want us to give him something. I don't know."

The soldier continued signaling and then reached in his pocket and pulled out a 100 Dinar Algerian bill. (Worth about $28). He then gestured like making an exchange of hands.

"OK. I got it. I know." John said. "He wants to trade money with us - black."

"Black-market?"

"Yeah."

Once we understood, we motioned to the soldier to wait a moment for us to decide. After taking a moment to consider it, I quietly asked John, "What do you think?"

"It's risky for us." John replied right away. "What do we do when we get to the border to leave Algeria?"

"Whattda you mean?"

"We'll have to show our bank papers and foreign currency. We'll be short. We're gonna have big problems with our papers leaving the country."

"You got that right."

During our brief talk the soldier continued staring at us. But now he wasn't looking at us with the same blank expression. He was now looking at us...almost hopefully. The longer, John and I talked over the situation, the more anxious the soldier seemed.

THE ALL NIGHT RIDE

Looking back over at John, I said in a hushed voice, "I think this guy really wants to trade money with us. He's probably never had a chance to get a hold of foreign currency before."

John took a quick glance at the soldier and said to me, "I see what you mean. I think we can cut a good deal - But what about getting out of the country? With messed up financial papers?"

"We deal with that when we get to it." I said, "For now we really need the money to get by. With no money we never get to the border…We never get back."

"Yep. That's a good point." John agreed. "Let's see what we can get."

John looked back over at the soldier and gestured thumbs up, meaning 'OK we'll trade.' The soldier at first seemed startled and offended by the thumbs up gesture. (I later learned it often had a rude meaning in the Arab world.)

But we quickly showed that what we meant was 'yes' we would trade black market with him. When he understood, he actually almost smiled. Six hours of no reaction and now he almost smiled…Not quite, but almost.

"What currency do you have to trade?" I quickly asked John.

"Not much. I think I've got a few French francs, some British pounds and some Lire left over. Plus the dollars"

"What about small bills? What do you have in small bills?"

"French francs and Italian lire. How about you?"

Sitting in the back seat I was able to look in my wallet out of sight of the soldier. "I've got a few French francs and a few Swiss Francs from when I bought those train tickets. Plus a couple large bills of British pounds and dollars. Uh, I also have 4 single pound notes."

By the way, 'large' bills meant bills worth only $10 or more.

So in a cramped car in the very early morning darkness, along an isolated desert road somewhere out in the Sahara, we started haggling with an armed Algerian soldier over trading some of our western currency black market for his Algerian currency.

We had a good idea of the official value of Algeria currency - from when we first had our money documented in Gafsa by the friendly customs official so we had an idea what terms we hoped to get. The negotiating all took place by gestures and handing money back and forth in the cramped car. The big soldier passed us his 100 dinar bill and then John and I would give him a few of our western currency. When he didn't agree, he took his money back and we took our money back. Then we would start over again with some other currency and hand the money back and forth. This went on for a long time...Back and forth.

He didn't want any Italian lire and we didn't want to give up any of our US dollars unless we had to. Even though we probably could have gotten a better deal with dollars, the dollars were in big bills so we couldn't really use them anyway. Eventually we were haggling over some British pounds and Swiss francs in return for his Algerian dinar. John and I were really holding tough in the negotiations. We needed to. Making extra money on the trade would really go a long ways for us.

We actually ended up spending over an hour in that hot, crowded car going back and forth with the money. With John and I holding tough in our negotiations, the big soldier was getting more and more irritated by the little money we were offering in return for his Algerian dinar. What we were willing to trade would have given us about 4-5 times the bank rate. (In other words, we wanted him to give us about 4-5 times as much dinar as any bank would give us for the same amount of western currency.)

After an hour of frustrating negotiating and haggling, the soldier had pulled out a second 100 dinar bill. He seemed to have forgotten about the other 100 dinar bill we had already been passing back and forth earlier. I was now holding the other 100 dinar bill in my hand, resting it on my leg in the back seat. Not hiding it, but out of his sight, just holding it during the continuous back and forth negotiations.

Then abruptly, the big soldier lost his patience and angrily terminated the negotiations. He roughly grabbed the few pounds and francs we had been offering and then put his other (second) 100 diner bill into John's hand. He then made an angry gesture like, 'That's it! We're finished. The trade is done."

He aggressively reached across John and pushed open the front car door on John's side. He then took John's backpack off the front floor, and flung it out onto sand next to the street. Next, he all but pushed John out of the car after his backpack. He then turned and while glaring at me made a threatening motion toward me to get out the car as well. He didn't have to do it twice. I hopped out of the car and joined John on the sand covered, narrow street. The soldier then angrily slammed the door and without a look back, sped off through the town and into the desert. We lost sight of him as the road curved out behind the little town out of our view. We didn't know where he was going.

THE ALL NIGHT RIDE

John looked over at me, as he was shaking the sand off his backpack. "Man, that was some tense negotiations. But I think we came out all right."

John then did some fast calculations in his head.

He then looked at me with a smile and said "We gave him, what, about $4 worth of Swiss francs and 10 British pounds ($16) for about 40 dollars worth of Algerian currency…So we made about $20 bucks on the deal. Not bad."

"That's not all." I responded with a big grin.

"What do you mean?"

"I've got another 100 dinar bill from him." I said showing John the bill in my hand. "We're actually up another 30 bucks."

"That's great." John said surprised, "How did that happen?"

"I was still holding it when he pulled out the second bill. And then when he threw us out of the car, it was added to the deal…I don't think he knew it was added to the deal – but it was."

"So we're up about 40 bucks." John said, "That'll really help."

"No kidding."

At that time, $40 seemed like a small fortune for us, and it was the way we were traveling. After all $40 was a fourth of the total money I had started with for the entire month long trip across Europe and Africa.

John and I quickly split the money we had made between the two of us. It felt real good to be *adding* money to my dwindling reserves for a change.

We then picked up our backpacks and started walking in the direction of the isolated, sleepy town. After an hour of haggling in the car it was now dawn and daylight was breaking over the horizon. The early morning sun distinctly and slowly edging over the desert horizon at daybreak was one of my favorite views in the Sahara. We paused for a moment to take it in. It was an inspiring sight.

As we started the short walk into the tiny town, I said to John, "Hey, what if he finds out he's missing the other 100 dinar bill and realizes we have it. That could be big trouble."

"You mean the soldier?"

"Yeah."

"Do you think he would come back to look for us?" John wondered.

"Who knows? Maybe he lives around here."

"Where?"

"I have no idea." I shrugged, "But if he does come back we're sitting ducks out here."

"Things got pretty intense in that car. If he thinks we intentionally ripped him off, he might be really angry."

"Yeah, and he's got a rifle and pistol with him. He could come back and shoot us. Who'd ever know?"

"Let's see what we can find in this town." John said, "See if there is some place we can lay low for a little while and stay out of sight."

"OK…Better safe than sorry. Let's go."

We started hustling into the little town to see where we could hide out for a while and maybe get a little sleep. We had been on the move for a full day and night now, with little rest and only one meal of couscous. Fatigue and hunger was finally catching up to me. It had been a very long but productive day, starting at sunrise with us backtracking about 150 kilometers from the Tunisian border town of Fierena to Gafsa to get our visas. We had covered a lot ground.

As we hurriedly walked through the dusty, desert town, the few streets and town square were completely vacant. It was just empty and quiet, as though the tiny town was still slumbering. With dawn just breaking, nobody had woken up yet it seemed.

We were genuinely worried the big soldier might come back for us if he found out he was missing money. The soldier's entire attitude, demeanor and actions changed dramatically when he lost his temper and threw us out of his car. He quickly changed from being neutral and passive to being a potential dangerous threat to us…A well armed, direct threat. At this moment, as we were for most of the trip, John and I were in an extremely vulnerable position. We couldn't afford to take any chances. The most basic rule to staying safe on the road was to immediately take action to remove a threat before it ever materialized.

"We gotta lay low for a while." John said, "Get off the road even for just a short time."

"I hear you."

"I figure, if he does come back he won't spend more than a short while looking for us. His temper should fade pretty quickly. But, still, we can't chance it…being out here in the open if he comes back."

"You got that right." I agreed. "We gotta find some place to get out of sight. But where?"

THE ALL NIGHT RIDE

After quickly looking around the sparse, little desert town, John frowned, "That's a good question."

We realized there was really no place to hide out in the town. You could almost see the entire speck of a town in one quick glance. Continuing to scan the town, John and I began quickly considering our limited options. But before we even had a chance to decide what our next move should be, a short, stooped, grey-bearded man wearing weathered robes and a turban appeared from one of the doorways.

He walked across the barren, sand-covered street directly up to John and me. He didn't speak but he smiled kindly and made a sleeping gesture by putting his hands under his head, and then pointed to us, like 'Do you want to sleep?'

We were shocked to see him and also by his offer. He just appeared out of the blue. But we quickly nodded, smiled and said, *"Shocurem sahab."*

The kind old man then signaled for us to follow him. He led us short way across the sandy, empty road to a door to his room. It was a compact, single room, with few furnishings and a kind of open washing area that he directed us to put our backpacks down and sleep in.

Within a matter of a few minutes of entering the town, we now had a place to sleep and stay out of sight. Through hand signals the kind stranger conveyed to us that we could stay and sleep for about four hours and then we would have to leave. It was another of the amazing and often timely acts of kindness that we experienced on the trip. The Algerian stranger had no idea of the difficult situation and potential danger we were in and how much his act of kindness helped us out.

By this time we had been on the road traveling continually by foot, bus and car for almost 24 hours straight. We had made a lot of tough miles and hadn't eaten anything since early in the previous day. We were dead tired, hungry and ready for a break. We thanked the kindly, old man again, got settled on the barren floor and quickly fell fast asleep.

CHAPTER **18**

Passing the Point of No Return

Before I knew it, the kind, old man woke us up and gestured that it was time for us to leave. I was still dead tired at that point and didn't really want to get up. I had only caught a few minutes of random sleep the night before, during the long car ride through the desert, but it was time to go. There wasn't much choice.

John and I gathered our backpacks and belongings. I didn't see any place to wash, and I didn't want to impose after the old man was so kind to us. So it appeared it was going to be another day out in the desert wind and sand with no washing, another day of many. To be honest, I didn't even notice at this point.

John looked over at me, while I was still arranging things in my backpack. "Time to hit the road again, Dennis. You ready"

"Give me a minute. My backpack strap is getting loose."

"How many miles have you put on that backpack. I think it's seen better days."

"No kidding. I've covered a lot of miles with it."

"You think it will last the trip?" John asked with a chuckle.

"Absolutely. It might be small and worn, but it'll last."

The backpack actually did last a long time. I traveled to over 35 countries with that same small, inexpensive backpack. It really served me well. Also, with the same chained wallet. I carried the backpack and wallet on so many travels to faraway places that they came to give me a little sense of home when I was on the road, especially when I was on my own. Just like having Coca-Cola out on the road gave me a little sense of home - so did having my trusty, old backpack and wallet with me.

PASSING THE POINT OF NO RETURN

I finished getting packed up, and John and I wearily stepped out of the room on to the dusty, village street.

"It's pretty quiet out here, isn't it? Not much activity." John said.

"It sure is a small town," I said, looking around the almost vacant, few desert streets of the little town.

There were only a few of the Algerian villagers out and about on the street. No cars or vehicles. Maybe half a dozen people, including a couple of women covered from head to toe with the flowing robes, along with a couple donkeys and one tired looking camel. I do believe that every single one of them, including the donkeys and camel, stopped dead in their tracks when my brother and I first came out onto the street. They hadn't moved since. They just stood and stared in shock.

"Do you have any idea where we are?" John asked, "That was a long ride last night. We covered a lot of desert with that soldier."

"Man, I have no idea. But we're no way near the Mediterranean. We're really way out here in the Sahara. We drove half the night straight through nothing but desert. That was some ride."

"We must be way south. I think on the entire ride we headed almost all south. After the first turn south that guy made, in that first town, we never hit another road. We never made another turn."

"Yeah, I think your right." I agreed. "We never passed another road anywhere. Just like in this town – There's only one road cutting through."

"Well, I'm starving." John said, "Let's see if we can find something to eat and then we can decide what's our next move."

"It's not going to be too tough to decide."

"Whatta you mean?" John asked.

"We don't exactly have many choices to decide from. We can either keep going forward, or go back the same way we came. That's it."

"Yeah, that's the truth." John agreed. "Let's get something to eat. I'm starving. We can try and find out where we are after we get some food."

John's priority was often food. Other concerns were often further down the list.

"OK." I said, "But I'm a little worried about the couscous. I love that stuff but the after-effects are still deadly for me. Maybe it will be all right this time."

John laughed and said, "For your sake, I hope so."

We started walking down the sand covered street looking for a market or something resembling a restaurant. The few people on the street still hadn't moved, and were just staring. As we walked past a short, middle-aged man, with a thick, black, unruly beard and a wind creased face, he smiled and motioned like he wanted to meet us.

So we stopped walking, smiled back and reached out our hand. After hesitating a moment the short, weary looking man shook hands and slightly bowed.

"*Aslama, saheb,*" John and I said.

"The man smiled brightly and said something in Arabic that I didn't understand.

"My name John." My brother said gesturing toward himself.

I introduced myself in the same way.

The man seemed to understand and pointed toward himself and said "Tareq. Tareq." His name was Tareq.

John then motioned like he was eating and looked around, "Where eat? Where food?"

Tareq acted like he understood and signaled for us to follow him. We walked a short ways down the little narrow sand covered street and then he entered a small kind of shop, with a couple old wooden tables and chairs along the wall. There was just one bearded, grizzled haired middle-aged man wearing western clothes working inside.

Well, not actually working. He was sitting in a chair leaning against the wall dozing. I think the breakfast rush probably wasn't something he had to worry about way out here in this town.

John and I sat at a table and Tareq ordered some food for us. It was couscous and bread. The shop owner brought the food over with a big smile. I looked at the couscous with a longing sense of hunger and…dread. Knowing I would enjoy the meal, but worried about the after-effects.

When we got our food, I asked Tareq for some Coke-Cola. I didn't expect them to have it in this isolated, desert town out in the middle of nowhere. But even way out here in this windy, dust of a village, miles and miles out in the empty Sahara, not only did the guy know what Coke-Cola was - he even had some bottles of it. The bottles looked like they were of a WWII vintage, from maybe about 1945, but he had them. It still tasted good to me.

John eagerly consumed his meal with great pleasure, while I cautiously ate mine concerned about what the meal would cause later. While we were eating a few other villagers had come into the little restaurant to take a look

PASSING THE POINT OF NO RETURN

at us. They were just kind of standing around, smiling and seemed very curious, but a little shy.

We tried to ask about where the road was heading that we had come into town on, but it was difficult to get any information because no-one spoke any English at all. At first the group was a little hesitant to approach us, but then one young man tried to help us. He was communicating via body language, gestures and drawings, and we thought we gleamed a little information from him about the road we were on.

"John, do you understand what he's trying to say?"

"I'm not sure." John answered. "It seems that the road continues south and west from here across Algeria. To where exactly…I'm not sure."

A couple other men of the group now became a little more animated and tried to give us some information. It seemed that the road did head further south into the Sahara and eventually in the direction of Morocco. But also, as best we could tell, they seemed to be trying to warn us about the road ahead that there was some problem or danger ahead. It wasn't very clear to us.

They kept gesturing that up ahead was danger and pointing a gun like there were soldiers or fighting or something. We also tried to ask about buses or any kind of transportation we could take from the town. There didn't seem to be anything at all.

John and I thanked the small crowd of men for their help, and walked out of the little restaurant back onto the lone street in the little town square. We stood out on the street with a warm morning wind blowing past, carrying the Sahara sand with it and, as usual, layering our clothes, hair and backpack with a thin coat of sand.

"Ok, so now what?" I asked John.

"I don't know." John shrugged, "What do you think?"

"Well, we have only two choices. We can keep heading on or go back the way the way we came."

"We came a long ways last night." John said. "That was a lot of miles we covered. It must have been close to 300 kilometers. Going back would be a lotta backtracking. We had one long ride last night – It could take a lot longer to cover the same ground."

"Man, I hate backtracking," I said.

"That's a long ways to be going backwards." John repeated.

"Those guys in the restaurant seemed to be saying that this road does head toward Morocco at some point. That's where we need to be going…I say we keep going ahead and keep moving forward."

"I hear you." John said nodding. "But those guys seem to think that there's some problem up ahead. I think they meant the road ahead is danger or we can't get through."

"Oh, yeah,…remember, so did that guy at the gas station last night. He kept gesturing the road is blocked. Go back." I said.

"Yeah, I remember. He did. What's up with that?"

"Who knows?" I replied. "I still think we came this far, we keep moving on."

"I'm with you." John said, nodding his head. "We came this far. It would be tough to turn around and backtrack and take the northern route, like we originally planned. Let's keep moving forward."

"Yeah. We keep making time. We'll deal with whatever lays ahead when we get to it."

With our decision made, John and I walked through the small village to follow the road out into the desert to see about making some mileage. To where? We weren't exactly sure. Actually, we didn't have a clue.

We had no idea where the road we were on was going. Actually, we didn't even know where we were; let alone where we were going. All we knew was that we were in Algeria, somewhere in the Sahara. And we knew we needed to head in the direction of Morocco. That was it.

Most everything was unknown to us. It was a true adventure into the unknown. We didn't know exactly where we were, and we also didn't know exactly where we were going.

With no buses from the town, as far as we knew, and with no trains anywhere within maybe a thousand kilometers, we decided to try our luck again hitching. We had no other choice. It was a rather novel idea – to hitch-hike across the Sahara Desert. It's not something we ever discussed or planned in advance. I'd never heard of anyone who had ever done it before. Like always, we were just doing what we had to do.

So we walked out about 100 yards past the edge of the town to start hitching where the lone road left the village and headed out into the empty desert. The road just continued out in front of us in a meandering way and disappeared into the endless Sahara sand.

It was still morning and the day was warming up into a partly sunny and windy day. After walking a short way out of the town, we stood next to the road waiting for a car or truck or some kind of vehicle to come by.

We waited a while with no vehicles passing by...none coming and none going. So we dropped our backpacks off our backs and sat down in the sand next to the road to relax and wait for a ride.

"Well, we'll see if we can get a ride out of here. There's not much traffic, is there?" John said.

"No. Not much."

"I wonder if anyone ever hitches out here."

"I doubt it." I said, "I don't think the locals hitch. We haven't come across anyone hitching the whole time we've been in Tunisia and Algeria."

"Yeah. We've covered a lot of road in Africa the past week, what, maybe about 1,000 kilometers, including the backtracking - And I haven't seen anyone hitching. Not a one. I've never heard of anyone hitching in the Sahara."

"I don't know if they even know what hitchhiking is out here in the desert." I said.

"We'll find out soon enough, I guess."

After sitting by the road a few more minutes with still no vehicles going by, John said, "It looks like it's going to be a nice day. The sun's coming out. It's beautiful out here."

"Yeah. It is kinda nice out here." I said, looking up at the clearing blue sky, and all around at the rolling, mountain waves of brown sand shimmering in the sun and wind. It was an impressive sight.

I laid back in the sand with my head on my backpack and just took in the desert sights.

"I'm going to get a little sleep." I said, "You mind watching the road first? Watch for cars?"

"All right. You sleep. I'll hitch first."

I closed my eyes and quickly dozed off in the desert sun…But not for long.

"Dennis. We got a ride. Wake up. Let's go."

"Huh?" I said, wiping the sleep out of my eyes.

"Time to move." John said hurriedly, "We gotta ride."

"Really? That was fast."

As I stood up I could see there was a dented, rust covered, small car stopped on the road just a little ways ahead. John and I ran up to the car. When we opened the door to the car, we were shocked to see what was inside.

Sitting cramped in the passenger seat of the car, next to the Arab driver, was a smiling mustachioed, sandy haired Westerner in his early 20's. He was traveling with a very big backpack and a lot of equipment, including an expensive camera and tent that was on the seat behind him. He was the first and only Westerner we saw on the entire trek across the Sahara. John and I stopped for a moment outside the car and just stared. We were so surprised - We now had the same reaction as everyone else had had with us for the past week. .

The guy sitting in the car continued smiling, and said in English "Hi. I'm Knut."

After a moment's hesitation, John said, "Oh…Hi. I'm John. This is my brother, Dennis."

We quickly shook hands with him as we climbed into the back of the little car. Without speaking the Arab driver then started down the lonely road into the desert.

"Man. We're really surprised to see you out here. Where're you from?" John asked.

Knut answered, "I'm from Norway. How about you guys?"

"We're Americans." John replied,, "From Michigan, near Detroit."

"What are you doing way out here?"

"Just traveling." I said, "Were heading to Morocco and then making our way back to England. How about you?"

"The same. I'm just traveling. Hey, it's great to see you guys. You're the first Westerners I've seen here."

"Yeah. Likewise." John said.

We spent that day traveling with Knut. He was a good guy. A friendly, tall, easy-going guy…A 'travelin man' just like John and I. He followed the same sense of adventure and code of the road that we did. He was also to be the only other foreigner we were to see anywhere in the Sahara.

We drove for a long time in the little car through the desert to the next town, passing the miles of desert sand with only an occasional car or more often, a truck or jeep going by in the other direction. Scattered occasionally throughout the drive, alongside the road, were the bones and carcasses of dead donkeys or camels, along with an abandoned, decaying car or vehicle here or there; for whatever reason, not having been able to make it to the next town or oasis. They were a fairly common sight on our trek all across the desert, and a grim reminder of the sometimes deadly, unforgiving nature of the Sahara.

PASSING THE POINT OF NO RETURN

When we arrived in the next town, John, Knut and I got out of the car and thanked the man who had given us the ride. This town was as far as the guy was going.

It was a bigger, spread-out town called Touggourt, with a wide paved, sandy street running through it, and many other side streets and roads winding among several two story clay buildings in and about the hilly town. There was a lot of activity and people out on the streets and a large market near where the driver let us out. Men were sitting at tables along the road playing cards and the board game with rocks, others were leading donkeys packed with sacks, and some covered women were walking through the market area shopping for food. Camels were being slowly ridden by or led by turban wearing bearded men carrying large bags of goods on their humped backs. Men were pulling old wooden carts of bread or other goods. There were even some old cars and rusted trucks rumbling by on the streets. After the almost ghost town like feel of the previous towns we had recently passed through, this town seemed the New York City of the Sahara.

The three of us walked down the street and stopped to buy some bread and Coca-Cola and watched the men playing their games. I had the runs again from my morning meal of couscous, so I was glad to have some bread to eat. People on the streets were friendly and always stared, just as they had in the other smaller villages we had passed through for the past several days.

We spent some time walking the streets, taking pictures and looking around. John and I went to look for a kind of phone bank where we were going to try and make an international call home, while Knut looked around the town. We wanted to try to call our parents and little brother Winston to wish them a Merry Christmas. This day happened to be a couple of days before Christmas Eve. We never would have known it except for the date. Both Tunisia and Algeria are Muslim countries, and as the friendly guy named Keridin told us on our first night in Africa, 'Christmas is not celebrated much here.' That was for sure.

By now it had been a couple months since I had communicated with anyone at home. They had no idea that we were now in the Sahara Desert or even that we were in North Africa. The only contact we had was a postcard we had sent from Italy, but that had probably not even reached home yet so we wanted to let them know where we were. Also, our younger brother Winston was only eight years old and was a great kid. John, who was always joking, planned to call Winston and joke with him that I had run off with an Arab princess and that I would not be coming back.

◄ TRAVELIN' MAN ACROSS THE SAHARA AND BEYOND

After a lot of checking, John and I did make our way to some kind of international phone bank service where we wasted time and also some money trying to get a phone call placed home. We never did get a call put through.

While John and I were at the phone bank, we met a rather dignified, elder Algerian man. We talked (communicated) with him while we were fruitlessly waiting to place our call. He gave us a bit of vital but ominous information. Through mostly gestures and drawings, he warned us about continuing on the road in the direction we were going. He told us we should go back. We finally understood why people had kept warning us about a problem or danger ahead of us. The man explained to us that we were going in the direction of a war, what we later found out was, the Sub-Saharan war. Fighting and battles were taking place between Morocco and Algeria in the desert up ahead. With gestures and pictures, he seemed to be saying that supplies were taken to the Policerio guerrillas from this road. There would be a turn up ahead (finally) and one turn headed toward where the Policerio were hiding out in the desert.

He told us no people were allowed through that way. We would be blocked. Only trucks taking supplies for the guerrillas were let through. He drew a picture of a full truck going along OK - and then a stick figure of a man that he put an X through, shaking his head 'No' and pointing to us. No. No. He was quite adamant about it.

That was very bad news for John and me...But that wasn't the worst of it.

When we were able to make the informative Algerian man understand that we needed to get to Morocco, he gave us some even more ominous information. He seemed to explain that the entire border between Algeria and Morocco was closed. All blocked. All closed off. No-one was allowed through because of the war. With this information he seemed a little less adamant. Not so sure...

After the older man left us, I said to John, "What do you think? What do we do? Man, we're way out here. We're a long, long ways from home. How we gonna make it back?"

"I don't know." John said, concerned. "I wonder if what that guy said is true. You ever read or hear about any war between Morocco and Algeria?"

"No, I don't think so. I remember seeing something on the BBC News in England one time about the Policerio guerillas, but I don't remember much about it. How about you?"

"No. Nothing."

PASSING THE POINT OF NO RETURN

After failing in our attempt to even get a call through to leave a message at home, John and I left the phone bank to go find Knut. John and I walked the streets for a few more minutes in silence contemplating our options. We were in a very dire situation. It was decision time. Big-time. Do or die time for us…And we knew it. We had a very important decision to make.

Finally, John asked me, "So, whadda ya think we do?"

"Well, we've only got two choices. We keep going forward and try to cross into Morocco and make it back to England that way. Or we give up our dream to cross northern Africa and go all the way back the way we came - all the way through Tunisia, cross the Mediterranean and travel back through Europe and cross the Channel to England."

"Yeah. That's about it. We keep moving ahead or we back track and go all the way back the same way we came."

'Not many options."

"That's for sure."

"How much money you got left." John asked.

I didn't have to take my money out and count it. I knew exactly how much money I had at any given time. "Between the Algerian Dinar, Swiss Francs and the pounds and dollars I've been holding, I've got 82 bucks. How about you?"

John on the other hand was less concerned about our money situation and seldom checked his funds. He ran low on money first and ended up asking me for money on the trip. I still have the little paper with the 3 dates and the amounts I loaned him – Three 5-pound British notes, a total of about $25.

John stopped walking and checked his money belt.

"OK…Let's see…I've got about 78 bucks with all the currencies I'm carrying."

"That's it? 78 bucks."

"Yeah. But it could be a lot worse. Think if we didn't make that money on the black market trade."

"True. That really helped us out." I said, "We'd be dead in the water without it….But still, how are we ever going to get back with about 80 bucks each. Either way we go, we still gotta cross the Mediterranean Sea. That will take a chunk of our money right there. And then we still gotta cross Europe and the English Channel."

"Uh-huh. Plus we gotta cover, what, more than a thousand miles overland."

"Man! It doesn't look good."

After a few more moments thought, John said, "I don't think it's possible to back track, and go back to England the way we came. We won't make it back. No way. With 80 bucks each. We've spent almost double that getting this far, plus the extra black market money we've used. There's no way we could make it back."

"Yeah, I agree. We'd never make it back with the money we have."

"Not a chance." John said.

I quietly added, "We've passed the point of no return."

"That's the truth. We gotta keep going… But if the Moroccan border is closed or we're blocked by the war - we'll have to turn around anyways and still go all the way back the way we came. That's a huge risk." John said.

"Yeah." I said concerned. "If were forced back, we could get stuck out in the Sahara with no money."

"But I still think we have to risk it. We've come too far to turn back"

"Alright." I agreed. "There's no turning back now. If we keep going ahead, we *might* make it. At least we have a chance. We just gotta hope the border is open. If Morocco is closed, we're dead."

During our entire conversation and actually during this entire trip across the Sahara, we never once discussed trying to get money sent from home. We never even considered it. It never came up. Ever. We knew our parents would do anything for us if we asked, but we just had that fierce grit it out attitude. Keep carrying on, using our wits and nerve, and making it on the road

At this time, 1977, in our situation, it would have been impossible to arrange for money to be sent anyways. So it wasn't an option. But it's something we never would have considered. On all of my trips and adventures around the world (and I think also for John on his), we never once asked or even considered asking for money or for any kind of assistance from home - to make it back from a tough situation. There were several times that it really would have helped. Later on in life with business and home situations I did get a lot of assistance, but never on my travels.

CHAPTER **19**

Losing the Road

With our decision firmly made to keep going forward toward Morocco, John and I walked through the streets and met back up with Knut. He had been looking around taking some pictures. After talking for just a moment, John glanced over at Knut and said, "You want to start hitching again?"

Knut looked back at John a little surprised.

John continued, "We need to be making some distance today. We heard the border might be closed with Morocco and there might be a problem with the road being closed up ahead because of the war zone. You hear anything about that?"

"Uhh, I heard a little something about some fighting but nothing for sure." Knut replied, "But if there's a problem ahead. We can always turn around and head back another way."

I added, "Yeah. I know…But we're getting a little low on money. John and I don't have much left to make it back with."

That was a major understatement.

"Oh, ahh…OK." Knut replied hesitantly, "I'm in no rush. But I'll hitch with you guys to the next town, and then I'll probably hold up and spend some time there. Maybe we can meet up later. I've got plenty of money and a lot of time to travel."

"All right. That sounds good." I said.

"Say, are you guys going to be OK. Do you have enough money to make it back." Knut asked, a little concerned.

"Yeah…Yeah. We're good. Don't worry about it." John lied.

"Oh, yeah. It's no problem." I lied too. "We just need to be making some distance while we can. That's all. No problem."

TRAVELIN' MAN ACROSS THE SAHARA AND BEYOND

After quite a tiring walk through the hot dusty streets we finally made our way to the edge of the large town to the lone road leading out of Touggourt into the Sahara. The sky had cleared and it was turning into a hot, dry day, the hottest day of the trip so far. With no shelter from the baking sun, it seemed even hotter to me. As I said before, frigid cold weather hardly bothers me at all, but in hot weather I melt.

I took off my jacket and outer shirt and put them in my backpack, making it a little heavier to carry, which added with the heat, and lack of sleep the past few days was tiring me out..

"Well, we'll we see how we do hitching, again." I said hopefully.

John nodded, "So far, so good."

"There sure aren't many vehicles out here, but, man, they almost always stop when they do come by." I added.

"I doubt if there've been many guys who hitched across the Sahara before." John said

With that said, the three of us waited just a short while looking out at the endless road leading out into the hard rock flat desert. The desert landscape had now changed from the rolling sand hills to a flat hard surface, with small rocks and stones scattered about. We had to wait for all of four vehicles to come by before a car stopped to offer a ride. It might take a little while for a car or vehicle of some kind to come by - But we knew there was a great chance that when it did, it would stop and offer a ride.

Completely unexpectedly, hitch-hiking in the Sahara turned out to be the best hitching I ever did. Like a lot things on our adventure, hitching across the Sahara was not something John and I had planned for or even discussed in advance – We were just improvising and doing what we had to do to get by…and to keep moving forward.

In my younger days I would guess that I hitched in about 30-35 different countries, about 10,000–12,000 miles. I actually started hitch-hiking regularly when I was in 8th grade. I would hitch from my home to Oakland Hills golf course where I was a caddie to earn money. Then when I was a freshman in high school before I was old enough to drive a car, I used to hitch to school every morning…

And hitching in the Sahara was the best hitching I ever did anywhere. Out in the Sahara, having more than half a dozen cars go by without a ride was unusual. Compared with my experiences hitching in many other countries where on a bad day, well over a thousand cars might pass by with none offering a ride. It wasn't uncommon for it to take 2-3 hours of cars endlessly going by before one stopped to give a ride. Or in one case, as you may remember earlier on this very trip, it took 22 hours to get one ride. Even on a good day, hundreds of cars might go by before one offered a lift. It came as a tremendous shock to me, but hitch-hiking in the Sahara was the easiest hitching I ever did.

When our ride stopped we ran up to the car and looked to see who was in the car. It was a balding, bearded Algerian man wearing western clothes driving a fairly late model car. One of the newer and nicest cars I had seen out in the Sahara. The three of us climbed in the car; Knut and me in the back seat and John in the front. Without much speaking, the driver quickly started off following the narrow, paved road deep into the desert. Very soon we were completely engulfed in the vast desert again.

After we had driven a short while, John turned around and looked at Knut in the backseat, "Do you know how far the next town is?"

"Uhh…I think at least a couple more hours drive."

"OK." John nodded, "I know we're all really beat…How about we take turns sleeping with one guy being lookout. I'll take the first lookout and you and Dennis can sleep first. I'll wake you after about 30-40 minutes and we'll switch."

"All right." Knut answered.

"Sounds good to me." I said. I was dead tired and definitely ready for some sleep.

Very quickly I fell fast asleep. I went out like a light. The slow rocking and humming of the car put me right to sleep. I was really tired and it was a very deep sleep, the best sleep I had had in days. The sleep was great but the waking up part, on the other hand, was not so good…rather disturbing actually. After sleeping, for I'm not sure how long, I started feeling a bumping and jarring sensation. It woke me from my deep slumber.

As I opened my eyes to re-adjust to my surroundings, I was looking over at Knut in the back seat with me. He was sound asleep. I then looked over at my brother in the front seat and his head was rolled to the side. He, too, was sound asleep.

Now came the disturbing part. I then looked over at the Algerian man driving the car. His head was facing down toward the floor and his chin was bobbing along with the bumps of the car. He, too, was sound asleep. It took a moment to register in my waking brain, but I soon realized something was not right here. <u>Everyone</u> was sleeping - but the car was still moving…Very fast…And bumpy…And as I looked out the front window of the car, I realized we were not moving along the road. We were bumping along through the hard rock desert at a blinding speed. The road was nowhere in sight, and there was no one driving the car.

When this rather unsettling realization finally hit me, I grabbed the drivers shoulder and shouted, "Wake up. Wake up. We're off the road. We're gonna crash."

After my heated warning, John was the first to fully awaken and react. He looked out the front window and said, "Oh my God! We're off the road."

He also looked over at the now slowly waking Algerian man driving the car, and jerked at the driver's other shoulder just as he was reaching for the steering wheel. The driver turned the steering wheel sharply to the right and the car started screeching in a violent, sharp turn with the car's tires hurling rocks and sand in every direction as the car fought to stay upright. I really thought we might flip.

The driver, seeing we might flip-over because of the sharp turn, then over reacted and yanked the steering wheel hard in the other direction. Now the tires were skidding and screeching across the hard desert sand in the other direction with the car again teetering almost on two wheels barely holding to the sliding desert rock and sand. Although the driver was fighting the steering wheel to keep us from flipping out of control - It apparently took him a while to consider that slowing down on the accelerator might also help our situation. Finally, after a roller coaster of a ride, the driver took his foot off the accelerator and the car began to slow and he gained control of the car. The car then settled to an abrupt halt in a cloud of desert rocks, dust and sand.

As soon as the car came to a stop, John, Knut and I jumped out of the car and hurriedly ran about 10 meters away from it. It was as though we were worried the car had a life of its own and might unexpectedly take off again. Once away from the car, with the immediate danger gone and the tension broken, we began to laugh and joke about what had just occurred.

"Did you see that? I thought for sure we were going to flip." Knut said laughing.

"That was some ride." I said, "It beats any ride I ever took at Disney World."

"You can say that again." John added.

"Yeah." I said, "You could sell tickets for that kind of ride. It would make a lot of money."

"Did you see that guy's face when he woke up." John laughed, pointing over at the driver who appeared shaken up and was now kneeling, checking out the tires and underside of the car.

"Yeah. He looked scared to death. Like he had woken up from a nightmare." I said.

After we stopped joking around, we walked back over to the car to check it out. It could be a serious problem if we had a car problem now - As evidenced by the abandoned, decaying cars I had been seeing often along the road through the Sahara.

Each of us briefly checked out the car and tires and found no serious damage. We felt a sense of relief although the driver still seemed very concerned about his car and our situation. He continued nervously looking around the car. Now we also realized we had another problem…We couldn't see the road. We had actually lost the road. It was nowhere in sight. We were shocked. We could see in every direction for miles and miles across the barren desert. The desert was a hard rock surface and appeared to be mostly dead flat with slight mound here and there for as far as we could see. But none of us could see the road.

We could make out some crazily winding skid marks for about a hundred meters, but then any markings or tire rut just disappeared into nothing in the desert rock. Under the blazing sun, we looked and squinted in every direction - but there was nothing. So John, Knut and I started heading out into the desert under the hot sun, each in a slightly different direction, looking for the mysterious road that had somehow disappeared on us.

After walking and looking for quite awhile, I shouted toward John and Knut, who now looked like a couple of tiny dark spots out in the distant desert. "You guys see anything?"

There was no response. So I shouted louder, "Hey, you guys see anything?"

After a moment, I heard John's voice faintly floating on the desert wind over to me. "No. Nothing but desert."

Then a moment later, John's voice again. "Knut doesn't see a thing either. We're going back to the car. We'll meet at the car."

So we all walked back over to the car and met up with the Algerian driver, who was still looking over his car and appeared very apprehensive and worried. Having lived in the Sahara, he was probably much more aware of the possible danger we were in if the car would not run.

We gestured to him that we could not find any road. He didn't respond. He still seemed shaken up from what had just occurred. After a moment, he just motioned for us to get in the car. We did, and the Algerian man started up the engine and let it hum for a moment to make sure there were no problems, before he put it in gear and slowly drove off. He started slowly driving across the desert, first following the general direction of the limited car skid marks and then in a zigzagging manner as John, Knut and I intently looked out the windows trying to catch sight of the road.

We still didn't see any road.

The driver then changed directions a few times and started zigzagging again as we all looked for the road. We had now driven quite a ways in various directions. I started wondering if we had somehow entered the twighlight zone or something. A road couldn't just disappear...could it? I was beginning to wonder.

During that short time that we were looking for that road, I gained a great deal of respect for the power, vastness, and emptiness of the Sahara. With no road or markings anywhere to follow to lead us back to civilization, the Sahara desert suddenly became a much more intimidating place. In the blink of an eye, it changed from exuding not only vastness and beauty - But a sense of extreme danger and concern for survival.

After more driving in what seemed to me to be a series of blind, aimless circles, I had the feeling we were getting lost. We had no idea what direction the road might be in.

Then suddenly Knut said, "I see a car. I think I see a car."

He was turned pointing in the almost opposite direction that we were heading. We all turned and looked behind us in the direction he was pointing.

"I see it. I see it. It's very far away." John said excitedly.

As usual I still didn't see anything.

The driver hurriedly turned the car and started driving in the direction Knut was pointing. He drove at a fast speed over the hard, bumpy rocks and flat desert in the direction Knut had seen the car...The same car, which by now had also somehow disappeared into the desert.

It turned out we were a long, long ways from the road. Even after we had seen the car, (or I should say, after Knut and John saw the car since I never did spot it) we didn't see the road until we were almost right on top of it. It would have been very, very difficult for us to find the road without seeing a car driving on it to mark the direction for us. So having made it back on to the lone desert road, we headed out again. This time nobody did any sleeping. We all had our eyes peeled on the road ahead, with continual nervous glances out of the corner of our eyes over at the Algerian driver… just in case.

It was mid-late afternoon when the next desert town appeared on the horizon and we drove into the town. It was still a hot and sunny with the sun shining brightly all throughout the day. After arriving in the town we thanked the driver for the entertaining ride, and wished him well. I think he needed it. It still didn't seem like he had recovered from our near crash. He had stayed on a nervous edge for the remainder of the ride to town.

After leaving the car and driver, we walked through town and found a dusty roadside eating place, where John and I sat down with Knut to get something to eat.

"Dennis, after we eat we should get back on the road and see if we can make some more distance today. What do you think?" John asked.

"Ok. Sounds good. We still have a couple more hours of daylight."

Looking over at Knut, I said, "What about you?"

"Ahh.. I think I'm going to take stay here and take it easy for a while. I'm tired out from all the travel the last couple of days. Maybe I'll meet up with you guys later. I've got time to kill."

"All right." John said.

"You guys are really traveling hard, huh?" Knut said.

"Yeah. We're trying to make it back to England." John replied, "We've gotta get back soon."

"Why? What's the rush? You guys have something to make it back for?"

In reality we had a serious cash crunch that was putting us on a tight deadline. We were in a race to make it back before our money ran out. It was a race we were losing. We had to make as much distance using as little money as possible, but we didn't say that. John had another reason for needing to get back soon, and that's what he told Knut.

"I've got a return ticket from England to the US that expires on January 3rd. I have to use it by the 3rd or it can't be used and I lose the ticket. So we need to get back."

"I see."

As soon as we finished eating, John and I said our goodbyes to Knut and headed out to the edge of town to start hitching. We never did meet up with Knut again. He was a good guy…a travelin' man like John and I.

CHAPTER **20**

Jeep Surfing in the Sahara Sand

Once again John and I stood out by the side of the road in the late afternoon sun, looking out at the endless Sahara sand in front of us, waiting for a ride. I looked over at John and squinted in the sun, "Let's see if we can make some more miles today while we still have some daylight."

"Yeah." John said, "Hopefully, our luck hitching will continue."

"It's sure been good so far. That's for sure."

"Man, it's hot standing out here with all this desert sand around." .

"Yeah." I said, as I wiped the sweat and ever present sand off of my forehead and face. "It's too hot to stand around out here with the sun glaring off the sand."

Fortunately we didn't have to stand around for long. After only a few cars and trucks went by, a very old, rusting, faded blue, dented jeep stopped. The beat-up jeep looked like it had just been KO'd in a bruising fight, and was in serious need of a car doctor. I was surprised it was still standing. John and I walked up to the jeep to see who was offering the ride. It was a slim, short, dark haired, dark skinned Algerian guy in his mid 30's. He was wearing torn jeans, a t-shirt and an old grease-stained, jean jacket.

We quickly got in the jeep, with John in the backseat and me in the front. As I started to get into the front seat, the driver quickly tapped my shoulder, gave me a look and pointed down to the car floor…Or I should say, to the lack of floor. Most of the front car floor was missing. It was rusted right through. He was warning me to be careful. There was only a small metal bar to put my feet on. Otherwise, there was little but open road under my feet. It was the same for the driver's side of the car – everything had been rusted

JEEP SURFING IN THE SAHARA SAND

through and there was very little floor under the gas pedal and brake. I was wondering how he could drive the jeep.

I looked over my shoulder into the backseat. "Hey, John." I whispered, "Do you have any floor back there? Be careful. There's no floor up here."

"Really? There's a floor back here. It's rusted through a bit, with some holes, but there's a floor."

John leaned up and looked over the seat at my feet. "Man, your serious. There really isn't a floor. Kind of reminds me of Fred Flintstones car."

"No kidding." I said with a laugh.

After getting situated in the car, the driver took off. We soon learned his name was Lahkdar. He was a real good guy. We ended up driving a long ways with him.

While we were driving through the desert, we were able to communicate fairly well with him. Lahkdar only knew a few odd words of English, but was very expressive with his gestures, expressions and body language. He was very serious but at the same time very animated...an interesting guy. We found out that Lahkdar was a mechanic. The reason he was driving through the Sahara that day was because he was following a supply truck somewhere in front of us. His job was to follow the truck on its route through the desert, and to repair the truck if it had any problems along the desert road.

He told us trucks carrying materials and supplies through the desert often had a mechanic like him following behind in a jeep or another vehicle. He said that if the truck has a problem on the desert road, it needed to be fixed on the spot - or it often had to be abandoned and the driver returned to safety.

There was no such thing as '911' or a car repair service to call out in the Sahara. I understood what he meant right away. During our trek across the Sahara, I had seen several abandoned, rusting cars, stripped and semi buried in the shifting sand along the side of the highway; Cars that hadn't made it to the next town. Also, the carcasses and the rotting skeleton remains of dead donkeys or an occasional camel were a fairly common sight along the single road that we had been traveling on through the endless desert.

They were grim reminders that despite its magnificence and endless beauty, the Sahara could be a very dangerous and unforgiving place.

During the long ride across the open desert in Lahkdar's old jeep, we passed through some areas with beautiful, towering waves of shimmering desert sand. It was getting later in the afternoon and the sun was slowly beginning its descent, showering the sky with streaks of misty hues of red and orange that seemed to shimmer off the gigantic waves of sand. It made for some breathtaking sights.

"John, do you believe this scenery around here?" I asked.

"Yeah. The waves of sand around here are just endless and untouched. It would be cool to take a little sand dune ride in the jeep, wouldn't it?"

"That's a great idea. Do you think he would go for it?" I said, nodding toward Lahkdar.

"Maybe...Nothing ventured, nothing gained. Let's try to ask him."

We did. With gestures and pointing, we explained what we wanted to do. Lahkdar seemed to understand and looked amused. He then shook his head OK.

After finding a good spot, Lahkdar suddenly pulled off the paved desert road and began roaring up and down some of the towering hills of desert sand. It was a thrill. The jeep was sliding, swerving and rolling up and down the sand hills. It felt like we were jeep surfing through the waves of sand. Thankfully, Lahkdar knew what he was doing. It would have been a big problem if we got stuck or flipped. But I think Lahkdar had done this kind of driving before. He seemed to get as big a kick out of it as John and I did, as we slid and surfed up and down the desert hills spraying a gusting wall of sand in our wake.

During the jeep sand surfing, Lahkdar stopped on the top of one of the desert hills and we got out of the old jeep and took some pictures. After the exciting jeep surfing in the Sahara sand hills, we headed on down the lonely desert road again. It was getting late in the day and dusk was approaching as Lahkdar drove the beat-up, floorless jeep through the endless desert.

John looked over at me in the front seat and said, "Hey Dennis, you have any idea how far the next town is from here?"

"Not a clue." I shrugged.

"We're gonna need to find a place to sleep. Hopefully, we won't have to sleep out in the open desert tonight."

"Yeah." I said. "We'll have to see what's up in the next town. Maybe Lahkdar can help us out."

We continued riding along the lone paved road for another hour or so through the vast waves of brown desert sand, just passing the miles away. Later the desert waves mostly flattened out into endless level sand with only

JEEP SURFING IN THE SAHARA SAND

minor mounds or ripples of sand out in the distance. Only a few cars or trucks came by during the entire drive. Like for most of our travel through the Sahara, the vehicles on the lone paved road were few and far between.

We drove on through the desert for a few hours when Lahkdar suddenly pulled off of the paved road and started driving straight out into the sand desert. I was surprised. He just turned off the paved road and started driving straight into the Sahara over some wavy sand hills. There was no road, only a vague, shifting sand path.

"Man, where are we going now? Where's he taking us?" John said surprised, leaning over the front seat.

"I don't know." I replied. "There's not even a road. He's just going out into the Sahara."

"What could be out here?"

"Maybe some Nomads or a Bedouin camp. Who knows?"

"Hopefully it's not a camp for the Policerio Guerrillas or something."

"Huh? What do you mean?" I said alarmed.

"I was just joking." John replied, trying to laugh it off.

But actually John's comment gave me pause. We had no idea where we were, or where we were going, or what was ahead of us.

Lakdar drove through the soft sand directly into the Sahara for some time, slipping and sliding until after descending a low sand ridge, we came upon an isolated desert camp of some kind. It consisted of a single, very small box-shaped, roughly made, two-room shack that was sitting out all alone in the middle of nowhere. The desert shack was surrounded by nothing but miles and miles of mostly flat, soft sand for as far as I could see in every direction. The ramshackle building stood out completely on its own and was barely tall enough to stand inside. I had no idea where the nearest civilization might be, but I figured it must have been at least a hundred miles in any direction to the nearest town.

We soon found out that, like Lakdar's jeep, the small shack was floorless with nothing but desert sand under it. It appeared to be haphazardly made of different materials with a mishmash of wood boards as a roof covering. There were a few small box seats and old barrels scattered around outside of it, with a couple donkeys standing by themselves, un-tethered out a ways in the desert.

The shack was the only man-made structure of any kind that I had seen since passing through the last town a few hours earlier. Actually, it was the only man made structure I ever saw outside of any of the desert towns since we had been in the Sahara, with the exception of some rare Roman ruins. Back in Tunisia I had seen some ancient Roman ruins along the desert roadside. I was very surprised because I didn't know they existed in the Sahara.

As we pulled up to the lone, desert shack, there was a very large, dented, loaded-down truck parked out nearby in the sand. Surrounding the shack and truck in every direction was nothing but the unending sand of the vast desert. Pointing at the big truck, Lahkdar explained to us that this was the truck it was his job to follow through the desert in case it needed to be repaired. He would be meeting the truck driver out here.

After Lahkdar stopped the jeep, we walked up to the shack and I saw the driver of the truck sitting on a little box in the sand next to the shack. He was a very large, very black man with a big, bald head and a jovial, friendly face. He was wearing dark, torn western style pants and a worn-out, long, black, coat. Sitting out a ways in the sand, under the fading but still blazing desert sun, was a group of about five, tough looking, leathered skin, bearded men wearing long, sand-covered robes and turbans. It was hard to tell with their turbans but four of the men appeared to be in their forties, with one older man, with curly, graying hair.

They had very rugged features and faces that were lined by the wind and sun, and looked to me like nomads who lived their life completely out in the desert. A couple of the tough looking men had all but their squinting eyes covered by their turbans, which were wrapped tightly around their heads and face to protect them from the blazing sun and blowing sand. They were sitting out on the desert sand in a group together.

As we approached the men, they seemed to recognize Lahkdar and slightly nodded at him. They then stared over at John and me with penetrating, intense eyes from behind their turbans. They did not gesture or speak or make any effort to communicate with us. The friendly, welcoming stares I had grown accustomed to since entering the Sahara were nowhere to be seen out here. The rough looking, desert men seemed to be making an unspoken appraisal of us.

"That's a tough looking bunch of guys over there." I said to John, as we sat down next to the little shack.

"That's for sure. I wonder what they're doing out here in the middle of nowhere."

"Who knows? They look like they nomads, like they live out in the desert…What is this place out here, anyways?"

JEEP SURFING IN THE SAHARA SAND

"I don't know." John said, "We're totally isolated out here. We'll have to be careful and stay on guard."

"That's for sure. We should stay close to Lahkdar until we see what's up."

We sat down outside the little shack on some small wood boxes and a stocky Arab man appeared from inside the shack and brought us over some tea. We sat with Lahkdar and the big truck driver watching the sun as it began its slow descent across the vast, open, desert skyline. Meanwhile, the other group of robed men stayed silently seated on the desert sand away from us, just warily eyeing us.

While we were sitting drinking our tea, the big truck driver smiled heartily and joked in Arabic with Lahkdar. Apparently they had made several drives back and forth across the desert together, with the big black man driving a truck load of supplies and Lahkdar, the mechanic, following behind in his beat up jeep.

With evening approaching, John and I were getting concerned about where we could sleep the night. John signaled to Lahkdar trying to find out if he would be driving on to the nearest town before nightfall. He was non-committal. I also tried to ask about where we could sleep. Again, he didn't give any kind of answer, and just kind of motioned for us to wait. We sat some more outside the shack, enjoying the explosion of brilliant bright lights layering the sky as the sun lowered near the desert floor. After a while, Lahkdar glanced toward us, got up and strolled over to the group of tough looking men sitting out in the sand. He sat with them on the sand for a few moments, talking in hushed voices. He then casually got up, meandered back over to us and sat back on his box leaning against the wall of the shack. He then gestured and explained to John and me that we could sleep the night out here in this little shack.

I looked over at John, "He wants us to sleep out here? In the middle of the Sahara? In the middle of nowhere?"

"Yep. I guess so."

"What do you think about it?" I asked.

"It's a place to sleep. But, man, it's really isolated out here. This is even more remote than the Algerian border post."

"That's for sure."

"And what about those desert nomads? You think we can trust them?" John asked, nodding in the direction of the group of men sitting in the sand.

"Lahkdar seems to know them. I trust Lahkdar. So maybe we can trust those guys, too."

"You think so?" John asked, not too convinced.

"I really don't know." I admitted.

"Well, I guess we got no choice." John said. "It's going to be dark soon. We can't leave here on our own. We'd need a ride through the desert sand just to get back to the main road, and then who knows how far it is to the nearest town."

After contemplating that for a moment, I spoke up with my concerns. "I wonder if Lahkdar is staying out here for the night? And how about all those other desert nomads? Are they all sleeping out here for the night, too?"

We tried to ask Lahkdar, but he mostly just shrugged his shoulders and didn't give us much of an answer. We weren't exactly sure what was happening, But whatever was going on, it appeared John and I were going to spend this night sleeping out in this little camp in the middle of the Sahara.

A short while later, at Lahkdar's direction, John and I walked over to Lahkdar's rusting jeep and took out our backpacks. We brought the battered backpacks over near to the shack and set them down in the sand. Soon the big truck driver stood up, said something to Lahkdar in Arabic and walked over to his truck. He gave us a friendly wave, pulled his heavy frame up into the big truck and started up the engine. He then rumbled in the truck through the sand back over the little sand ridge across the desert and out of sight.

It was now getting dark as Lahkdar walked back over to the group of desert nomads, who were still sitting out in the desert off a ways by themselves. He sat in the sand with them again for a while and they quietly talked together. While Lahkdar was talking to the desert men, John and I got up from our wood box seats and wandered around the small shack and took a look around the desert camp. There wasn't much to see. Just the lone, little make shift shack, a couple of donkeys standing quietly out a ways behind it, and Lahkdar's beat-up jeep parked about 30 meters away. Otherwise, there was nothing but unbroken, soft brown, Saharan sand surrounding us. With the bright sun giving off its last burst of light as it disappeared under the distant horizon, I could see for miles and miles across the desert sand. It was an awe-inspiring and spectacular sight. The sand just seemed endless.

"Quite a sight, huh?" I said looking out at the desert horizon.

"It's something else. No doubt about it." John replied softly.

After standing for a few moments watching the sunset, the light started quickly fading as I said to John, "Well, it looks like we're staying out here for the night. This is going to be some night out here. Do you believe this?"

"Not only that." John replied, "It's going to be quite the Christmas morning to wake up to."

"Hey, that's right. Tomorrow's the day. I never imagined a Christmas like this. Out here. Man, we're a long ways from home."

"Home?" John asked, "We're a long ways from anything. Home seems like from another life time."

"Yeah." I said, "But what an adventure, huh? We're living our dreams. You can't beat that. This is the adventure I was dreaming about during all those long hours working at Peabody's back in Michigan. Working and saving money. I wouldn't trade this experience for the world."

"Me neither." John said, nodding.

CHAPTER **21**

Christmas Sunrise in the Sahara

We walked back over to the other side of the desert shack to find the desert men finally standing near the shack, and Lahkdar heading toward his jeep. John and I hurried to catch up to him.

"Hey, Lahkdar, what are you doing? Where you going?" John asked.

Lahkdar stopped and turned. He gestured and communicated to us that he was leaving.

We were surprised and a little leery to be left out here on our own, out here in the middle of the Sahara at some isolated desert camp, with a group of rough looking desert nomads. Men we hadn't even met yet or spoken to. We still didn't know who they were, or where they lived, or if they would all be staying with us at the little desert camp for the night. There were a lot of unknowns.

Seeing the concern in our eyes, Lahkdar gestured for us to stay. That it was OK. He also seemed to communicate that he would be back the next day. We weren't really sure about that last part. And with that, he quickly climbed up into his floorless jeep, pulled the jeep around in a cloud of sand and swirling tires, and headed off back over the small sand ridge out of sight.

John and I were now on own.

We stood for a moment in the dimming light watching the familiar dented jeep disappear over the ridge, before turning back to face the desert men, who were now standing in front of the forlorn shack and intently looking at us. As far as I knew, there were six of them; the five nomads, who had been quietly sitting out in the sand, plus the one guy who had served us the tea from inside the little shack.

"So, what do we do now?" I whispered to John, without turning away from the group of desert men, who were still eyeing us.

"I'd say it's time to get acquainted." John said, as he started walking directly over to the men.

I followed behind.

John approached the men, smiled broadly and said, "*Aslama Saheb.* My name's John. Me John. *Sahab.*" He said again, pointing to himself.

The men at first didn't react; they just stood their ground and cautiously looked on straight-faced. Finally, after a few tense moments, the one older man with a white-streaked beard stepped forward, touched his chest, raised his right hand and nodded slightly. John smiled and put out his hand. The old man did the same and they shook hands.

The old Arab man said his name to John but I didn't hear it. He gestured to me, as well. John and I then briefly introduced ourselves to the other desert men as well. They all made the same gesture with their right hands but didn't offer their names or smile. They were all cordial, but very serious, peering at us from behind their turbans with sun red, squinting eyes. They remained quietly stoic and reserved.

They still seemed to be withholding their judgments about John and me, as though we hadn't proven ourselves yet. They didn't seem too impressed with these two young American travelers, who had suddenly appeared out in their midst. I believe they were willing to help us out because of Lahkdar, and also probably because of the desert code that says you never refuse a request for assistance. But any friendship to be offered beyond that would have to be earned.

After briefly introducing ourselves to the desert men, they wandered off into the distance, sat down in the sand and intently watched us, while John and I walked over to the little shack and sat back down on the same boxes. It was pretty dark now. The desert shack had a little generator that connected to a single light hooked up on the wood roof. The only other piece of equipment I saw was a small refrigerator with a little plate stove on top of it. That was it. No TV, radio, phone, lamps, or toilet. Also no floor, just sand. Very basic, but suitable for us. It provided us cover for the night and a place to sleep. And as far as we knew it was free.

The single low powered, roof light lit up the area around the little shack for only about 10 meters in every direction, and then its beams just faded into the shadows and was absorbed by the desert night.

"Well, this is going to be a quiet night out here. That's for sure." I said to John as we sat by ourselves in the still desert night.

"No kidding. It's really peaceful out here. "

"Yeah. It should be a good night's sleep. It'll be good to be off the road tonight and have the entire night to rest and sleep. No worries about making distance or where we're going to spend the night."

With nothing else to do, we sat out under the night sky for quite some time just relaxing and taking in the desert. As it got later, the night brightened with an amazing display of stars dotting the canvas of the vast sky. It was a clear night and the stars created a spectacle of starlight that seemed to reflect off the soft desert sand, allowing us to partially see across the misty desert landscape for a long ways.

"I wonder if they have space for us to sleep inside or what." John said some time later.

"We'll find out soon enough." I said standing to stretch. "Where are those desert nomads, anyways? I heard them talking out a ways in the desert a while ago, but I don't hear anything now."

"I don't know. Let's take a look around. It's pretty quiet around here."

We walked around the little shack and wandered quite a ways out into the sand desert keeping the shack light within sight. We looked all around, but didn't see anyone or anything outside. It was just dead quiet, dark and empty out there. When we returned to the shack, we heard some low noises from inside.

John and I leaned into the low shack through the small opening and took a look in. There were two, middle-aged, Arab men, wearing the long robes but without their turbans, seated on the desert sand floor inside. They were both older, maybe in their fifties, heavy set, with round faces and several days growth of dark whiskers. They both had wind and sun weathered faces with lots of creases. They were drinking tea and quietly talking.

One man was the guy who served us the tea when we first arrived with Lahkdar. The other man we didn't recognize. All of the tough desert nomads were nowhere to be found. They had somehow earlier disappeared out into the desert.

The two men looked up at us with little expression, and politely gestured for us to go out and wait. Looking surprised, I said. *"Aslema, Shocercum"* and we backed out of the opening.

"John, where are all the desert men, the desert nomads? What do you think happened to them?" I asked.

"I don't know. But they're long gone. I have no idea where they could have gone or where they're spending the night."

Looking all around out into the vast empty desert night, John replied "Yeah, there's nothing out there but sand for miles and miles. Nothing at all. I wonder how they live out here."

"Hey, you know." John continued after a moment, "Those two donkeys that were around back are gone, too. They mustta taken them."

"Yeah. They must be nomads, living off the desert. They looked like tough, fearless guys, didn't they?" I said.

"Yeah, they sure did. They just had a quiet toughness about them."

"Well, as long as they're not the Policero guerillas, we should be OK." I said with a grin, but also a trace of truth.

John and I sat outside the shack sitting on the small boxes looking at the desert sky and Sahara sand. It was actually very relaxing and enjoyable to spend a while just sitting out in the night air with no worries about our next move. We had been traveling hard and fast for days now with no let up. This was the first time in a while that we had a chance to unwind and not be worried about making time. With the clear, starlit sky, the desert night was fairly bright and just beautiful. As it got later, the starlight from the vast sky seemed to dance off of the soft, brown, desert sand and create a wavy, ghost like mist rising from the desert sand floor. I loved the feel of it.

Later on the Arab man who had served us the tea, came out and signaled for us to come in the shack. He showed us an area where John and I could sleep in the corner of the cramped front room next to a bunch of boxes of supplies. He had cleared off a little area directly in front of the opening to the shack. There were also two sheets laying folded on top of a large rug that had been laid out on the desert sand floor for our use. The rug covered much of the sand, but not all of it.

We thanked him for his hospitality.

Before he left, he signaled for us to be careful of spiders when we slept. After making some drawings in the sand floor, we understood. He wasn't just saying spiders. He was warning us to be careful of scorpions. He became very serious. He communicated that a scorpion bite meant death, and for us to shake our boots, all our clothes, sheets, backpacks and everything very carefully before going to sleep. He told us we should also do the same in the morning when we woke up.

After giving us that warning, he flicked some kind of switch shutting off the generator and the lone outside light and went into the second small room, pulling a thick rug cover over the door opening behind him. It was now quite dark in the room, with just a little starlight filtering in from the shack opening. It took a few moments for my night vision to kick in.

"Did you hear that?" John said nervously, "Scorpions! Man, that's not a good thought to sleep on."

"No kidding." I said as I started shaking out my sheet.

"I'm sleeping with my shoes on tonight."

"Why don't we put our backpacks outside." I said.

"Good idea. The fewer places for scorpions to hide in here, the better."

After shaking all of our things out and getting more situated in our little corner of the desert shack, John said, "Who woudda thought this is where we would end up tonight."

"You just never know hitching out on the road." I replied.

I grabbed my backpack to take outside and said to John, "I'm gonna step out for a while to take in some of the desert night."

"Sounds good. I'll join you."

So we walked outside and set our backpacks a few meters from the shack opening. I then picked up one of the old small boxes and headed a ways out into the desert away from the shack. I didn't want our voices to bother the hospitable guy sleeping in the other room. Also, I wanted to get a bit out into the desert away from the shack to get a good feel and taste of the vastness of the desert night. John followed suit.

About 50 meters from the shack we stopped and sat down on our little boxes.

"Man, this is a great night, isn't it?" I said quietly.

"Yep. As long as we don't meet any scorpions or snakes out here."

I chuckled and said "A Christmas Eve to remember. That's for sure. Say, I wonder what time is it?" I continued. "When will it turn Christmas?"

"Hard to tell time out here. I think it's still early." John said, "It doesn't matter much anyways."

"True. The only thing that really matters is the miles and the money."

"Yep." After a pause, John continued, "And that's something we can talk about later."

CHRISTMAS SUNRISE IN THE SAHARA

With that said we stopped talking and just enjoyed the peaceful desert night. It wasn't the time to talk about our situation, our plans, or our next move. We just weren't in the mood.

After a while, John got drossy and went back to the shack to sleep. I stayed out by myself in the desert, just enjoying the peacefulness and the starlit sky. Ever since I was young, I've always had a strong affinity for the stars at night. They've always been a source of motivation for me. Also, when I was on the road traveling, seeing the big dipper in the night sky always gave me a sense of comfort. And just like having Coca-Cola made me feel closer to home, so did knowing that the same stars I was looking at were the same stars I looked at since I was a boy back home in Michigan.

Later I made my way through the darkness across the sand to the little desert camp and shack to sleep. It was a little cramped in the small room, but it was a very quiet, peaceful sleep since for some reason John was hardly snoring at all. He was probably still awake thinking about the scorpions or snakes that might be about. I was too tired to think. I quickly fell asleep. It was a long, deep sleep.

I didn't awake until the next morning, just as the sun was breaking over the desert horizon. From the open door of the little shack the bright morning sun came streaming in upon me at dawn and woke me from my sleep. John and the other Arab men in the next room were still sleeping. I sat looking out the little doorway for a while watching the sunshine slowly creep over the edge of the distant horizon as it made its way across the desert toward me. It was a spectacular sight.

It was Christmas morning in the Sahara.

I stood up slowly shaking out my sheet and clothes as I rose from the rug and sand floor. I then quietly went out of the low, little shack opening and walked out a little ways into the desert to take in the morning sunrise. I stretched a bit and tried unsuccessfully to shake off the sand that was still in my hair and thinly covering my clothes. The sand was everywhere. It was never really cleaned off.

As I walked out in the desert, the night coolness was just beginning to burn off and it was beginning to slowly warm. The morning had the makings of a bright, beautiful, sunny day. After a short walk, I just sat down out in the desert sand taking it all in. A while later John and, a short time after that, the two Arab men came out of the shack, brushing the sand off of their clothes, shaking their heads and stretching. I walked back over and the one Arab man offered us some tea.

We sat out along the side of the shack and as we sat drinking the tea, John said to me, "I wonder if Lahkdar is coming back? If he doesn't, how we gonna get out of here."

"I don't know. We'll have to wait and see what happens."

"We're a long ways from any town."

"That's true." I replied, "But you know it's still really early. Maybe he'll show up."

"Maybe…But I wouldn't count on it."

"You don't have to worry about that. I don't count on anything out here."

We finished our tea and a short while later as John and I were getting our backpacks put together inside the little shack, four of the desert nomads showed up, seemingly out of nowhere. They didn't really acknowledge John and me, other than a quick glance in our direction.

I never saw them coming. I don't know where they came from or how they approached our little camp without us noticing them off in the distance. You could see for miles and miles across the mostly flat, sandy, endless desert in every direction. They seemed to appear and disappear into and out of the Sahara at will.

The desert nomads had with them one straining, sweating donkey, with a heavy sack over its back. One of the turban covered men pulled the heavy sack off of the donkeys' back and took it into the little shack. He came back out and stood talking with the bearded man, who had served us the tea and who had slept in the other room during the night. The other desert men joined them and they then sat together in a circle in the sand outside the shack for quite some time.

They all were covered with the long robes and turbans wrapped around their heads partially hiding their faces. Looking at the rugged, bearded men with their long blowing robes, sitting out in the sand with the sun rising and shimmering in waves off the desert; it looked like some kind of meeting of the sultans of Arabia or something. Occasionally as they were talking, they would peer over at John and me as we sat on our boxes out next to the shack. I had the feeling they were talking about us.

"They're having another serious discussion out there." John said.

"They sure are." I answered, "I still wonder where they went last night. It was pretty dark when they disappeared out into the desert."

CHRISTMAS SUNRISE IN THE SAHARA

"Who knows? They seem to know this land quite well."

After a moments pause, John continued, "Man I'm really getting hungry. You have any food left on you?"

"Whatta you mean?"

"You have any bread left, or any of those breakfast cereal packs left like you had back in Switzerland?"

"Huh? I haven't bought any bread in a couple of days. How would I have any bread left?"

"I don't know. How about those breakfast cereal packs? You got anything like that left on you?" John asked again.

"What are you talking about?"

"You know...The cereal packs. You holding out on me?"

"I had those cereal packs a couple of weeks ago, back when we were in the Alps, in the snow and cold…Now were in the Sahara. They're long gone. I've got nothing."

"Just checking." John said, "Well, I'm starving. I need some food. I wonder if they have any food out here. They must have something to eat. "

Looking out at the group of rugged Arab men sitting in a circle out in the desert sand, I said, "When they finish their talk out there, you can try and ask them."

When it came to food, John had quite the appetite. Food was often a top priority for him when we traveled no matter what our situation. He would be thinking about food, when it still hadn't even become important enough to cross my mind. Other considerations often put food way down the list of concerns for me.

John also enjoyed eating and trying different foods more than I did. He really enjoyed his food. For me on this trip, I had the 'runs' much of the time we were in the Sahara, so that also took the edge off of any appetite I might have. While I enjoyed eating and I liked the food, eating often left me with serious and not so pleasant after effects.

Eventually the desert men stopped talking, slowly stood up, and walked back over to the shack where John and I were still sitting on our box seats. As they approached us across the desert sand, John and I stood up and looked at them.

This time one of the desert men walked right up to us. He was a slim, solid looking man in his 40's, with a face deeply lined by the sun. He had his turban down and his face exposed. His skin was like tough leather and darkened by the wind and sun, and he had a furry beard that covered much of his face. His teeth were stained and browned like many of the people I saw in the Sahara.

He smiled and put up his right hand and said something in Arabic that I couldn't understand. While speaking, he lightly tapped his chest with the fingers of his right hand and gestured toward us. Although I couldn't understand the words, I could understand the intention and meaning behind them. He was offering us friendship.

John and I copied his gestures using only our right hand and smiled earnestly back at him. He then bowed slightly and reached out and shook our hands. We did the same. The other tough looking desert nomads standing behind him stepped forward and each did the same. They then led us over to the area in the desert sand where they had been sitting before and had us sit down with them.

As we walking over with them, I quietly said to John, "I guess we've been accepted by them. I'm not sure why."

"I don't know. Maybe the guy who stayed in the shack said something on our behalf, or maybe we passed some kind of test or something."

"Yeah. I don't know either. But for whatever reason, I'm glad."

"Me, too. I sure wouldn't like to have these guys as enemies."

To be honest, I was impressed with them. I had a good gut feeling that they were not a danger and that they were trust worthy. It seemed to me that these were tough desert men, nomads, who lived a hard life living on their own off the Sahara. They had their own ways, their own code for doing things and for surviving. Their strong, stoic manner and quiet toughness reminded me of the image I've always had of the American cowboy.

In my heart of hearts I've always wanted to be a cowboy. I've always wished I had lived in the days that the American West was being discovered, explored and settled…In the days of the American cowboy. I guess this travel adventure across the Sahara was one of the times that I got somewhat close to living the life of a roaming cowboy.

Later in life in my early-thirties, I did take up horse riding. By chance I happened to take a horse-riding lesson once and fell in love with it. With the help of a girl friend who knew horses, I bought a registered Arabian horse two weeks later, before I even knew how to ride or before I knew anything about horses.

CHRISTMAS SUNRISE IN THE SAHARA

The horse's name was Cody – short for 'Code of the West'. He was a spirited, rugged but good-natured horse. I kept Cody at a buddy's farm in the country and I would go riding every chance I could. I loved being on that horse out in the open countryside riding over that next hill or river.

It's something I really missed living in Asia. So when I lived in Asia I rode motorcycles to discover and explore the country. I rode with an international group of riding friends based in Korea. There were riders from Australia, Canada, Russia, the US, Korea and New Zealand. We took an overnight trip once a month or so to all different places around Korea. It gave me a little taste of the road and a chance for some adventure, and to do some exploring.

John and I sat down in the desert sand with the wind blowing past, and for the first time we talked with the desert nomads. It was a bit difficult because they spoke no English and they were men of few words and even less emotion. But when John and I were finally able to convey to them that we were on our way to Morocco, the desert men's expressions took on a look of concern, and they began murmuring among themselves.

When they concluded their private discussion, one of the tough, leather-faced men leaned over and pulled his turban away from his face. He looked to be in his 50's, with a hawk nose, a long, curling, grey beard and piercing eyes. He proceeded to draw a rough map in the sand using the index finger of his right hand, showing Algeria and Morocco.

He then casually put a little X in the sand in Algeria to show where we were now. It was a very, very rough drawn map in the shifting sand. But it was the first time since entering Algeria that I had any idea where we were. It was fascinating to see that X in the sand. I was momentarily mesmerized. I just stared at the X in the sand for few moments. Up until that moment I had no idea at all where I was. All I knew was that I was in the Sahara, in Algeria.

I believed that for the past few days we had headed a long ways south and maybe a little ways west through the Sahara Desert, and I estimated that we had traveled close to 800 kilometers since crossing the border into Algeria. But that was all just based on intuition and a rough sense of direction. Everything was just totally unknown at this point. All of John and my decisions had been based on what we believed about our location and situation, not what we knew.

Until that moment, I couldn't visualize any location or diameters of the country and had no reference points – until seeing that X mark. That rough X in the shifting sand gave me the first real idea of what we were facing. According to the X, we had traveled further south than I had imagined. We had come a long ways but we still had a lot of desert to cover before getting up north and near the Moroccan border.

Unfortunately, that wasn't the bad news. The bad news came quickly after the X. One of the other desert nomads grimly proceeded to draw a line in the sand down the entire length of the border between Morocco and Algeria. And then he crossed it all out. With a few more gestures we understood what he was telling us. The nomads believed the entire border with Morocco was closed. There was no way through.

If that wasn't bad enough, the other desert men, using body language and drawings, and now actually getting a little animated for the first time, went on to explain that there was fighting up ahead; Soldiers and fighting, and danger.

They drew in the sand the road we had been traveling on, and what was up ahead. They showed at a further point there would be a split in the road, with one way going south deeper into the fighting and the other direction heading north away from it. John and I understood it to mean that the Policerio guerrillas we had been hearing about were up ahead. When we gestured asking if the road we we're on now was blocked, they kind of shrugged and pointed ahead. They didn't seem to know. They were telling us to be careful.

I looked over at John and said in a low voice, "Doesn't look too good, does it?"

"No it doesn't."

After a moment's thought John continued, "But we've come way too far. With the money we have, we know we can't make it back the same way we came. It's not possible. We gotta keep going forward."

"Yeah." I agreed. "It's already a done deal for us."

"We'll just have to hope the border is open for us to cross into Morocco."

"Maybe it's only closed for Algerians and Moroccans because of the war. Maybe they'll let other nationalities through."

"Let's hope so." John replied, "If not, were dead."

For John and I, the die was cast. We had already passed the point of no return. We had made our decision to try getting past the guerillas and crossing to Morocco, and there was no turning back.

CHRISTMAS SUNRISE IN THE SAHARA

A few minutes later, the man who lived in the shack, came out, smiling and carrying plates of some kind of food. It looked like some variation of couscous. He made a couple of trips out and gave all of us a plate. So we sat out in the Sahara sand, with a group of desert nomads in the Christmas early morning sunshine, eating our first meal in a long time. The meal was in some ways different than what I had eaten before. I'm not exactly sure how, but it was different. Although it was different, it was still delicious and unfortunately still had the same deadly after effects for me.

John really enjoyed it and ate a couple of plates full which the desert men seemed impressed with. Having had his breakfast, John was now in a better frame of mind. We were also given some tea to drink with the meal. It was a good start to Christmas day.

"Well, how we gonna get out of this desert camp and make some mileage today?" John asked as we finished eating.

"Man, there's definitely no transportation around here - That's for sure, unless you count that old donkey over there." I said jokingly as he pointed at the tired old donkey in the distance.

"I guess," I continued, "Maybe we'll have to walk it back to the main road and start hitching from there."

"That'd be a tough walk." John said, "Especially in this soft desert sand."

'Yeah, that's for sure. It'd be slow walking in the sand. Maybe we could walk it in a day, maybe a half a day at best."

"If we walk it, we'd have to be careful to find the main road." John cautioned, "That sand trail from the main road out to here wasn't very clear. With the shifting sand and wind, I doubt there's much of a path to follow. I'd hate to get lost out in the Sahara."

"Yeah. That could be deadly. We'd have to be real careful walking it."

"The problem is," John said looking around, "there're no landmarks or reference points to follow out here. It's all just the same empty, sandy desert landscape."

"It'd be a tough walk. No doubt about it. We'd also have to hope that our hitching luck holds up once we reach the paved road."

"No kidding." John replied. "We wouldn't be hitching from a village or town this time. Once we reach the main road, we'd still be out in the desert, in the middle of nowhere. I think it's a long, long ways to any town from where we're at."

"Yeah, and we need to make it to a town today…Wherever that is?" I said, "We got lucky last night to have a place to sleep. It'd be tough spending the day and night out in the open desert."

"We'll also need to get some food and Coke-Cola before the days out." I added.

The more we talked about walking it, the less enthused we were about it. It wasn't a very appealing option and, in fact, was quite dangerous. Of course, in the end we'd do what we had to do. But just the same, we were hoping we wouldn't have to do it.

"Well, it's still early." John said, "Why don't we wait a while and see what's turns up. Then we can head out a little later if we have to."

"Sounds good."

A while after we finished eating, John and I approached the desert nomads and offered some money to pay for the meal and for their hospitality. Our offer of money was quickly and strongly refused by the desert men, who seemed offended that we had even offered.

It was not the first time since being in the Sahara that our offer to pay for some hospitality or assistance was quickly refused. I learned to be careful and very respectful about offering to pay for any assistance I received.

CHAPTER **22**

Back On the Road Again

Later as we were sitting out in the sun next to the shack with the group of desert nomads, I saw a familiar vehicle come into view over the sand ridge in the distance. It was the old beat-up, floorless jeep that we had ridden into this isolated little desert camp the day before. It was a sight for sore eyes.

"Hey look, he came back. It's Lahkdar." I said excitedly.

"I don't believe it.' John said, "He actually came back."

"It'd be great if he could give us a lift again. I wonder where he's heading today."

We had only met Lahkdar the previous afternoon, but already he seemed to us like a returning long, lost brother. Out here in the Sahara I trusted him completely, more than some people I had known for much of my life. Such were the ways of the road.

Lahkdar drove through the soft sand and pulled up in his jeep in front of the little shack. John and I walked up to his beat up jeep to greet him. He climbed out of the floorless jeep, smiled sheepishly and shook our hands.

"*Aslama saheb.*" John said smiling at Lahkdar

"Aslama saheb. Good to see you." I added.

We asked him if he would be going our way and would he be able to give us a ride. Lakdar smiled and communicated that he would take us further down the road a little later. He motioned for us to just wait. So we did. Lahkdar wandered over and sat out at the little desert camp and talked with the desert nomads drinking tea. They sat out in the sand as before and had a quiet conversation under the morning sun. After a while two of the desert men stood up, slowly walked over to where John and I were sitting, gestured, took each of our right hands and seemed to say goodbye. They nodded and then started slowly walking out into the desert. They were heading away from the direction of the paved road, straight out across the sand into the middle of nowhere.

"Man, I wonder where they could be going." I said, watching the two Arab men slowly disappear out in the waves of sand.

"I have no idea." John replied. "There's just nothing out there."

We stood, fascinated, watching the two men slowly walk away until they became nothing but small dots shimmering on the sand, in the heat. Then they just seemed to fade and slowly disappeared into the desert sand.

It was now time to go, time to leave this little isolated desert camp in the Sahara. Lahkdar came back over and communicated to us that he would drive us farther on across the Sahara in his jeep. We weren't sure how far he was going or even where, but there was only way to go and that was to continue following the single paved road west in the direction of Morocco.

The remaining desert nomads, along with the other man who seemed to live in the little shack, all walked over and stoically said goodbye to us as we put our backpacks into the old floorless jeep. We thanked them for their hospitality, as each of the grizzled men shook our hands, tapped their chest lightly and made a little gesture towards us. They then moved back toward the little shack that had been our home for Christmas.

We climbed back into the beat-up jeep and Lahkdar noisily threw it into gear, quickly spun the jeep around and headed out into the sand back toward the paved, lone highway. Lahkdar drove through the soft sand until we finally reached the main road and then turned toward the west. We headed on our way down the highway. As always, the road was mostly vacant and endless. Just a lone strip of unmarked pavement running endlessly through the desert sand, with very, very few other vehicles, passing by only occasionally.

"Well, that turned out to be a nice little break out there. It was good to get a full night's sleep." John said to me as we drove on down the highway.

"Yeah. It was. It was good to get recharged. That little shack and desert camp was a quiet place, wasn't it? It's the most isolated place I've ever seen anyone live."

"That one guy must have actually lived out there. There was another guy who was there when we went to sleep, remember? I wonder what happened to him? I never saw him the next day, did you?"

"No." I said, "He just disappeared and never came back again."

"Yeah.."

BACK ON THE ROAD AGAIN

"Who knows?"

We tried to ask Lahkdar how far it was to the next town, which turned out to be called Ouragla. He told us it was still a long ways. He explained to us he had driven to the next town the night before to follow the truck driver for his delivery. He then spent the night there.

Early this morning he drove all the way back to our remote desert camp from the same town just to pick us up. At the next town, he was going to be meeting up with the same truck driver from the day before to follow the driver back through the desert carrying his next load. They would be heading back the same way we had come from the day before, back to Tourregot. It was Lahkdar's job as a mechanic to follow the truck back and forth through the lonely desert and repair it if necessary.

As Lahkdar drove us down the highway, I sat back, being careful not to stick my feet out onto the pavement because of the missing jeep floor, and just watched the pavement roll by through the empty desert. It was a long ride.

When we finally pulled into Ouragla, it was early afternoon. It was a pretty good size town. There were a few paved streets running haphazardly through the hilly town, with several smaller sand and dirt streets and alleys winding in and about the streets. Several dry clay buildings lined the streets, mostly single story but a few that were two floors. There was a lot of activity and Arab men out on the streets; Some walking, some carrying sacks, some selling goods on the streets, some pulling wooden carts, others leading donkeys or camels down the road. Other men were also seated on little chairs along the street or leaning against the buildings playing cards or talking. Mostly men covered with the long gowns and turbans wrapped tightly around their heads and faces to protect them from the sand and wind..

A few women were also about, but not so visible or noticeable. The rare few, who I ever saw in public places, seemed to me to always be in the shadows and in the corners; covered from head to toe with the white gowns, hiding all but their eyes. And they never spoke to me. Never. Not once. No woman ever said a single word to me the entire time I was in the Sahara that I can remember. Heck, they never even made eye contact with me.

Actually, there was only the two times I ever made eye contact with a woman during the entire trek across the Sahara. As I said, one time was with Muhammad's mother in his home in Habjib, which was OK. The other time was with the young woman on the bus in Tunisia. That wasn't OK. And that didn't exactly turn out so well. Actually it could have turned out much worse, but I was lucky it didn't.

It was strange. But women just were not part of my travel experience in the Sahara. It's like they didn't really exist for me, which was very odd since I've always enjoyed the company of women. I always enjoyed being around woman and had many female friends or girls I dated when I was young. But in the Sahara, they just didn't exist.

Lahkdar stopped and parked the beat up jeep along the roadside in the town. We all got out of the jeep onto the street among the chaos and activity of the street. We wanted to find some place to eat. It was hot, dusty and quite breezy with the desert sand blowing across on the wind. The sand was getting in my hair, eyes and clothes. I turned the collar of my coat up and wrapped an old t-shirt around my neck and mouth to keep the ever-present sand out.

Lahkdar communicated he would have to go soon and meet the truck driver to follow him across the desert with his next load. Before he left, we quickly found a little food stand out on the dusty street where a young Algerian man was selling food. John was quite excited about that and, with Lahkdar's help, spent time picking out some type of meat sandwich to eat. He really enjoyed the food.

I, on the other hand, didn't eat anything. I was still recovering from the breakfast at the desert campsite. After the morning meal I had spent about 20 minutes out in the desert sand again with the runs. I won't go into details but it wasn't pleasant with no toilet or TP. I hadn't had access to a toilet or TP for several days now. So for a lot of the time, I wasn't exactly thrilled about eating much food because of the after effects.

After John's meal, Lahkdar said it was time for him to leave. We stopped on the street among the hustle and bustle of the small town, and shook hands with Lahkdar. We made the same gesture with our right hands that the desert men had made to us when they left. Lahkdar did the same. When he finished John and I smiled, shook hands again, slapped him on the back, American style, and wished him well.

He had been a very big help to us, and really looked out for us. Plus he took us jeep surfing in the Sahara - How many people can say that's something they have ever done? Before he left John and I exchanged addresses with him. I still have Lahkdar's address in my old address book.

Bedouin Camp
Somewhere out in the Sahara
We spent Christmas Eve sleeping at the camp. John is sitting between the 'truck driver' and Lahkdar, with several nomadic tribesmen.

Dennis next to Lahkdar's jeep that drove him and John to remote Bedouin camp in Sahara

Algeria
John watching men playing popular traditional street game. We never figured it out.

Feriana, Tunisia - John waiting for bus to Gafsa... We had to backtrack 100 miles to Gafsa to get visa for Algeria.

Dennis' Algerian bank paper. Algerian dinar was a controlled currency and was worthless outside Algeria. During journey; Dennis and John traded black market with an Algerian soldier. They made some extra money- but it put them in a dangerous situation.

Moroccan money

Tourgout, Algeria
Dennis and John ready to get back on the road to start hitching again.

*Dennis on board packed ship... Leaving Tangiers harbor on way to Gibraltar.
Later on open seas Dennis, John and almost all on board got sick from rough seas.*

*Dennis in front of the Rock of Gibraltar
Moments after crossing the Strait of Gibraltar by ship from Tangiers, Morocco.*

CHAPTER **23**

Danger Ahead - End of the Line?

John and I then spent some time walking around the town taking in the sights. Like usual, we were intensely stared at everywhere we went. Mostly friendly stares, but also some of the utter shocked reactions we had sometimes gotten since entering the Sahara. Although I had grown accustomed to the intense stares and attention, it still made me feel a bit uncomfortable.

Eventually, we found a little market area, where some bearded, robed men were hawking bread and other items off of scraped wooden carts that were being pulled by donkeys. John stopped one of the men and gestured that we would like to buy some bread. Quickly a friendly, small crowd of robed men gathered around us to see what was going on with the two young strangers. The group of men smiled and joked among themselves, as we got our bread. We took our bread, paid a few dinar, smiled at the men, waved and walked away down the road.

We wanted to find out where the road leading out of town was so that we could start hitching again. We hoped to make some more distance since it was fairly early in the day and we still had a lot of daylight left.

We stopped and asked a couple of bearded, older men on the street for some directions for the road to Morocco. It took a moment for them to understand, but when they did they gave us concerned looks and shook their heads no, no. They motioned for us to go back, that the road was closed up ahead. When we tried to ask why and insisted that we needed to keep moving forward, the men gestured like fighting and shooting was up ahead. But they eventually shrugged, and pointed the way we needed to go to get to the outskirts of town on the road to Morocco.

TRAVELIN' MAN ACROSS THE SAHARA AND BEYOND

It took some time but we made our way through town passing a large market area where there were many little stands and carts pulled by donkeys loaded with various items and a lot of activity as people moved in and about the hot, dusty market. Just past the market the town butted up against the harsh desert and the road continued past into the open Sahara sand.

We walked a little way out of the town into the desert and set our backpacks down in the sand along the desolate roadside to wait for our next ride. Based on our previous hitching experience in the desert, we weren't expecting many vehicles, but we expected to get a ride as soon as one drove up.

We had been spoiled by the incredible luck we had been having since we inadvertently started hitching across the Sahara. Very few cars or vehicles were ever on the road, but we never waited more than a short while for a ride. I don't think that more than half a dozen or so cars ever went by without one stopping to offering us ride. The Sahara was like hitchhikers heaven.

But now at this spot outside this town, suddenly no one would give us a ride. Very, very few vehicles passed, but when they did none stopped. After awhile one of the drivers slowed his truck, gave us a concerned look and gestured for us to go back to town. The vehicles were now very, very few and far between. There was very little traffic, even by the standards of the Sahara.

After a couple hours with no ride and very few cars, I said to John, "What do you think is going on here? Why no ride? And where did all the cars go. There are no cars out here. Only a few old loaded up trucks."

"I don't know." John answered, "I think there is some problem up ahead, maybe the guerillas we've been hearing about It's a big change from all our hitching before."

"Who knows? Let's just keep at it. We're bound to get a ride soon."

But we didn't. We stayed out there for another hour or so with no ride. We also got more of the concerned looks and signals to go back to town from the few drivers passing by.

Finally, one dilapidated truck stopped. We ran up to the truck expecting our first ride from town. Instead an older man with a thick beard, wearing a dirt-streaked turban leaned out the truck window and using a lot of gestures and body language explained that the road was closed up ahead. He seemed to explain that the road was blocked to people going through. It led into a war zone or something, and there was a soldier checkpoint.

We thanked him for the information and he headed on down the road into the desert, while John and I started slowly walking back towards town.

DANGER AHEAD - END OF THE LINE?

"If it's true, that's some bad news." I said as we walked along, "What are gonna do if there's no way through? We are way, way out here. There's no way we can make it back the way we came."

"That's for sure." John agreed, "We've come way too far to turn around now."

After a few more minutes walking, I said, "Let's find out in town what's up. Maybe we have some other options, maybe the truck driver is mistaken."

When we got back into town, we walked into the marketplace and looked around. There was a lot of activity, with men and donkey's pulling wooden carts full of foods and bread, kicking up the ever present desert sand as they passed by. Men and some teenage boys were standing in front of outdoor stands hawking different items, with a lot of hustle and bustle everywhere. I even saw a couple of women shopping, carrying bags of food. They were, of course, covered from head to toe with the white flowing gowns concealing everything including their faces and a few were wearing sunglasses. But just the same I was surprised to see them out on the streets.

As we walked into the market, John's attention quickly turned to food. No matter how dire our situation, it was often his top priority.

"Let's see if we can find something to eat. We can try to get some information while we have a meal. Sound good?"

"Yeah. That's OK with me. We can grab a bite and figure out a way to get through."

Up to this point, John and I were never really too fazed by any obstacle or problem we faced. At 19 years of age, and my brother 21 years old, we were both quite seasoned travelers way beyond our years. John had started his traveling adventures shortly after graduating high school, and I had quickly followed in his footsteps a couple of years later.

By this time John had been to over 30 countries. Barely 19 years old, I had already traveled to about 15 countries and counting. More than just the number of countries we had crossed, was the rugged method and means by which we had traveled.

Any danger or difficulty we came across, we mostly took it in stride. We just assumed we would think of something, and would do whatever we had to do to make it. And right at this moment we were indeed facing some serious danger and a major obstacle, but we didn't blink twice. We just stayed intensely focused on finding a way and, like always, doing what we had to do.

TRAVELIN' MAN ACROSS THE SAHARA AND BEYOND

I like to think it was the fearless confidence of youth, but then again, I'd say it probably had as much to do with the inexperience of youth. In reality at the time, we had no idea what was ahead of us…or what we were in for… or the actual challenges and dangers we would soon have to face. Whether we could actually meet those challenges and overcome them remained to be seen.

John and I eventually found a little food stall that was selling some kind of sandwiches. It was out on the dusty roadside and had a few, rough, wooden chairs to sit on. While the food was cooking in some kind of stone pot, John and I took a seat and waited for the food to be prepared. It didn't take long. I wasn't surest exactly what our meals were made of, but it tasted real good. While eating our food, several robed, Arab men meandered over from the crowded, hectic market and gathered around us, looking at us with curiosity.

We began asking them about getting a ride to the next town in the direction of Morocco. It took a moment for them to understand. When they did, their expressions changed from ones of friendly curiosity to concern and apprehension.

The men signaled, 'No, no. You can't go that way.' John and I kept gesturing and pointing that 'Yes, yes. We must travel that way toward Morocco.' They reacted with stern hand signals, 'No, no it's not possible.' This gesturing battle went on for some time, until one clean-shaven, dark haired man in his mid 20's stepped forward and addressed us.

He was slim and boyish looking and wore western style clothes. Speaking in broken English and pointing to the men gathered around us, he said. "They say – you not go. Cannot go that way. Road closed. War and fighting that way. No-one go."

"Why?" I asked "We've traveled a long, long ways on this same road. Why can't we go that way?"

The young man hesitated a moment and then said, "I'm sorry. Not possible. Policerio guerillas control the road. Can't go." Pointing to the group of men he continued, "Also, they hear Morocco border closed. Can't cross border."

"But we must." John replied strongly. "We must go that way and get to Morocco."

The group of men gathered around us began murmuring, nudging and whispering to the young man. Everyone seemed very concerned.

DANGER AHEAD - END OF THE LINE?

The young men then spoke up again and said, "This road closed. There is war that way. Many fighting. Only soldiers and supplies for Policerios can go. Trucks with supplies go. No other people."

"Uh huh." I said, listening with a sense of growing dread.

The young guy continued, "There soldier check and road block that way. You go back. You must go back."

With this information John and I were at a loss. We stepped aside away from the crowd out on the street to talk by ourselves.

"Man, what do you think?" I asked John. "It looks like this is the end of the line. What're we gonna do."

"I'm not sure. It seems to be true – what they said." John replied.

"Yeah. Must be. They all seem to agree."

We stood in silence for a few moments along the busy roadside with donkeys, camels, carts and lots of people coming and going from the market, contemplating what our options were. It did not look good. In fact, the more we stood there thinking about our situation the worse it looked. It looked downright desperate. If we had to go back and couldn't keep going on the way toward Morocco, there was no way we could make it back before running out of money. We were dead, and we knew it.

"I feel like I got the wind knocked out of me. I didn't really think the road would ever get blocked." I said, still in disbelief.

"I know what you mean." John answered quickly. "We gotta come up with something. Turning back is not an option. We'll never make it back."

Doing a quick calculation in my head, I said, "If we go back, we don't have enough money to even make it across the Mediterranean. We'll run out before we even make it to Europe. We'll never get outta north Africa."

"No kidding. Going back is not an option. We gotta keep moving forward somehow."

"Yeah." I agreed. "Just do what we gotta do. Whatever it takes."

"That's for sure. The question is - What's it gonna take?"

"There must be something we can do." I said. "There must be some way we can get through."

We both thought for a moment, while the group of men who had been talking to us earlier stood silently in the desert wind, watching us with concern. After a few moments, I said, "Hey, what if we somehow walk it."

"Whattdyya mean? Walk it? How?"

"I don't know. Maybe we could walk the highway and when we get to where it's blocked or where there's a guerrilla checkpoint – we walk around it through the desert."

"You serious?" John asked in disbelief.

"Yeah. Why not?"

After another moments thought, John replied, "That'd be real dangerous. We have no idea how far it is to the guerilla check point? How far it is past the checkpoint, or where the road's blocked, or how far it is to the next town? Or what kind of check it is?"

"Uh huh."

"Who knows what's out in the desert and how we gonna find our way through the open desert off the road? It'd be real easy to get lost out there. That could be deadly."

"Umm." I grunted, somewhat annoyed with his logic.

"Plus they probably have patrols out in the desert. We could easily get shot."

"OK. OK. I see your point. Bad idea."

Our only road through was now blocked and we were out of ideas, desperate and appeared to be at the end of the line.

CHAPTER **24**

Guns, Guerrillas and…Gas

We both thought some more, trying to think of any way through, anyway at all. After a time, John spoke up. "If we can't hitch to get a ride, how about if we pay a truck driver to drive us through the checkpoint?"

"You mean bribe a driver for a ride."

"More or less."

"Yeah. That might work." I said. "At least get us through the check point, through the guerrillas, or whatever's blocking the way."

"Think anyone would take us?" John questioned. "It'd be real dangerous."

"I don't know. There's usually someone who'll do what's needed if the price is right."

"And once we get through," John continued, "We can head north away from the war area…away from the Policerio guerrillas. Remember the map those nomads drew in the sand for us at the desert camp?"

"Yeah. What about it?" I asked.

"This road we're on splits at some point and one way continues south into the war and the fighting…The other way heads north."

"Yeah. That's right." I said. "OK. Let's see if we can find a truck driver that we can bribe to take us through."

"Sounds good. It's worth a try. We've got nothing to lose."

As I started to move, John said, "But wait. How we gonna pay a driver to take us? We're really low on funds. I'm down to about 80 bucks total. How much we gonna offer him?"

After a moment's thought, I replied, "Whatever it takes. Hopefully not more than a few bucks…But whatever it takes. We got no choice."

That was the truth. We had no choice. No other options. We were desperate.

With our plan set, we walked back over to the group of Arab men who were still standing motionless in the street watching us among the donkeys, camels, carts and people moving about the outdoor market. We motioned we wanted to meet a truck driver. They didn't understand what we wanted. We pointed down the dusty road going out of town into the desert and gestured like driving a truck. They still didn't understand. The young guy who spoke a little English was now gone.

We gestured some more like paying money, paying a bribe, to a driver to get us through the guerrilla checkpoint and pointed down the road. It took a while but they finally seemed to understand. Two tall, slim, bearded men wearing loose robes with turbans covering their faces pulled us aside, and signaled they could help us. They signaled for us to follow them. I was a little apprehensive, but we did.

They led us away from the crowds and out of the market area through some narrow winding streets. We followed them to an isolated, side-alley area, where there was one small stand with a few, beat-up, wood chairs and tables set up.

One man was working at the stand, and another man was sitting at one of the chairs sipping some kind of drink. No-one else was around. The seated man wore robes and a turban, and they both had scraggly beards on their dark faces. The seated, drinking man slowly looked up as we approached. Unlike most people we encountered in the Sahara, he did not smile. He was stocky, with a weathered face and lifeless, hooded eyes. With his turban pulled aside, he appeared to have some kind of wicked looking scar across the side of his jaw, cutting through his beard and down his neck. He was not a friendly looking guy. He just peered at us with wary, appraising eyes.

The two Arab men we were with timidly walked up to him and, while still standing, spoke to him in Arabic. They spoke for a few moments. They seemed a little nervous and a tension filled the air. The seated man with the scarred jaw listened, grunted something and then made a brusque hand gesture. The two men, who had brought us, then turned and signaled for John and me to come over and sit at the table.

As we walked over to the table, the two men who had brought us here bid us goodbye and hurriedly left. John and I looked over at each other and made eye contact. My instincts were definitely kicking in and going on alert.

Without speaking, we both knew what each other was thinking. "This is crunch time. Stay alert. Be careful and aware."

I quickly looked around before sitting, to see who and what was in the immediate area. I made a mental note of two different exit points from the little area we were in. I then pulled a chair aside and sat so that my back was nearest the wall, giving me a full view of the area without anyone being able to walk up to me from behind. John sat next to me.

'Scarface', the seated guy with the vicious looking scar, waited a moment, looking us over. Then he gestured about driving a truck and taking us with him. Using a little French and a lot of body language, we all came to understand that John and I wanted a ride past the soldier checkpoint to the next safe town. It was also understood that the guy was driving a truck full of supplies for the guerillas and could take us there.

With that quickly understood, it now it came down to the money…the payment…the bribe. Now it got serious.

We started haggling with the tough looking truck driver over the price. The negotiations were quite heated and went on for a while. We were talking US dollars. It's the only currency 'scar face' would negotiate in. I don't think he knew the value of any other currency.

He was a tough negotiator. John and I tried our best to hold firm, and at one point we stood up and acted like we were going to walk away. 'Scarface' reacted angrily and shouted something in Arabic, but he did become a little more flexible after that.

Finally, we settled on a price of $15. An awful lot of money for us at the time. Much more than we hoped to pay, and much more than we could afford. But like we said before, 'We had no choice.'

When we agreed on the price I was speaking in French. Well, not really speaking in French. More like kind of mumbling about incoherently in French. We agreed to the number 15 in French.

Like I said, my French was not at all fluent. Not even semi-fluent. Not even remotely semi-semi-fluent. My French was one, disinterested, college semester of French fluent. Nothing more, and maybe less.

So when the agreement was made, John counted fifteen fingers in front of the driver and flashed his 15 fingers to him to make it clear we both understood. Scarface agreed. I then took out my pen from my backpack and wrote the number 15 on the palm of my right hand with a dollar sign. I wrote '$15' in big dark print, showed it to Scarface, had him look at my palm and agree again. Then I shook his hand with it. Now I had proof of our agreement.

I whispered to John, "We should be OK now and avoid any rip-offs later on."

"Uh-huh, yeah…Sure." John said, not at all convinced.

With the terms set, the truck driver finished his drink and got up. It was time to be on our way. The truck driver walked over, paid the owner for the drink and pulled his dusty turban up over his scarred face so that only his squinting, flat eyes were peering out. Then he signaled for us to follow him. He walked through the windswept, side streets and soon met up with another man who joined up with us.

The other guy was a slim, slightly younger guy with a long, flat beard, wearing a dirty, brown robe and turban. They seemed to know each other quite well. He made no introductions for us. We later learned that he was the guy's driving partner.

John and I followed them through the dusty streets and markets until we came upon a big, heavily loaded-down truck parked along the side of the road. The truck had a big, scratched and dented cabin in front and large, lightly treaded tires that seemed to be sagging under the weight of the load. The rear of the truck was very large and had sides up about 3 feet high. A thick, heavy green colored tarp was covering the entire rear area of the truck and the load it was carrying. A thick rope was tied down over the tarp to keep the tarp and load from sliding or blowing off.

As we approached the truck John and I took a quick walk around the sagging, old truck, while the two drivers were discussing something about the trip. The truck looked like it had seen many a rugged mile through the desert.

While we were away from the truck drivers on the other side of the truck, John asked me, "Whattda ya think of these guys?"

"I don't know, man. I don't trust em. They seem like traders and hustlers. Especially 'Scarface', the guy with that wicked scar. He's stone cold."

"Yep."

"They remind me of a couple of convicts. I think they follow the green." I said making the hand gesture for money. "Whatever way the cash is coming from that's where they'll be. That's where their loyalty will be."

"You probably got that right." John replied. "It's good we didn't pay the money yet. Not until after we get through the guerrilla checkpoint…Make it to the next town. It'll give us a little leverage."

"Yeah. It should."

After a moment I continued, "Man, it's some dangerous travel were heading into. It's do or die time for us…."

'No kidding." John replied.

"I wonder how they're going to get us past the soldier checkpoint or road block?" I asked.

"No idea." John replied back. "If they sell us out at the checkpoint or we get nailed, we could find ourselves going to the front lines. We could be going to fight with the Policerio guerrillas."

"Or worse." I said grimly..

"Yeah. I guess there's always worse, isn't there? They could shoot us."

"Yep. But we got no choice. We do what we gotta do."

"The code of the road, huh? Do what we gotta do and keep moving forward."

After the two, tough, Arab truck drivers finished their inspection of the old truck, they hurriedly gestured for John and I to get in the front cab. We climbed up into the cab where there was a kind of long, tattered, rolled-up rug for us to sit on up behind the driver's seat.

We sat down and tried to get comfortable, as the two, grizzled drivers climbed in and sat in the front seats. We were sitting up high with a good view of the road ahead out the front window. 'Scarface' got in behind the wheel, while his friend road shotgun. He quickly fired up the tired, old truck and we started rumbling down the road out of the small town into the isolated Sahara.

Not long after leaving sight of the town, we hit the same hilly, hard rock desert we had sometimes seen on previous days. As we started out, the two drivers ignored us and went about their business like we weren't there. They seemed like hard guys, who had made this or other dangerous trips through the war zone before.

After leaving town, for the first time since we had started our trek through the Sahara, the desert road changed. The single paved road we had been following for days now had been the same strip of unmarked, smooth, flat pavement endlessly cutting through the desert. While the desert landscape had often changed, the lone road we traveled never did. It had been endlessly the same. But now as we left town it quickly changed into a rocky, potholed, partially unpaved, broken strip of road, jutting its way through the harsh desert. The desert road and the ride got rougher and rockier as we went along, and the driver's pace slowed considerably as he tried to work his way through the ruts and breaks in the road.

Sitting high up in the cab behind the turbaned Arab driver and his partner was quite uncomfortable. It was cramped and stuffy with a thin wave of desert sand continually blowing in through the partially opened truck windows, filling the air with a hazy layering of sand.

"Man, I'm really getting thrown around up here with all the bumps in the road." I said to John, as I banged my shoulder on the side of the truck compartment again.

"I know what you mean." John replied. "I feel like a squash ball getting smacked around."

John and I were continually being bounced around inside the cabin as the old truck hit and maneuvered through the rough road and potholes.

"This sure isn't doing much for my condition."

"No kidding. I can smell it. Man, you must be passing enough gas to fill a gas station fuel tank."

I just laughed. What could I say?

"I'm surprised the windows haven't fogged up." John continued with a chuckle.

"I can't help it. I've had the runs for days, ya know."

Having had the runs for several days, the bouncing in the cab was causing me to pass gas, repeatedly. I couldn't control it. After a short while, the smell in the truck cabin got quite bad.

Sitting up behind the driver and his partner, I noticed them making faces from the smell and talking back and forth about it. They seemed to be getting quite concerned about the strange smell filling their truck.

'Scarface' repeatedly reached under the dashboard checking the vents looking for some problem. Any vehicle problem or breakdown in the Sahara could be very dangerous, so they weren't taking any chances. They were paying close attention to the strange smell.

This went on for a while as I kept bouncing around the cab and kept passing gas. The more concerned they got, the more John and I had to keep from breaking out in laughter. It was quite comical for John and me to be sitting behind these two, tough, desert drivers watching them getting more and more concerned about their truck because of the smell of my farts. They didn't have a clue what was the true cause of the strange smell, and there was no way I was going to try to tell them.

Finally, after about half an hour of my continual passing gas and their continual checks and discussions of a possible problem with the truck, they suddenly stopped the truck in the middle of the road. They didn't bother or need to pull over to the side. There was virtually no traffic coming or going down the isolated desert road since we left town. We were completely surrounded by nothing but endless desert.

The two truckers then climbed down out of the cab, walked to the front of the truck, opened the hood and started checking and arranging things with the engine of the truck. With John and I looking on, they spent a good 15 minutes working under the hood checking the wiring, fluids, belts and adding coolant to the radiator. When they finished they smiled, brushed their sleeves and slapped their hands like "Job well done. We got that fixed."

While we were watching them work, John and I tried to stop from bursting out in hysterics and just stood aside, laughing as quietly as we could to ourselves.

"I can't believe it. Your farts are going to be legendary. They put a stop to two, tough, desert truck drivers." John said laughing.

I didn't respond. I just continued chuckling uncontrollably.

"I've heard of smelly farts before, but I've never heard of them stopping a truck dead in its tracks."

I still didn't respond. I just kept laughing.

"Man, wait till we make it back and I tell everyone. You're never going to live this one down." John continued between breaks in laughter. "Those farts oughtta be in the Guinness Book of World Records."

I still didn't respond. I just kept laughing. What could I say? As a claim to fame, John had his snoring. Now I had my smelly farts.

Before jumping back into the old truck, I walked way out into the desert sand away from the truck and took care of business. I was hoping it would cut down on my passing gas. It did a bit.

With the engine smell problem now fixed (not in the way that the truck drivers thought) we started heading on down the bumpy, broken road again. It was slow going as we made our way through the rugged empty desert into the guerrilla war zone area. It was also hot and uncomfortable sitting in the little cab as we bounced through the desert, with the choking dust and desert sand continually blowing through the truck cab.

After another couple hours or so of slow travel through the Sahara, we still had come across very, very few vehicles on the road. The only vehicles were a rare truck with supplies. The road was just empty.

When we got further from town and hit a certain stretch of desert, things changed. Suddenly, there was a different feel and mood to everything. I could sense it. It put John and me on alert. I kept my eyes peeled to the road, continually scanning the surrounding desert area.

The drivers had become more focused and tense. The banter between them had stopped and they became intensely focused on the road, and whatever lay ahead of us. We drove on with a nervous silence filling the truck cab. The two drivers were continually glancing around the desert area outside, as if looking for some sign or landmark. Occasionally, they would exchange some hushed comments between themselves.

"We're getting close. I can feel it. It's time." I whispered to John.

"That's for sure. These guys are really tense." John said quietly, as he nodded at the two, tough truck drivers sitting in front of us. "We must be getting close to the soldier checkpoint. I wonder how they're going to get us through."

"I don't know." I replied. "I sure hope they know what they're doing."

"I hope so. They seem like hard guys, but as long as they don't sell us out to the guerrillas..."

We drove on a little further, when suddenly the truck driver with the gruesome scar turned off the road and drove a little ways into the desert behind some sloping hard rock hills. He stopped the truck, cut the engine, jumped out of the cab and brusquely gestured for John and me to follow him.

John and I looked at each other and shrugged. We didn't know what was going on. We climbed out of the cab and followed 'Scarface' around to the rear of the old truck. His partner joined us. They then undid the rope holding down the tarp and yanked the tarp back. Filling the rear of the beat-up truck, there looked to be stacks of military type uniforms and clothes, along with some boots.

'Scarface' then aggressively gestured and half pushed us up onto the back of the truck. John and I quickly climbed up on top of the clothes in the back. The two drivers then pulled over some of the clothes and made spaces for us to crawl into. They then looked at us and made the gesture of 'shh, shh, quiet. Don't talk.'

The two, hard guys gestured for us to crawl under the clothes. John and I hesitated a moment, but 'scarface' impatiently began pushing and shoving us to hide under the piles of clothes. It wasn't a request. It was a command. We did what he wanted.

Everything then went dark as the two drivers piled clothes and materials on top of us, covering us completely. It was hot, cramped and suffocating. I was surrounded by darkness. I couldn't see John at all.

I then heard the tarp being pulled over top of us as the two truck drivers moved around the truck securing the tarp's rope.

Very soon after, the truck started to jostle and bump along with us hidden in the back. While we were bumping along, John and I didn't talk or move. We didn't dare. The only way I knew John was there was from hearing his breathing from a few feet away as we laid in the back of the old truck like we were frozen in place.

My heart was thumping so hard that I was sure it could be heard from outside the truck and across the desert for miles. I was also perspiring a steady stream of sweat - from the stifling heat, but even more from the unbearable tension. We were now heading to the check point for the Policerio guerrillas - No civilians allowed.

If we got nailed or the drivers sold us out, I could soon find myself heading to the frontlines to fight, or taken prisoner or shot. Who knows what the guerrillas might do if they found a couple of Americans hiding in a supply truck going through their checkpoint. Out here in the remote Sahara…they could do anything they wanted and no-one would ever be the wiser.

John and I hid in silence, unmoving. I had no sense of time but it seemed like we waited hidden in the back for hours as the truck slowly bumped and rocked along the road until, finally, it came to an abrupt stop. I tensed up. I could hear the driver jumping out of the truck and the truck door slam shut. I then vaguely heard the sound of footsteps approaching the truck. It sounded like several sets of footsteps. There were then muffled voices. Several voices.

The voices and footsteps circled the truck and stopped near the rear. My heart came to a stop. I waited. I strained to hear any additional sound or movement. I waited some more. I feared the tarp was going to be pulled off, with a rifle pointed at my face. There was some more muffled conversation and then what sounded like footsteps. The footsteps moved away from the rear of the truck and then disappeared. After a time I could then hear the truck door open and someone climb into the truck and slam the door. I was hoping it was the truck driver with the scar and not some soldier. The truck started slowly moving again and I also started breathing again. John and I remained unmoving, waiting, silent. We still didn't dare speak or move.

The truck bumped along for what seemed like ages. I didn't know what had happened or if we were safe. It was very dark, tense and hot waiting hidden covered in the back of the old truck.

The big, beat-up truck continued to drive on for quite some time, while I stayed silent and motionless hidden in the intense heat under the military clothes and tarp in the back of the truck. I didn't know what had happened at the soldier checkpoint, or where the truck was being driven now, or who was driving the truck. I didn't know if we had made it through, or if we were safe, or in immediate danger.

I didn't know a lot of things. I was in the dark. Literally. All I could do was stay hidden, wait and hope.

Finally, the truck stopped moving. For a moment I thought my heart also stopped as I waited and heard someone getting out of the cab and moving to the rear of the truck. Then I could feel the tarp being moved and suddenly blinding light appeared as the clothes and supplies were pulled off from me. Breathing the open air and getting out from the suffocating heat was a huge relief.

A much bigger sense of relief was soon to follow. After blinking from the direct light, I looked to see who had removed the tarp and covering... It was the truck driver with the scar and his driving partner, both sneering arrogantly. There were no soldiers or anyone else anywhere around; just the vast open desert. I gave a sigh of relief, and started breathing normal again. A moment later, John also staggered out from under the coverings. Like me, he was soaked with sweat, dirty and grimy, even more so than usual, but also like me he was now smiling.

"I guess we made it through OK." John said looking around.

"Yeah. Man, that was hot and tense."

"No kidding! I thought I was going to suffocate. How long do you think we were hiding under there?" John asked, pointing to the back of the truck.

"I don't know, at least a few hours , a long time." I replied wiping the dripping sweat and dirt from my forehead and face.

"When we first stopped and I heard all those footsteps around the truck, I thought for sure the tarp was going to be lifted at any moment."

"Me too. I kept expecting to see a soldier and the barrel of a rifle pointing at me or something."

John and I stood for a few moments and caught our breath as the two drivers rearranged the truck's supplies and replaced the tarp and tied it down. Before tying it down with rope, they pulled out our backpacks from where they had been buried and hidden under the supplies and tossed them to us.

John and I took them and climbed back up into the cab of the truck, as we were directed by the truck drivers. The two drivers followed us in and sat down in the front seats.

John and I both said "*Shocaren sahab.*" "Thank you, friend. Thank you."

The younger driver just sternly nodded back at us as he fired up the old engine and started chugging on down the rough road. It was another long ride with the rough, rocky road eventually getting a little flatter and in better condition. We drove and bounced our way through the empty desert, while both John and I kept our eyes peeled looking for any sign of soldiers, or military vehicles or guerrilla camps.

"So far so good." I said quietly to John as we bumped along in the cab of the old truck.

"Yep. So far…But were not safe yet. I still don't trust these guys."

"Me neither. Especially, ol 'Scarface' there." I whispered, nodding in the direction of the guy with the scar down his neck.

"Who knows where they're really taking us." John said eyeing the two desert drivers warily. "They're dangerous guys. The only reason they took us is because of the bribe."

"You got that right. They'll follow the money…take the best deal."

"Who knows what their real intentions are or what's up ahead."

"Let's just hope they didn't cut a better deal back there with the guerrillas… Were totally isolated and vulnerable out here." I said looking out at the endless, shimmering desert that completely surrounded us.

It was a long, tiring drive through the vast empty desert as John and I stayed very alert watching for any signs of danger or any unexpected activity from the two drivers. I was very tired and it was draining staying so focused and alert. It had been a tense several hours since we started this drive.

Finally, we came upon another road and a split where we had to choose which direction to go. It was one of the few, rare times we came across another road in the Sahara, actually it was the first time in days. From what the desert nomads had showed us with their sand map way back at the desert camp, we knew if we turned left we would go further south and west directly into the war area. If we turned right we would head north and west back up toward the Mediterranean coastline and away from the fighting.

As we approached the split John and I both got very alert and held tightly to our backpacks ready to move. We kept our eyes on the driver, hoping he would turn right towards the north. If he didn't, John and I would have to try and get out of the truck somehow. I didn't want another repeat like our mistaken overnight ride south into the Sahara with the soldier at the Algerian border. One wrong turn in the Sahara could mean hundreds and hundreds of miles before we could change directions and from what we had been told by the nomads with their sand map, a wrong turn here and we would be heading directly into the war with no way out. It was a very important moment for us.

With John and me sitting in the cab back behind him, 'Scarface' momentarily came to a stop at the desolate crossroads. He looked over at his partner, nodded, said something in Arabic and then turned the big, old truck to the right and started heading north up the road. John and I both let out a big sigh and grinned. For the first time in a long time, I really relaxed.

We had apparently made it through the guerilla checkpoint and were now heading north out of the Sub Saharan War zone area.

While we were rumbling down the road, I looked over at John. He looked as exhausted as I felt, "It looks like we got through, huh? We should be heading away from the war zone area now. I think we're safe." I said.

"Yep. I think so. Finally! Man, what a relief."

"Yeah. That's been hanging over us for days. We finally did it. All those villagers and nomads…for days…telling us we couldn't get through the guerillas."

"We proved them wrong, didn't we?" John said.

"Sure did."

"Man, I'm really beat. It looks like we're OK now. Why don't we take turns catching some sleep?"

"Sounds good." I answered. "Why don't I sleep first."

"Ahh…No…Why don't I sleep first."

"No. That's alright. I'll go first. I know how much you enjoy looking at all this desert scenery." I said grinning and gesturing out the window.

"No, that's OK. You can keep your pal 'scarface' company and I'll snooze first." John replied.

"Alright." I grinned. "How about I'll flip you for it?"

"OK. You got a coin?"

GUNS, GUERRILLAS AND...GAS

"I think so." I said, as I started digging through my pockets. "Yeah. Here I got one."

It was an Algerian coin. I held it in my hand and said, "You call it."

I flipped the coin in the air and John called out, "Heads."

I looked. It was heads.

"OK. You sleep first. I'll wake you in a while." I said.

And with that John very quickly fell asleep. Despite my best intentions of trying to keep my eyes on the road ahead, within a matter of minutes, I too fell asleep. I was dead tired. We both were. With the stress and immediate danger gone, we couldn't stay awake.

I slept for I'm not sure how long. The next thing I knew John was nudging me, saying "Wake up. Wake up. We've hit town."

I looked up out of the truck and we were approaching a fairly big sized town that was spread out directly in front of us up on an elevated sand ridge. The wide spread town had some larger, two-floor buildings and a few sand covered, paved roads heading in different directions with several side streets and a few thirsty looking trees and some vegetation along the streets.

There was not a lot of activity in that area of the town from what I could see. There were just a few old trucks and cars rumbling along on the roads and only a few people with donkeys in sight. The weather had also changed and the sky had turned dark and cloudy. It must have been late afternoon and it felt like it might rain.

'Scarface', who was now riding shotgun, looked back over at us and pointed up ahead like we would be getting out soon. He then also gestured about the money. It was time to pay up.

"I think this is the end of the line for us." John whispered to me, "We need to pay the 15 bucks to these guys. You got it."

"Yeah. I got the ten dollar bill and five ones."

"OK. Keep it ready."

"Yeah." I said, "We'll pay when he stops."

They drove up a little ways into town and then stopped along the side of the wide road with some larger buildings off in the distance. The guy with the scar then turned around in his seat and looked back at John and me. He said something in Arabic that we didn't understand. We assumed he was asking for the money.

"Give him the 15 bucks." John said to me.

I took the 15 bucks and handed it over the seat to him. He quickly grabbed it out of my hand and showed it to his driving partner. John and I thanked them for the ride, and started to get our backpacks ready to get out of the big truck. But the two guys didn't move.

Scarface then looked back with a menacing expression and communicated that we owed him $50, not $15. John and I thought we misunderstand at first. He gestured again...He wanted $50 and he wanted it now. He was dead serious.

I looked over at John and angrily said, "He's trying to rip us off."

I then counted 15 on my fingers and gestured that $15 was the deal. The guy with the scar quickly and strongly shook his head no, no and gestured 50. It was 5-0....$50.

John then remembered I had written $15 on the palm of my hand, and said, "Show him your hand. Show him your hand with the $15 in ink."

"Yeah. That's right. That will do it. We got proof."

I held my hand with the palm up and showed him the $15 I had written. John then gestured and pointed that we agreed to the $15 and had shook hands on it. John and I kept strongly motioning and communicating that the deal was $15, but the truck driver wasn't having it.

"We gotta hang tough." John whispered to me, "He's trying to rip us off."

"Absolutely. We can't budge. The deal was 15 bucks. There's no way were gonna pay 50 bucks."

"Not a chance." John agreed.

There was no way we could afford to pay $50, and we didn't intend to. It was a blatant attempt to rip us off. We had to hold tough no matter what.

So what happened? We quickly paid him $50. Why?

Well, our intentions for holding tough were quickly defeated by one threatening gesture from the guy with the scar. He made an intimidating gesture and then just pointed over to the large building across the street from where we were parked.

Upon a closer look, John and I could see that it was some type of military building. There were some military vehicles parked off to the side and I could see a couple guys with rifles in some type of uniform, standing off in the distance against a wall.

That stopped John and I dead. We went absolutely quiet. Right then the idea of any contact with the military scared the hell out of us. We had just secretly crossed through the policerio guerilla checkpoint to pass through the war zone area, which we had been repeatedly warned was off limits to all civilians. A few days earlier we had traded currency black market with some Algerian soldier. We were now in some town way out in the Sahara somewhere, and we had no idea whether we should even be in this town or what else the truck driver could pin on us.

We immediately stopped any attempts at negotiating and as quickly as possible rummaged up $50 between the two us. We got the bills together and just gave it to the guy with no comment. Scarface smiled deviously, counted the money, proudly flashed it to his driving partner and then opened his cab door and let John and I out of the big truck.

We quickly climbed down out of the truck without a word, and started urgently walking away from the truck and away from the military building across the street. We hustled down the street into the seemingly deserted town without a look back, trying to get as far away from Scarface and the military post as fast we could.

"Man, 50 bucks. That hurts." I said to John as we hustled along.

"Yep. They really ripped us off bad. 50 bucks in one shot. It's gonna be tight makin it now.".

"That's the truth. At least they got us through the checkpoint."

"That was a relief." John said, "Now we just gotta make it to the Moroccan border and get through it."

"Hopefully the borders open."

"We'll see." John said.

"Things can't be any tougher than what we went through getting past that guerilla checkpoint."

"Yeah, hopefully. But its gonna be really tight from here out."

We walked through the town looking for a place to hole up and get off the streets. We were nervous about the military post nearby and wanted to get off the streets as soon as possible. After walking a while through the mostly quiet town we didn't see anything resembling a hotel. It was a pretty big town with wide paved streets. There was sand blowing though the mostly empty streets and some two or three floor, wind-scarred, clay buildings lining some of the roads, but very few people out or about and only a few vehicles passing by. The town seemed vacant, quiet and deserted. .

"Not much activity in this town, is there?" John said to me

"No, not much. It's sure a quiet place."

"I wonder where everyone is."

"I don't know." I answered. "There might be a curfew or maybe everyone fled. I think we should get off the streets as soon as possible."

TRAVELIN' MAN ACROSS THE SAHARA AND BEYOND

"Good idea. It's getting dark, too."

We walked a while longer and still didn't find anything resembling a hotel. Eventually, we found a place that we thought might be a boarding house. It wasn't. The young Arab man who answered the door seemed shocked and slightly taken aback to see us at his door. He nervously sent us on our way as quickly as he could.

After some more walking down a few different streets, it had now gotten dark, which just added to our unease about the town. There were a few lights on the streets but not much, and almost no people. Finally, we found a two-story clay building that appeared to be a hotel. This time it was. The older Arab man who owned the little hotel was flabbergasted when he saw us come in to the dark, little lobby. He looked like he couldn't believe his eyes. He was friendly enough, but just seemed so shocked that he didn't know what to do with these two foreigners. He just stood in the little lobby looking at John and me in disbelief.

The lobby was a small, single room with a long, beautiful rug on the floor and one dark hallway leading away from the back of the room. There was a picture of, I assumed, the Algerian president on the back wall. I was surprised to see on the other side of the room a picture of American boxing champion Muhammad Ali.

The man at the hotel eventually recovered from the shock of having two, young Americans standing in his small hotel lobby, and he took us to a room. It was a small, dark room with no beds, just a couple of sheets and a wooden chair. No toilet or sink or window. It reminded me of a pleasant jail cell minus the bars. We paid the man with Algerian currency. It cost about three bucks. The room was small and cramped and had no lights, but it did just fine.

During the trek across the Sahara, I saw pictures of boxing great Muhammad Ali hanging on the walls of buildings in several different towns. There would be the picture of the country's president and somewhere nearby a picture of Ali. Ali's persona definitely transcended sports, even at that time. I also imagine he was also so popular across Tunisia and Algeria because he had converted to Islam.

This was 30 years ago, long before any globalization or international communications. Aside from the few pictures of Muhammad Ali and the availability of Coca-Cola, there was almost nothing visible or known from America or the West. The world was a very big place in those days with very limited communications and little, if any, information available in some parts of the world.

Throughout my trip across the Sahara, there was no direct information of America or the West I ever came across…No movies, newspapers, TV shows, magazines, books or pictures. I never saw or heard about a single TV or even radio, and definitely no movie theaters or local newspapers. No contact with any Westerners, just no direct information.

The only bits of information seemed to be passed along from someone who had maybe been to another neighboring country or big city, or had seen a movie or magazine or something. That was it. It made for some very odd or outdated perceptions.

I remember in the village of Habjib being asked if I had ever been in an Indian fight. One night in Habjib, one of the villagers asked if John and I had I ever been in a shootout with Indians. The crowd of men around us at the time all waited with much anticipation for our answer, like they expected it to be true.

The reason they asked was because some men from the village had once seen old American Western movies or a book with cowboys and Indians. I actually was asked about being in an Indian fight a few different times, once with little kids mimicking shooting arrows.

I also remember being asked by two Algerian men, if the streets in America were really paved with gold. The men actually believed the streets in America were literally paved using gold. I heard that same thing a few times over the years from different people in different countries. A girl I dated in high school, who grew up in Sri Lanka (Ceylon), told me that all her life growing up in Ceylon she had been told and believed the streets in America were paved using gold. She told me it was a commonly held belief.

Another fairly common perception in the Sahara and elsewhere was that America was full of gangsters and there were shootouts on almost every street corner across the country. The image of Al Capone and old time gangsters, toting machine guns from the 1920's and 30's was a perception some people had in the Sahara. I guess from old black and white movies of Edgar G. Robinson and James Cagney.

A few people in the Sahara also didn't understand when I said U.S.A. They sometimes didn't understand when I said I was from the U.S.A., or I wanted to mail something to the U.S.A., etc.

They didn't recognize the term U..S..A., saying each individual letter. They pronounced it like it was a word spelled usa (spoken like "oohsa").

TRAVELIN' MAN ACROSS THE SAHARA AND BEYOND

They had never heard it spoken U-S-A. They just saw it written and pronounced it like it was a word, not an abbreviation. So when they spoke it, they spoke it like the word usa (oohsa). It took me awhile to catch on to what they meant when they kept saying 'usa' this and 'usa' that.

It made for some interesting and enlightening moments for me.

CHAPTER **25**

Moving Faster than a Sahara Sand Storm

After sleeping the night in the cramped, dark room, John and I awoke early at sunrise to try and get an early start. As John was stretching and yawning to wake up, I said "We need to make some distance today. That rip-off yesterday really set us back. 50 bucks, man. That hurt."

"Yep…It did. It's gonna be real tough now to make it back." John answered, "But we should be able to make some good time with no more checkpoint problems. It's good to get past the soldiers and guerillas."

"That's for sure. Did you believe that? Hiding in the back of that truck. That was something else."

"Sure was." John answered. "It was hot back there. I couldn't breathe."

"Me neither. I was too tense to breath. I thought for sure we were going to get nailed."

John and I got our backpacks together and headed out into the street in the early morning with the sun just rising over the horizon casting long shadows off of the buildings onto the empty streets. We walked through town looking for a road that might lead north.

In the morning sun we could see the mostly empty town was fairly big and spread out. Like almost all of the desert towns we had passed through, there were very, very few, if any, buildings over one floor high. While walking through the town we didn't see anything that resembled a restaurant, which was bad news for John since he was looking for some food to start the day. There were very few shops open or people on the streets. No-one pushing carts with bread or other goods. It was pretty quiet.

When we got to the edge of town we found a single, empty, paved road leading out of town into the desert. Like every other town we had passed though since entering Algeria, there was one road into town and one road out of town. That was it. We never had to worry about deciding which road was the correct road to take. We walked a little ways out onto the road and set our backpacks down in the sand to wait for a ride.

"Well, since we've made it through the soldier checkpoint and we're finally heading away from the Policerio guerrillas and the fighting – maybe our hitching luck will pick up again." John said hopefully.

"Yeah. It's nice to be finally heading away from the war, not into it."

"That's for sure. I wonder how far it is to the Moroccan border from here? Whattya think?"

"I don't know." I answered back.

"I think we got a long ways to go."

"Yeah. Me too. At least 600 or 700 kilometers. Maybe a 1,000. Algeria's a big country. One of the biggest in Africa."

"Yep. And we're taking the long way across it." John said.

"Man, you got that right. We sure went a long ways south. I think we have to go almost all the ways north and then east to get to the border. We're not exactly taking the direct route across. It's been quite a detour we've taken across the Sahara."

"We got an early start today." John said after a while. "It'd be good to make some mileage today."

And we did. It was a very productive day hitching, one of the best on the entire trip. Our luck hitching in the Sahara never failed us. We spent the entire day out on the road hitching across the Sahara and we covered over 400 kilometers as we made our way north, a ways out of the desert.

When we started hitching in the early morning hours, we got our first ride very quickly. It was a man driving a huffing-puffing, small, ancient truck. He was a short, middle-aged man, with a scraggly beard, friendly, squinting eyes and a kind smile. He was wearing a turban that was hanging loosely around his face and a western style jacket. He beckoned us into the old truck with a wave and a smile.

We hopped in and he quickly headed down the highway out into the Sahara. The man driving the truck spoke no English, but he was friendly and animated. He communicated well with us using a little French and body language. He explained to us that he was going to visit his friend. He also explained that he had three different wives waiting for him at home. When John and I reacted with surprise, he seemed amused and assured us it was true.

We drove with him for a couple of hours through the empty desert, before he suddenly turned off the main paved highway onto a small semi paved side-road. He didn't try to tell us where he was going or why. We didn't ask. We were along for the ride.

After a ways, the side road seemed to kind of parallel the main highway. It then quickly led down into a little, narrow, desert valley with vegetation and trees mixed in with the sand. It was like a long hidden valley oasis. You never would have known it was there unless you were right on top of it. There was a widely dispersed village spread out along the rolling valley road. A few homes and little markets dotted along the hilly road for several kilometers. The friendly Arab driver followed the road a ways and then stopped his old truck along the road in front of some kind of little shop or restaurant. He hopped out and signaled for us to follow him into the shop.

The shop turned out to be his friends place. We spent some time in the little shop where we were served tea and some bread. While we were there, a few other villagers wandered in to see us. They were only men, of course, along with a few youngsters. Everyone was very friendly and low key. They seemed to be intrigued having two young foreigners show up in their village. Intrigued but not overly impressed. It was a slightly muted reaction, which I rather enjoyed after the constant stares and shocked reactions we had been getting for so much of the time

While sitting in the shop, the man who drove us here offered for us to stay the night in the little roadside village with him and his three wives and several children. While it was an interesting offer, there was still a lot more hours of daylight left. John turned to the friendly Arab man and motioned thanking the man, but that we would be leaving. The man smiled and wished us well.

So we bid him and his friend's goodbye and walked back out to the small, slightly paved side road he driven us onto. As we walked out on the road, I gestured asking which we way we should go – back the way we came in off the main road or keep on heading down this side road.

The man pointed down the road away from the way we came in, so that's that the way we headed. We started walking down the road. The road ahead continued winding down the small desert valley with some sparse trees and vegetation growing in and among the hilly sand. The road led down into the valley then back up in the distance and over the distant sand hills. It was a warm, sunny, late morning and the sun shone bright in the sky. I was quickly getting hot and sweaty.

"Man, it's hot out here." I said as I wiped the sweat and sand off my forehead.

"No kidding." John replied. "I hope we get a ride soon. It's too hot for much walking."

"We've sure done our share of walking on this trip."

"Yep. We have." John said with a grin and a shrug. "The ways of the road, huh?"

"Yeah. The ways of the road. Walk till you drop and then walk some more." I said with a grin.

As we walked at a slow pace along the road there was no traffic at all coming by. Just a few, small, single-level desert clay buildings scattered here and there set back a ways from the road. There were also some sand paths leading away from the road heading up and through the valley hills with a few more buildings and trees in among the valley in the distance.

Unlike most of the desert villages we had passed through, these homes and building were spread out and scattered out all along the road and in the valley for a great distance. After walking down into the valley and partially up the next hill without any cars or vehicles passing by, we saw a man on a big tractor come barreling down from one of the sand hill roads leading down onto the paved road we were walking on.

John and I stopped walking and stared in awe as the big tractor came rumbling down the sandy hill at what seemed to be an incredible speed. It was sliding and swerving and seemed to be going way too fast. I expected it to flip at any moment, but it didn't. The guy driving the big tractor made it down the hill and drove right up toward us.

As he approached, John and I put out our thumbs in the gesture for hitching for a ride. The big guy on the tractor didn't seem to understand our hitching attempt. He just drove up to us and stopped. He was a big, strong looking, middle-aged, guy wearing western style work clothes. He had broad shoulders, a strong jaw covered with whiskers and short graying hair. He looked down at us from the tractor with a beaming smile. We just stood there and smiled back. After a moment, he signaled for us to climb aboard his tractor.

So without a word John and I quickly climbed up. It was a very, very big tractor, but it didn't really have any spare seats for passengers. We tried as best we could to find a space to sit and something to hold onto. Before we had a chance to find a place to get situated, the guy took off like a shot. I was surprised how much pick up the tractor had and how fast it could go. John and I were holding on for dear life as the big tractor rumbled and bumped its way down the road. We were flying up and down and being heaved every which way as we tried to stay on the tractor. Actually, it was a thrill. I loved the ride. It felt like I was riding a wild, eight-foot high, bucking bull.

The smiling guy driving the tractor gestured like 'are you OK?' We both grinned back. We didn't dare try to give a thumbs up or some other gesture, since we were tightly holding onto the tractor itself to keep from falling off.

He drove us a little further down the paved road and then suddenly turned off onto a sand side path leading up one of the hills out of the valley. He pointed over the hill like it was some kind of short cut or something. It was a narrow sand path that led directly up the hill at a steep angle, and then followed along the winding edge of the hill at the top of the valley. There were a few trees and vegetation along the path and scattered through the hills.

We rode up to the top of the hill while spinning and sliding in the sand, where the big guy then wound along some hair-raising turns and curves along the steep edge at the top of the hill. It was quite the ride. That big tractor got going fast, with the wind and sand blowing across us as we weaved through the valley. We were really hauling through the hills and valley.

After coming down the steep backside of the valley leading back onto a paved road, the smiling driver brought the big tractor to an abrupt stop. He smiled again as John and I caught our breath. The big driver then gestured that this was the end of the ride and we needed to get off. John and I jumped off and took a couple of pictures before the friendly guy rumbled off with his tractor.

I quickly shook the sand and dust off of my hair, face and clothes. I was covered with it. It was rimming my eyes and in my teeth and ears. But I didn't care. I looked over at John and excitedly said, "Man. That was an amazing ride, wasn't it?"

John was grinning as he answered, "I couldn't believe how fast he got that big, old tractor going. We must have been going at least 40 or 50 mph."

"Yeah. I thought we were going to fall off the edge of that one hill, for sure. He was riding it right on the edge."

After getting our breath back, we took a look around. There were a few single, clay building or homes off in the distance, with the same limited vegetation growing in the area. The small paved road we were standing on wound on down a ways and then disappeared around a bend ahead of us. There were no vehicles passing on the road. We could see an old truck parked out in the distance in front of one building, and a couple of men strolling out in the distance among one of the hills - but that was it.

We started walking down the small road along the valley. As we were walking, a couple of old cars came rumbling by. We put our thumbs out to hitch. The drivers of the cars slowed and gave an astonished look at us but didn't stop. I don't think they know what hitchhiking was.

A short while later a large, dusty, tarp covered truck drove up the road. It looked almost like an old military truck with a huge 6 foot high tarp covering the open back of the truck. Again John and I put our thumbs out to hitch. The truck stopped in front of us and out jumped a friendly looking, dark-skinned, young guy wearing a worn blazer and jeans. He had thick curly hair almost like an afro, black stubble on his chin and a bright smile that never left his face. He smiled expansively at us and we smiled back.

John then gestured that we wanted a ride. John said "Morocco." He tried to explain that we wanted to go in the direction of Morocco. The driver nodded that he understood. He waved for us to follow him around to the back of the truck.

We walked around to the back of the truck and were astonished to see that the truck was loaded with smiling, laughing school children. There must have been at least 20 of them crammed in the back of the covered truck. They looked to be elementary school kids. They were all boys. Many of them were wearing caps and holding schoolbooks. They were sitting on benches on both sides of the truck under the tarp cover. They seemed as surprised to see us, as we were to see them. The kids were being driven home after their school finished.

The school kids soon started laughing, and squealing, and talking excitedly among themselves, while gesturing towards John and me. John quickly took some pictures of me with the smiling kids and then he hopped onto the truck with me. The driver then drove us on down the road, with the kids laughing, making faces and trying to joke with us. John and I joked back with them.

The school bus (truck) drove down, around and through the little valley, making stops to let groups of kids off the bus. After riding a ways further, with almost all the kids off the bus, we came over some hills and out of the valley area back out into the open endless desert. The friendly driver then stopped the bus and came back to the backside of the bus. John and I jumped off the bus to greet him. We were now back out into the open endless desert heading in the direction of Morocco.

MOVING FASTER THAN A SAHARA SAND STORM

We shook hands with the driver and we wished him well. He climbed back into the truck and after he turned the big old bus around, he headed back down the road the same he had just come from.

"Well, that was a couple of interesting rides, wasn't it?" I said.

"Yep. Sure were." John agreed with a laugh."

It was now early afternoon and the sun was beating down hard, shimmering off the waves of sand, with very little wind. I wiped the sweat and dirt from my face with a t-shirt that I had in my backpack. Now that I was standing, I started getting hot very fast. The sweat started to quickly soak through my shirt. The same shirt I had been wearing for the past 3 weeks... continuously.

I didn't notice it. But I'm sure by now my clothes had a definite and distinct smell to them, as well as a thick coating of sweat stained dirt. As I said before my clothes could just about stand up on their own if they had a mind to. My hair had also taken on the characteristics of barbed wire...That is barbed wire coated with a thick layer of sand and dirt.

But who was there to notice. John and I certainly didn't. Nor did any of the local people we met throughout our desert travels. It also wasn't like there were any women around that we wanted to impress or be concerned about. Clean clothes and hygiene just weren't issues for us in the Sahara. Other things such as finding food and shelter, managing our money, staying safe, making distance and finding a way through to Morocco and across the border were the issues that we were focused on.

John and I slowly walked over to the main paved road and set our backpacks down along the roadside to wait for some cars and our next ride. As usual out in the Sahara, it didn't take long at all for our next ride to stop. For the rest of the day we got rides and made great mileage at a steady pace with little, if any, down time. There was very little waiting between rides. It was great hitching. The best rides of the day, however, were the first three; the friendly guy with three wives, the wild tractor man and the school bus.

During the course of the day, we passed through the big town of Laghouat, and then a little, dusty speck of town called Aflou as we made our way north through the desert. The next ride with a quiet, heavyset Arab man wearing western clothes was a long four-hour, stretch to a town called Tiaret.

It was a 4 hour stretch of endless desert with nothing in between. We drove over four hours with the quiet driver, through nothing but unending sand, desert and white sky. It was our last stretch of real Sahara travel.

TRAVELIN' MAN ACROSS THE SAHARA AND BEYOND

As we approached Tiaret, the landscape started to change slightly, with the endless desert sand and rock being occasionally overtaken by some patches of green grass, rolling, green-brown hills and a few trees. Tiaret was the first town since we left Tunis that had many buildings higher than two stories. It appeared somewhat modernized, and had a different feel to it than the numerous windswept, desolate desert towns we had been passing through for the past several days. It was also the first town in many days that had more than one road leading out of town. We actually found out there were two roads heading out of town. Two roads certainly aren't many, but it's more than one. John and I didn't spend much time checking things out. We immediately decided to take the road heading due north. So we made our way through the expansive city and started hitching again along the road heading north toward Oran. We had been told Oran was not too far and was as far north as we could go before hitting the sea. So for almost the first time since landing in Africa, we had a destination point of an actual city.

We were trying to get to 'Oran' and not just 'the next town.' For our entire trek across Africa we were always just trying to get to the 'next town.' There was rarely a name or location we knew – it was always just the 'next town' down the road.

As we stood by the road outside the town of Tiaret to hitch, John said, "It's getting late. It's gonna be dark soon. You wanna lay low here? Find a hotel or sleep out here?"

"Nah." I answered. "We've had great luck hitching today. We still got, maybe, 1 or 2 hours of daylight. I say we keep going while the goings good."

"I'm with you."

We continued hitching and our luck held up. After leaving Tiaret, the traffic picked up a bit. There were sometimes more cars on the road and actually an occasionally sign or markings on the pavement. It took a few rides but we passed through the towns of Zimmora, and later a town called Sig.

(I like that name. Just 'Sig.' It sounds like it's my buddy's town or something. 'This is his town. Just call it 'Sig.'")

We finally made it into Oran later that night. When we drove into the city, it was something of a shock after the many days crossing the endless Sahara. Oran was a very large, fairly modern city with several wide, well-marked streets, numerous, steel, high-rise buildings, bright street signs, billboards, neon lights, etc.

MOVING FASTER THAN A SAHARA SAND STORM

It was quite a shock to be back in civilization. After being in the unrelenting sameness of the Sahara desert for weeks, the bright lights of the city were overwhelming.

There were two things that stood out the most. First, all the different bright colors; the greenness of the grass and trees, the bright colors of the signs and billboards, the colored neon lights, and the bright colored clothes people were wearing. It was like a visual overload. In the desert everything had been a dull gray or brown. The endless desert sand, the low clay buildings, the robes and turbans were always the same dull brownish color.

The second thing, and most eye-opening for me were the women, seeing all these women walking the streets in public. And not just out in public, but walking the streets at night wearing western shape-fitting clothes with their hair free flowing and their faces exposed. After the women-less Sahara, it was like some kind of fantasy land to see all the attractive women out on the streets.

Arriving in Oran was also the first time in weeks that I had a sense of my bearings and an idea of where we were. Oran was next to the Mediterranean Sea, and I *knew* where the Mediterranean Sea was. I finally had some reference point. Morocco was now directly west of us, to the left. We estimated a couple hundred kilometers would get us close to the border.

When we first hit the streets of Oran, John and I just spent some time wandering about soaking up all the sights and sounds of a modern city again. We spent a couple of hours walking the streets, and got something to eat before we started looking for a place to sleep.

Later in the evening, after some looking, we found a cheap place to sleep. It was in some kind of boarding house on a narrow, dark, side road. As we walked into the shadowy, confined building, I immediately had a bad gut feeling about the place and the guys hanging around inside. I quickly scanned the room to locate who was where, and get a lock on the situation we were getting into.

There were two young guys with dark features wearing western clothes in the back of the small lobby room, causally leaning against some kind of wooden counter. To my right, two other young, bearded guys were sitting slouched on a bench and I could feel the presence of someone behind me, who I couldn't see. There was a stairway leading down a dark hall out of the room near the counter. The only way out to the street was the way we came in.

I immediately had a strong gut feeling that it was a bad situation…danger. I took a quick look over at John and I knew he felt the same. So like always, we followed our gut instinct and right away started attempts to get out of there and avoid a confrontation or a dangerous situation.

When we walked into the room, the two guys leaning on the counter looked over at us and smiled. They were smiling, but their eyes were flat, cold and calculating. They had the look of predators. The two, sitting guys to our right stood up and stayed standing in an aggressive manner. I glanced behind me, and some other guy had moved between John and I and the door out.

It only had been moments since we entered and we had only walked a few steps into the room, but we were already in a vulnerable situation surrounded by a group of 5 menacing guys. We tried to stay casual and controlled. And like always in that kind of situation not show any fear or aggression…just project a strong, but neutral stance and attitude.

John and I gestured like asking about a room. The two guys by the counter made some comments in Arabic about the price, and motioned for us to come further in and get a room. We acted interested and communicated OK, but gestured that we were going to get something to eat first. We didn't hesitate. Before they really had a chance to make a move, we immediately started moving back towards the door out. We kept gesturing and talking like it was OK, we were coming back after eating, and kept moving. The guy behind us didn't move aside, but he didn't try to stop us.

Before things had a chance to go south, within a few moments John and I were out of the building and moving down the street. We got as far away from the place, as fast as we could. We never looked back…

As in this situation with the guys who confronted us in the little boarding house, not hesitating and maintaining a strong, confident but non-aggressive posture and attitude was important for neutralizing and looking down a potential threat. In many other situations I had done that.

It was really a matter of will. Many times I didn't feel confident. On the contrary I often felt very threatened and vulnerable, but I always tried to force myself by habit to maintain that strong, confident, non-aggressive appearance and attitude. It worked well in many different situations for me.

One such experience was later when I was in my early 30's, I took a part-time job in the evening teaching college business courses at Jackson State Prison in Jackson, Michigan. I was told Jackson Prison was the largest walled prison in the world. It's a huge, ancient, maximum-security prison, with most prisoners serving 25 years to life. I was told they put the long-termers and lifers in Jackson, behind 'The Wall' because they were a higher threat and a high risk for escape.

I was hired on very short notice to teach college business courses three nights a week in one of the maximum security cell blocks at the rear of the prison. I didn't really need the job. I had a business at the time, but I took it as a challenge for myself. I wanted to test myself and see if I could do it. See what it was like. I had no idea what to expect. I was told by Mr. Williams, the guy who hired me, that it was important to not show any weakness. If I did, he said the inmates would walk all over me and I wouldn't last…like the guy hired before me. He also said it was important to not show aggression or disrespect. Just maintain a strong, confident but neutral, non-aggressive posture and attitude. It was good advice. It had served me well in many prior threatening situations out on the road, and it also did while I was teaching in prison.

Later that night John and I tried to find another place to sleep, but we ended up spending the night sleeping out on the street along a doorway and later in a little park area. We never really decided to spend the night sleeping out on the street, it just turned out that way. As we moved about the city, it kept getting later and later and the next thing I knew the sun had already risen. It was a cold, uncomfortable night.

I woke up first and nudged John who was still crumpled up on the pavement beside me with his backpack under his head.

"Hey, it's morning in the big city. Time to get up. Let's get moving."

John slowly came back to life. He yawned, stretched and the first thing he said was, "I'm hungry. Let's find something to eat."

We headed out into the big city to find some food. It took us a while and some walking, before we found a little, street-side food stand that was just opening up. An older, whiskered, dark haired guy was just getting set up for business. John walked up to him and gestured about ordering some food. The guy smiled and showed a sample of some kind of meat sandwich with sauce. It looked good. There was a sign in Arabic saying 'Two Algerian Dinar.' (Less than $1)

John smiled back and ordered a sandwich. I did the same. They were quickly prepared for us. We stood along the road-side and ate them. They were delicious and John quickly ordered a second while I waited.

After he finished eating, we took out our money and handed over 6 dinar for the three sandwiches. When we did so, the attitude of the guy selling the food quickly changed. The smile was gone and replaced with an angry scowl. He put up his hands and demanded 20 Dinar. He crossed his hands over the 2 Dinar sign and pointed to the sauce and sandwich like it was some kind of special, expensive sandwich we had eaten.

It took John and I barely a second to come to the same conclusion…rip-off. We just looked at each other with the same tired expression. We were getting ripped off and we both knew it. We also knew there was very little we could do about it at this point since we had already eaten the food. We could argue and complain, but we had no leverage. We knew we were going to be paying up sooner or later.

"First thing in the morning and we've already been ripped off. Not a good start to the day, Huh?" I said with contempt.

"What a jerk. He set us up…all smiling and friendly. He saw us coming a mile away." John said as he looked for his money.

"Yeah. That was a stupid mistake. We shouldda known better."

After walking a while I asked John, "So how much Dinar do you have left?"

"I should have some dinar left. Let me check."

John went through his pockets and found only some Algerian coins. He then searched his wallet...Nothing. He then searched his backpack. Again nothing. He searched some more…Nothing.

"I'm tapped out." John said surprised. "I've got no Algerian money left. How about you?"

"I don't know. I'm low. Let me check."

I went through the same search routine as John.

"Man, all I got is one dinar."

"One dinar!! That's less than a buck." John exclaimed.

"Well, we gotta change some money again." John said. "To get us through the border into Morocco. Maybe we can find a bank."

"Maybe. First…What kind of funds and currency do you have left to change? After paying off that truck driver we bribed with the dollars, the smallest bill I have left is a British ten pound note. ($16). That's way too much to break. That would be a huge hit to exchange ten pounds just to get through one day."

"Whattda ya mean?"

"Once we exchange the ten pound bill for Algerian money, the money's gone. We can't get any of it back. Algerian currency can't be exchanged for any other currency. It's worthless. The Algerian currency we have left over can't be exchanged in Morocco or anywhere else."

"Oh.. Man, that's right. We lose the whole ten pounds."

"What's the smallest bill you have?"

John did some checking and the smallest bill he had was a $20 US bill. We were in a tough spot. There was no way we could afford to break and spend $15 or $20 for just part of one day. That was a lot of money for us at that time. In fact it was a fortune. It would mean we would arrive in Morocco with $15-20 less to make it back on.

As I mentioned earlier, managing my money and currency transactions was often critical when traveling on such little funds. The timing of bank exchanges and having small denomination bills available was sometimes very important, as in this case.

"Well, I guess we got no choice." I said, "We can't spend any money until we get into Morocco. We make it into Morocco today, or we spend the night sleeping outside, and we go with no food until we get there."

"That's gonna be tough, especially no food." John replied.

"We got no choice."

"Well, let's hope we can make it to the border today." John said.

"Yeah. And let's hope the border is open when we get there."

"It better be open. If it's not - breaking that ten quid note won't make any difference. We'll be dead no matter what we do."

"You got that right." I said..

So we were now on a deadline to get to the Moroccan border. Getting to the border today became very urgent for us. If we didn't make it, it meant we would have no food or shelter that night. Actually, it wasn't urgent that we just get to the border - It was urgent that we get *through* the border and enter Morocco. We still didn't know if the border was even open. We had been told repeatedly that it was closed because of the war.

It was 'do or die time' for us and we knew it. But to be honest we weren't that fazed. We had already been through so much, and made it so far. We had a kind of unspoken fearless faith - that we would just do what we had to do to get the job done.

We figured we had already made it through the worst of it. What could possible happen to us that would be tougher than what we had already been through?

Well, as it turned out…Quite a lot, actually. Despite all the difficulties and challenges we had already overcome, we couldn't have imagined what was still in store for us. Little did we know, but things were only just starting to get exciting. Both of us making it back in one piece from this incredible and ill-conceived adventure was far from certain and would depend on a number of factors, some beyond our control.

CHAPTER **26**

The Moroccan Border: Moment of Truth

We made our way through the city of Oran to the outskirts of town and a road heading west toward Morocco. It took about an hour of walking since Oran was a big place, but we got lucky and had some good directions. It could have taken much longer.

It was still early morning when we started hitching. There were more cars passing on the road than what we had been used to in the Sahara, but still it took us longer to get a ride. We had gotten used to getting a ride with one of the first half dozen cars that passed by us all across the Sahara. Now we had to wait sometimes for many cars to pass before one stopped to offer us a lift. It was still great hitching, though. We couldn't complain. We rarely waited more than 20-30 minutes for a ride.

Through the morning we slowly but steadily made our way across northern Algeria in the direction of Morocco. The rides now were often shorter and slower since we were not crossing huge open slabs of desert with each ride. People still stared at us, but it didn't seem to be as intense as in the Sahara.

By early afternoon, John and I found ourselves sitting alongside the road on a slightly grassy stretch of a hill halfway to the town of Teclemcen. It was a two lane paved and marked road with a fair amount of cars passing by. We had been let out by our last ride and we were just beat. We just sat down right where we were to take a rest. We were too tired to stand and hitch out in the afternoon sun. It wasn't really that hot, but the sun was draining. Even just standing required a lot of effort.

With all the walking about and the cold, we had slept very little out on the street the previous night. We had also been on the road hitching for over 15 hours the day before and had been traveling hard and fast for quite awhile now. We needed a little break.

"You wanna take turns hitching?" John asked me. "One of us can stand and hitch, the other one can lay down and rest. Then we'll switch."

"Sure. Why don't you go ahead and hitch first." I replied as I laid down on my back and stretched out.

"No. You first."

"Nah. You go right ahead. I'll hitch later."

"No. You first, little brother…Your older brother needs his rest." John said grinning as he also laid down on his back.

I laughed and said, "No, no. Go right ahead. The older brother should take charge and lead in this type of situation."

The friendly brotherly banter continued for a few minutes. Neither of us got up. After a time we both quit talking and just rested. It felt good to take a break. While resting by the roadside, I took out my journal and wrote for a while.

After getting our second wind, John stood up first and said, "We better get back to it. We gotta make the border today. We don't eat until we get to Morocco. And I'm starving."

"Yeah. I hear you. I also don't want to sleep out on the streets again tonight. Let's do it."

We stood by the road and started hitching again. It took a tiring 30 minutes of standing and hitching before we got the first ride, but the rides came at steady pace all throughout the day. They were generally shorter rides, so we had to spend more time standing out next to the road hitching. By mid afternoon, we had made our way to within about 20 kilometers of the Moroccan border. We were getting close.

For the last stretch, we learned we needed to head for a Moroccan town called Oujda, which was near where we could cross the border. After a short wait, we got one last ride with an Arab man and his son. It didn't take long riding in their truck before we got close to the border. We could see some markings and military placements along the road as we approached it. The guy driving us then abruptly just stopped and said this is as far as they were going, and pointed down the road toward what appeared to be some border buildings.

THE MOROCCAN BORDER: MOMENT OF TRUTH

John and I jumped out of the truck and thanked him for the ride. He quickly changed directions and with a wave and a shout headed on down the road, leaving John and I facing the border just about a kilometer ahead of us.

The road ahead led to the border where there was a big gate pole blocking the road and some soldiers standing near the gate. Off to the side a ways was a fairly large single-floor building with some signs and markings written in Arabic. It appeared to be the Algerian customs building. There was a slight hill and some trees and vegetation around and near the building. We couldn't see past the Algerian customs building, but we knew the Moroccan border building lay in wait just a little ways past it.

As we stood looking at the border, I said to John, "Well, this is it. I almost can't believe we made it here."

"Yep, me too." John replied. "It was a long, tough road getting here, that's for sure."

"Do you think the border is open?" I asked.

It was something we had discussed probably ten times over the previous week or so. Even though I knew John didn't have the answer, I just had to ask anyways.

"We'll see soon enough, won't we? There's sure not much activity though."

"Yeah. I don't see anyone coming in or going out." I said, looking at the border building up ahead. "Maybe we should just wait and see if anyone passes through before we try to cross."

We waited about 10 minutes carefully watching and hoping to see someone pass through, but there was no activity of any kind at the border building. All was quiet.

Finally John said, "This is a waste of time. Either the borders open or it isn't. Waiting here's not gonna change a thing. Let's go for it."

"Yeah…OK. But we should double-check our papers and money statements first. Get everything ready." I said.

I was the one usually aware of the money.

Earlier in the day when we had checked our funds we went through all our official currency exchange papers comparing it with the cash we had on hand…We had a serious problem. We were way short and way off. The western money we traded black market with the big soldier was not accounted for. We had no bank currency exchange papers to account for it. In addition, the 50 US dollars we ended up paying to bribe the truck driver wasn't accounted for. It had never been changed at a bank. While $50 wasn't much money, it was a large portion of the total funds we brought into Algeria.

We began checking our money and got our passports and everything ready and accessible.

As we were getting ready, I said, "Remember if there's a problem with our money statements and funds – We just say we lost the bank exchange paper...We tell em we exchanged 50 US dollars, ten British pound and eight French Francs back in Tourreget."

"I got it."

"50 dollars, ten pounds and eight francs." I reminded John.

"OK."

"Remember...We exchanged the money and just lost the bank papers. We don't say we lost the money. They'll never believe we made it this far with so little money."

"Yep. I know."

"We also don't say it was stolen. That could cause other problems."

"No kidding."

The reason we thought saying our money was stolen might cause other problems was based on very good reasons. When traveling I generally avoided any authority such as police, soldiers, or customs officials like the plague. Once you approach a person of authority you are putting yourself under their control, even when you have a legitimate complaint or need assistance. It's still a vulnerable position - one I avoided at all costs. This was based on my own experiences and stories I had heard from other travelers. When traveling in my younger days I met and exchanged stories with hundreds of other travelers about cheap places to stay, places to avoid, dangers and rip-offs, etc. It was like an underground network of information.

So with our story set about why we were short on our Western currency and why our bank transactions wouldn't match with our funds, John and I started walking up to the Algerian custom building. If we were able to clear customs and allowed to exit Algeria we would then walk over to the Moroccan custom building further down the road and attempt to enter Morocco.

John and I walked up to the low, Algerian immigration building. There were some armed uniformed soldiers standing in loose groups around and near the building, and along the road leading up to the building. At one point before we got to the building two soldiers stopped us and asked to see our passports. After a quick look the soldiers waved us on.

THE MOROCCAN BORDER: MOMENT OF TRUTH

"Well, at least they didn't send us away. That's a good sign." I said as we walked away from the soldiers.

"Yep. Maybe the border is actually open." John replied.

"It better be."

We then entered the customs building. Inside there were a few different rooms with tables and uniformed men and soldiers in and about the rooms. Unlike the desert crossing at the Tunisian border, the men in this immigration building seemed active and somewhat organized.

After a couple of moments trying to figure out where we should go, an official looking, dark-skinned guy in his 40's wearing a fairly clean uniform, waved us over to a table. When we walked to the table a second official joined us and they asked for our passports. They were both very serious and stern. They gave a surprised look when we pulled out our American passports and put them on the table.

Each of the officials picked up a passport and carefully went through them page by page with several intent glances back at John and me. After going through the passports, without saying a word, they set them on the table and gestured that they wanted to see our backpacks. John and I set our backpacks up on the table in front of the officials. Again, each of the officials picked up a backpack and carefully went through the items we had inside…mostly just a lot of extremely dirty and smelly clothes. Unlike at our other border crossings during this trip, the custom officials didn't get disgusted with our dirty clothes and give up. They carefully looked through everything in our backpacks.

Our backpacks also had a few scraps of papers that John and I had picked up along the way, some with drawings of camels, buses etc. from when we were trying to communicate or get info. The custom officials carefully set the papers aside and looked through each of the papers and scraps. The officials seemed dead serious, and concerned about everything we had, but it seemed that things were going OK…

That is until they asked for our money papers and statements. My stomach tightened. I tried to not show any concern…just maintain that strong, neutral attitude.

John and I first took out our official money statements that were stamped by the Algerian official when we first got our visas. It detailed all the funds we brought into Algeria, which was incredibly little. The two officials looked carefully at the statements in disbelief. They appeared shocked at how little money and funds we had when we entered Algeria. They briefly spoke to each other and then held the papers up and gestured like 'Is this for real? Is this it?' John and I both nodded our heads 'Yes, that's all.'

The two men then seemed to look at us with a heightened respect and their attitude lightened a bit. The one guy asked us in broken English where we were trying to go. I explained we were heading back to England. He seemed very surprised and gestured how? I kind of shrugged, smiled and shook my head like I didn't really know. The two custom officials glanced at each other with a bemused expression.

They then asked for all the money we had, our bank receipts and transactions from during our time in Algeria. John and I made a quick nervous glance at each other as we pulled out our money and official papers and set them on the table. The two custom officials picked up the papers along with the money and carefully went through them making some notations, while John and I stood across the table waiting with apprehension. When they finished, the one official asked us if we had more money that we didn't show them. He communicated we were short on our funds. There were some funds not accounted for. Both John and I shook our heads no.

We then tried to explain that we had lost one of our bank receipts when we exchanged for Algerian currency. The two custom officials talked together for a moment and then looked back at us. We continued telling them the story John and I had agreed on, explaining that in Tourregot we exchanged money at a bank, and lost the bank paper. They recognized the name Tourregot. I then said that I thought we had changed 50 dollars, ten British pounds and eight francs just like John and I had discussed earlier. They listened carefully and had me write the amounts on a piece of paper. They took the paper and did some calculations, looking at all our papers and money while John and I stood waiting. After a few tense minutes the two officials spoke together for a moment. They then pushed all our papers and funds back across the table to us. John and I quickly picked our money and papers and put them away. Apparently our story held up.

The one official then picked up both our passports and rifled through them. He picked up a stamp and stamped both passports, pushed them back to us and off-handily gestured toward the door. Before we could ask anything, he then turned away from us and went about some other business ignoring us.

John and I looked at each other.

"Is that it?" I asked unsure. "Can we leave Algeria?"

"I don't know…I guess so." John replied.

THE MOROCCAN BORDER: MOMENT OF TRUTH

"Does that mean the border is open?"

"I don't know? I'm not sure what's going on. I don't know about entering Morocco, but I guess we can leave Algeria."

John and I picked up our backpacks and left the building. We walked outside under the late afternoon clouds and started heading towards the fence behind the building where three soldiers with rifles slung over their shoulders were manning a gate through the fence.

One soldier stopped and asked us for our passports. He carefully looked through them and found the pages with our exit stamps. He then checked our passport photos, looked at each of us and gave our passports back to us. He then said something in Arabic to another soldier and the gate was lifted allowing us through the fence.

We walked through the fence and a ways over to the Moroccan customs building.

"Well, this is it." John said. "We'll finally find out if the border is open… If they'll let us into Morocco."

"Yep. This is it." I replied. "We've come a long way to get here, huh?"

"No kidding. It's been a long haul."

And with that we walked into the Moroccan customs building to find out our fate. The building contained a large, open room with several closed doors and a low counter separating us from the soldiers and customs officials inside. There were about a dozen men inside and there was a slight sense of chaos, with a lot of movement and activity.

When John and I walked in through the door most of the activity came to an abrupt halt. Many of the men inside stopped what they were doing and looked at us with wary expressions. We walked in and went up to the counter. After a moment, a slim, sweating, bearded custom official in a faded and sweat stained uniform approached us. He was accompanied by a couple of other tough looking, unshaven men who appeared to be soldiers.

From behind the counter the custom official demanded our backpacks. He took them and handed them to one of the soldiers to go through. While the soldier looked through our backpacks, the custom official took our passports. Seeing the American passports seemed to throw him off, and slightly confuse him, like he never expected to have Americans attempting to enter Morocco from Algeria.

He held the passports for the other two soldiers standing by to see. They looked as surprised as the customs official. They spoke together in Arabic for a moment. It was obvious John and I we're a unique case for them, and they didn't seem sure how to proceed.

After a moment's hesitation, in broken English the custom official began asking us a lot of questions about our trip across Algeria...how we got to Algeria...where we went... who we saw...what we did, etc. He then asked us our intentions for entering Morocco. We told him we were just quickly passing through and returning to England for my university study and for John's flight back to the US from London.

The custom official's attitude was not friendly. He seemed very wary and antagonistic. After one of the soldiers directed us to sit on a small wooden bench near the counter, we nervously waited as the custom official picked up our passports again and carefully went through them page by page making some notations. It took quite some time. He then began speaking with one of the soldiers while John and I waited some more. It was hot and uncomfortable in the windowless, cramped custom building.

"Man, this doesn't look so good, does it?" I whispered to John as we waited.

"Sure doesn't. But at least he hasn't sent us back, yet."

"Yeah. He seems to be considering letting us enter."

"Seeing our American passports really seemed to throw him off." John said. "I don't think he knows quite what to do with us."

"Yeah, that's for sure. But as long as he hasn't said no, we got a shot."

When the custom official finished talking with the other soldier, he motioned for us to come back over to the counter. When we walked over, he demanded to see John's ticket for the flight from London to the US. John rummaged through his money belt, found it and handed it to the custom official. He looked at it carefully and showed it to the other soldier pointing at the date of the flight.

When the official checked the dates on the ticket and saw the flight was for only some days later on January 3rd, he seemed to lighten up and lose some of his apprehension. I started getting a better feeling about our chances. Unfortunately, the custom official's lack of apprehension didn't last long. He asked to see our shot papers for our vaccinations. I quickly reached into my chained wallet and pulled it out and handed it over to him. But John, on the other hand, couldn't find his shot paper. He was looking through his wallet, then his pockets but no luck. With the soldier and custom official impatiently looking on, John checked and re-checked everywhere but couldn't find it. Finally, John gestured that he had lost it.

THE MOROCCAN BORDER: MOMENT OF TRUTH

The custom official reacted with a very irritated expression and commanded John and I go back and sit down on the wooden bench. He then stormed away and spoke to some other men while we waited again.

"Where's the paper?" I asked John.

"I don't know." He replied. "I had it at the last border crossing from Tunisia."

"Yeah, I remember. But how about now?"

"No clue. I mustta lost it somewhere along the way."

"Man, now what?" I said frustrated. "It just started looking good…Like we mightta had a chance to get in."

"I can't believe I lost it."

Like I said earlier, it was often critically important to keep track of passports, papers and money when on the road. As we were now finding out it could be risky to lose anything.

After a long, slow wait, the custom official returned with a couple of soldiers. They walked around the counter over in front of John, and signaled for John to come with them. John hesitated and one soldier grabbed John by the arm and pulled him to his feet. I began to stand up and the other soldier directed me to sit back down.

The soldiers were not threatening or overly aggressive, but they made sure we did exactly as we were directed without any problem.

In the blink of an eye, John was escorted out of the room into another side room, the door was slammed closed and I was left alone on the bench. I wasn't sure what had just happened or what was going on. I just knew I had been forcibly separated from John, and had no way of getting to him or making contact.

I sat on the bench for quite some time, wondering what could be happening to John…was he being arrested, detained, transported somewhere, deported back to Algeria…I had no idea.

I waited for what seemed a long time. Then another heavy-set, bearded soldier wearing an old uniform approached me and directed me to follow him. I was led into another smaller, windowless, stuffy room where I was told to sit on a little wood chair. I sat down on the chair, as the soldier left the room and closed the door behind him.

I was alone in the dank back room feeling very isolated. I waited, trying to figure out different options or actions I could take. After some thought, I came to one simple conclusion. There wasn't much I could do. Things were not looking good…Not good at all.

◄ TRAVELIN' MAN ACROSS THE SAHARA AND BEYOND

Here I was, 19 years old, with barely any money, sitting alone in some little Moroccan customs building near the tip of the Saharan desert, with an armed soldier standing guard and no one having any clue where on earth I was. That is, except of course, for my brother, who at this time was being held and who knows what else.

I waited and waited some more in the heat, in the closed little room. Finally, the door sprung open and there was the same soldier standing holding the door. He led me back to the same bench out in the main room and I sat down. I wasn't told anything, and I still had no idea what was going on.

Soon after, John was pulled out of a side room and led over and put on the bench next to me. I was surprised but relieved to see him.

"Man, what happened to you? What'd they do with you?"

"They took me into that other room and held me for awhile." John answered. "They then took me across to some other small room, where another guy pulled out a needle and gave me a couple of shots."

"Gave you a shot? Are you serious?"

"Yep. I couldn't stop him. It was quick. I think he gave me two or three shots."

"Are you serious?" I asked again in disbelief.

John just nodded in reply.

After a few more minutes wait, the custom official walked over behind the counter and gestured for us to approach him. He was accompanied by a soldier.

As we approached them, John leaned over to me and said, "Man, now what?"

I just shrugged.

We got up and walked over to the counter. The custom official then pulled out our passports and set them on the counter along with our backpacks. He picked up our passports, handed them to each of us and pushed the backpacks across to us.

He then said, "You granted visa. Enter Morocco. OK."

Those were the magic words. I looked over at John and we both just gave a tired, shared look of relief. After days and days of uncertainty, we were being allowed to cross the border.

"We actually made it in, huh." I said quietly, as we picked up our passports and backpacks.

"Yep, we did, didn't we?" John answered.

THE MOROCCAN BORDER: MOMENT OF TRUTH

Pointing at the same door we had originally entered the customs building from, the custom official then said, "That way, go."

So John and I walked out the door into the cloudy, late afternoon, crossed the border and finally headed into Morocco.

CHAPTER **27**

Hey Joe! What do You Need?

It was getting dark as we walked down the lone paved road into Morocco toward the town of Oujda, which we had been told was the closest town to the border on the Moroccan side. Before we left the border area, we exchanged some of our western money for some Moroccan currency at a small currency exchange office. So we now had a little Moroccan money to use. But with this last money exchange, our money supply was really dwindling fast. We were getting seriously low on funds.

It could have been worse though, because when I exchanged my money the guy at the currency exchange office tried to short change me. Fortunately, I had been alert and stayed right at the counter and counted in front of him the money he gave me in the exchange. It was way short, so I demanded the correct amount. He grudgingly had to give it to me because I counted it right at the counter in front of him. If I had moved away from the counter even a few feet and then counted the money, I would have been ripped off with no recourse.

There were many times at banks or currency exchange offices when people tried to short change me. It happened in Hanoi, Manilla, Communist East Germany, Warsaw, Bratslavia and at Kimhae Airport in Korea. It happens quick; you exchange some money and then start to walk away and count your money. If you walk even a couple of steps and then come back and say your money is short, it's too late. They won't return it. I made it a habit to always count my money right in front of the person who exchanged it...

We found a little food shop along the way and bought some bread and Coca-Cola. It wasn't much food, but it was the first time we had eaten since early morning and it was great to get some food in my stomach. Also, having some good ol' Coka-Cola from the classic American style bottle cheered my spirits a bit and made me feel a little closer to home, at least for a few moments.

We walked and hitched for a couple of hours down the winding road heading to the town of Oujda. There were a few, scattered trees and some skimpy vegetation growing in among the desert sand along the isolated road. It took us only a few rides to make it into Oujda. The last ride dropped us off just a little ways in the town.

As we drove into town I could see the fairly, big-sized town was a hilly, spread-out, hectic place. There was a paved road running through the town with several side streets and winding roads weaving between the one and two floor buildings, which seemed to be in some disrepair. There were several cars rumbling by, with donkeys and lots of people out and about on the street, only a few wearing the long robes and turbans. The narrow paved streets were full of commotion and activity.

When John and I were let out of the car, we began walking down the street through town. Almost immediately, we were approached by a scraggly, skinny, bearded man in a dirty jeans and a long jacket. Unlike our previous experiences in Tunisia and Algeria, the man did not have a friendly smile and welcoming manner.

On the contrary, he was very aggressive, grabbing at our arms and trying to pull us somewhere. He was trying to sell us something or trade money or something. John and I were taken aback; especially after the extremely hospitable treatment we had received the past couple of weeks during our trek across the Sahara.

Before we even had a chance to react to the first guy who had approached us, within moments, we were surrounded by a group of about 6-7 other men of various ages. They were pulling at us and blocking our way and very aggressive. They were in our face and kept pulling at us saying things like, "Hey, Joe. What you need? You need hash? You need weapon? Come with me, Joe. Come. You need change money? I get you anything. Come now, Joe. What you need Joe? ...."

I don't know where they got the name 'Joe' from – But, man, everyone was calling us Joe. The only thing I could think of was from GI Joe.

It happened very fast. Before we even had a chance to get a lay of the land or a look at the town, we found ourselves in a very dangerous and vulnerable situation. We were completely surrounded on the dark street by the group of aggressive men and we didn't have any idea where we were in the town or even where we were going. It was very unsettling and difficult to keep my cool, as we were getting pushed and pulled and jostled about among the crowd of men. When we stopped moving to try and confront them or talk to them, it just made matters worse. We were completely outnumbered and on their turf.

John looked over at me through the jostling crowd and I caught his eye, "We gotta keep moving, man. Don't stop…and don't let them separate us." John said.

"You got it. Watch your wallet and pockets."

"I will."

Glancing around to try and get a look through the crowd to see what was around, John shouted over to me, "Keep your eyes open for someplace we can get off the street and hole up."

I nodded as we continued pushing our way through the crowd. We began walking at a brisk pace with the crowd of men hustling to keep up. They didn't give up and maintained their relentless pursuit of us as we walked though the winding dark streets.

We walked for quite a while with the crowd still aggressively surrounding us. I was trying to keep my composure and not push back. It was tough. My basic instinct was to push and shove them out of my way and get some space. But that would have been foolish and dangerous. I was way outnumbered and had no clue where I could head for safety, or what options I had for getting out of the situation.

The only thing I could do was keep moving. And that's what John and I did. We walked for quite a while with the men continuing to try and hustle us or sell us something, and get some of our money.

"What you need Joe? Come with me, Joe. Come now. I get what you need. Me friend, Joe. Come with me."

We kept walking and saying, "No thanks. No. We don't need anything. No thanks, man."

It had no effect.

Finally, after a lot of pushing and walking, we came across what looked like a little bus station. As we were pushing our way down the street we came right up to it. There looked to be a small area where a few buses could park, and a little office or station set back from the road.

HEY JOE! WHAT DO YOU NEED?

We struggled our way through the group of men and walked into the station's open one room. We closed the door behind us. A couple of the men following us and looked in through the office door, but didn't come in.

There were two men in the small station. One man was about 40, tall, with dark stubble on his chin, wearing a long brown robe. He was the guy in charge. The other guy was younger, dark skinned with a thick black beard and beady little eyes. He was wearing jeans and a turban.

John and I tried to ask about a bus. They spoke no English, but we quickly learned that the place we were in was indeed a bus station. It took quite a while longer, but we found out there was a bus leaving the station about 3 hours later in the evening going in the direction of Tangiers. We knew it was going in the direction of Tangiers, but we weren't sure exactly how far it would take us.

That didn't matter to us. We said 'yes, yes'. We would take the bus when it came. With the group of men still hanging around outside the little bus station, we needed a place to hold out and stay off the street - just as much as we needed a bus.

John signaled to the tall guy in the brown robe that we would sit against the wall in the station and wait for the bus. The tall guy gestured OK. So John and I sat down with our backpacks and leaned back against the wall for the long wait for our bus to pull into town.

"Man, at least we're gonna get a bus out of this town. Do you believe those guys?" John said, gesturing in the direction of the small mob of men who were still lurking outside watching us.

"That was something else out there." I replied. "I thought I going to lose it. They wouldn't let up."

"No kidding."

"Those two big guys with the beards and long hair just kept pushing and pushing."

"Yep, and did you see that one kid who came up when we walked around that corner."

"You mean the little kid?" I asked.

"Yep." John replied. "The kid looked like he couldn't have been much more than 10 years old. Did you see that big bag of hash he kept trying to sell us?"

"Yeah. That's a pretty sad situation, isn't it? The same thing sometimes happens back home and in a lot countries.."

"Well, at least were off the streets and we got a bus coming to take us out of town."

"Yeah. We just gotta wait it out till the bus gets here."

We sat and waited in the little bus station for well over 3 hours until almost 9:00 PM. The bus ended up being about an hour late. It was a long wait. John and I sat on our backpacks leaning against the wall of the little station during the long wait, with the older bus clerk sitting and watching us.

I had some bread and Coca-Cola left over from earlier, so we ate that rather than venture out to find some other food. We weren't really looking forward to facing the aggressive crowd out there. Besides, we couldn't afford to spend any money on more food for the day. .

While waiting, John had talked about maybe trying to go to Tangiers by way of Casablanca. John thought maybe we could stop along the way in Casablanca before making it to Tangiers. But by well before this point, I knew we were already in a desperate race to get back before our money ran out. And more importantly I knew, without a doubt, that we were losing the race. It had become evident that no matter what we did we were going to run short. So any money we spent now - was money we would have to make later - to keep going.

When we arrived in Oujda that early evening, I was down to my last $69.

To make it back we still had to; travel all the way across Morocco, cross the Strait of Gibraltar by ship, travel across the length of Spain, travel across much of France, cross the English Channel by ship to England and make it the last 110 kilometers up to Grantham, England.

All told, we still had about 2,500 kilometers and two ship crossings standing between us and England… and I had $69 to make it with. It just wasn't possible. We couldn't make it, no matter what we did. We were going to run out of money. I knew it, but I still didn't really believe it.

After a few hours of waiting in the little station, people starting wandering into the bus station and I could see them waiting outside for the bus to pull in. Fortunately, no one paid much attention to John and me sitting in the corner near the bus clerk's desk.

Finally, later in the evening, about an hour behind schedule, a big old bus rumbled into the station; several of the people milling about hurried over to the bus and started climbing on board. There were already a lot of people on the bus when it pulled in and only a few of them got off. John and I followed the crowd over to the bus and went to climb on.

Just as we were approaching the bus, the bus clerk who had been sitting in the station with us for the past 3-4 hours came over and pulled at my arm. I turned around surprised. He started gesturing and speaking in Arabic. The other people around us pushed past us onto the bus, as the clerk continued gesturing and talking.

It took a few moments, but I finally understood that he was telling us that the bus was sold out. There were no seats for us on the bus! At first we were stunned and then furious.

We had spent the last 3-4 hours sitting in that little bus station with that bus clerk watching us. He knew we were waiting for the bus and he never said a word to us about there being no seats for us. Many of the people getting on the bus were people who had come into the station long after we did.

We couldn't believe it.

"Man, do you believe this?" I said angrily. "All that time wasted."

"Four hours wasted for nothing."

"Whatta we gonna do now?" John asked. "It's getting to be late night and we're stuck in this town."

"I don't know. We're gonna have to hit the street and see what's up. See what we can find. Find a place to sleep or another way out of here."

Feeling angry and irritated, John and I walked out of the little bus station that was now being closed down and headed out into the night. We walked onto the narrow, winding, dark streets to check things out and see what our next move would be. It was now mostly quiet with only a few people lurking about.

There were several shops and low-down buildings lining both sides of the street, with a few streetlights shining at intervals breaking up the darkness. A few men were walking the streets and some shady characters were standing off here and there in the shadows. I was very alert and began scanning the area around me as walked down the street. We didn't have a clue where we needed to go. We just started walking.

Very soon after we headed out down the street, a couple of men stepped out of the shadows and approached us. One tall, lanky guy was wearing a long, worn-out brown coat, and the other guy had a thick beard and wore jeans and an old turban covering part of his face.

They started saying, "Hey Joe. What you need, Joe?"

John and I stopped walking and looked at them. Trying to keep a few feet of distance from them, we gestured and said we needed to get to Tangiers. After a moment the one guy with the beard and turban understood.

He said, "OK. Joe. OK. I take you, Joe. Come with me."

We gestured back like "Where? Take us where?"

The bearded guy then said something to the other guy and they exchanged some harsh words. The other guy then stormed off and we were left with the one bearded guy. He turned to us and gestured about a train station.

When I understood, I said, "Train station? There's a train station in this town? Train station open now?" and acted like I was pointing to a watch. The guy signaled back that, yes, there was a train station in town, and using his fingers, told us that there was a train leaving around 11:00PM. John and I were very surprised and didn't really believe there could be a train station in the town, let alone one with a train leaving so late at night. We had never seen a single train, let alone a train station during our entire trek across Tunisia and Algeria after we left Tunis.

Also, we didn't trust the guy.

Seeing our mistrust, the guy motioned again and said. "Come Joe. Train soon. Come now, Joe. I take you."

We finally said, "OK" and started following the guy down the confusing narrow streets through town. It was very dark on the empty streets. There was very little light except for an occasional streetlight here and there and the streets were winding, with a lot of corners and sharp turns. Very soon we were completely lost. Actually, we were lost the moment we walked out of the little bus station and hit the street. We had never had a chance to get a feel for the town.

I was on guard and aware of my surroundings in case this guy was leading us into a set up. I tried to make note of landmarks and look for anywhere that would offer shelter or a place to get off the street in case we needed to get away quickly.

On my travels, I've learned you have to be aware and careful of setups when someone is taking you somewhere, especially at night. A friend of mine was traveling in Bangkok, which is a place I've been to several times and really enjoy, and late one night he hired a taxi to take him back to his hotel. He wasn't familiar with the city, had been drinking and wasn't paying much attention. The taxi driver took him to some isolated area where a couple other guys were waiting. They beat my friend up pretty bad breaking his nose, and stole all his money and passport. He was set up from the moment he got in the cab. It can happen in any city anywhere, if you're not careful.

Still not trusting the bearded guy leading us, John and I kept following the guy through the dark quiet streets as he continued badgering us, trying to sell us things. A few other men approached us from the shadows as were walking with him, but he quickly shooed them away.

After about 10 minutes of walking through the dark streets we came upon a very large, domed building with what appeared to be a train track running behind it. It was a very expansive building and there seemed to be lights on inside. He pointed to the tall circular building up the street ahead of and gestured that it was a 'train station.'

John and I were surprised.

"Hey it looks like a station." I said in disbelief. "This town actually has a train station. Do you believe it?"

"Amazing. I wonder if there is actually a train leaving tonight."

"I don't know." I answered, "It's really late. It'll be midnight in a couple hours or so."

We thanked the guy who led us here and I pulled out some coins I had in my pocket and gave them to him. As soon as the bearded guy had the money, he quickly took off leaving John and I alone. We walked up to train station to the two, big, metal front doors that were closed shut.

As we approached the doors I could hear a lot of noise; kind of like a low rumbling roar, and what sounded like chaotic activity inside. We walked up to the building and pulled open the big door. What happened next is something I've never forgotten.

When we opened the door I could see the entire train station. It was one huge, open oval room full of all kinds of people making a lot of noise and commotion. The expansive train station appeared to be bigger than the size of an NHL hockey rink. It was big and had high, gold painted walls with a rounded dome type ceiling, very few furnishings visible and a large open area in the middle. At the very opposite end of the room across from us was a small wooden counter with a single station clerk behind it. There were no chairs or benches that I could see anywhere.

The huge room was packed and full of activity and noise with the Arabic music playing, vendors walking around shouting and hawking bread and drinks, little kids squealing and running around chasing each other, women in the full flowing white robes with their entire body and face covered holding babies that were screaming and crying, groups of young men sitting on the floor playing cards and smoking hash and other drugs, a few people walking around begging, older men drinking tea, talking and arguing.

There were at least a couple hundred people in the station and many of them were sitting or standing crammed along the walls of the room. There were also all kinds of bags and luggage crammed everywhere around the room as well. It was a chaotic scene that we had stumbled into.

As John and I slowly entered the room, more and more people started noticing us, and the noise and chaotic activity started to recede as everyone stopped what they were doing, looked over at us and stared. By the time we had walked about 10 steps into the building, the huge room had gone completely silent. Everyone in the room was dead quiet and staring at us with a look of wariness, unease and some hostility. Mothers were pulling their children close to them, the vendors stopped moving and stared, while men put their cards down and stared. Everyone stopped what they were doing and just stared at us.

A tense, unbearable silence had quickly spread across the building. I felt very uneasy, like an unwelcome intruder going somewhere unsafe that I didn't belong. I had a <u>real</u> bad gut feeling. John and I slowed our walking and started to hesitate as we got to the open area in the middle part of the room with the masses of people all around us. All around us…and all silently staring at us.

We didn't know what to do.

We were already into the station and part ways across the big room. We didn't want to walk any further into the room, but we didn't really want to walk out either.

It was incredibly uncomfortable and a very unsafe feeling being in the big room surrounded by a few hundred people who did not seem to appreciate our presence…But going back out into the dark street and empty town was not exactly an appealing option either. There was nothing outside for us.

We hesitated again, trying to figure out the situation…As we very slowly made our across the room, I glanced over at John and out of the side of my mouth said, "Man, it's tense in here. What's going on?"

Looking around at the hundreds of people in the room, John commented, "They seem angry and fearful of us."

"Yeah. Why? What did we do?"

"No clue." John answered, "Man, this is not a good place to be…But what can we do?"

"We just gottta get to that counter over there and get a ticket." I said pointing to the little counter all the way across the huge room.

With our slow walk and the tense stares, the ticket counter seemed to be about a mile away. We continued slowly walking across the room with the stares and unnerving stillness following our every move. After regaining my composure a bit, I tried to give off that strong, confident non-aggressive attitude.

I tried, but I'm not sure how many people were buying it, especially the confident part. When we finally reached the station ticket counter, the lone clerk was standing back from the counter leaning against the wall. He was a stocky, middle-aged man, with dark stubble on his face and deep-set eyes. He was wearing frayed, black pants with his arms tightly crossed over an old, dirt stained official looking coat. As we approached the ticket counter, the ticket clerk's facial expression and body language displayed nothing but open hostility toward us. It didn't change when John and I tried to ask for a ticket to Tangiers.

We stood at the counter and in a friendly voice I asked, "Ticket. We need ticket, Tangiers. Ticket, please."

The man stayed leaning against the wall with his arms crossed glaring at us. He didn't move or say a word. Everyone in the building was still silent and staring intensely as the drama with the clerk played out.

Next John leaned over the counter pointing to a little sign with some prices and Arabic written on it, which I assumed was ticket information, and said politely, "We need ticket to Tangiers. Tangiers, Ticket."

Still no movement or response from the defiant clerk; he just continued glaring for a moment and then slightly turned away from us, deliberately ignoring us. Now I felt incredibly uneasy, and again didn't know what to do. Hundreds of people all around the huge room were still staring at us with a mixture of wariness and hostility…as John and I stood there looking like helpless fools. What could we do?

John and I both looked at each other with an expression of 'Now what?' We both just slightly shrugged.

The silence and tension across the huge room seemed deafening to me. We were momentarily frozen in place. We didn't want to be there, but we didn't want to leave either. It was a long walk across the room to get to the door out of the station, and besides once we got out - then what would we do? It was the middle of the night. We had nowhere to go.

So we continued standing there and the guy behind the counter continued deliberately ignoring us. Time seemed to stand still. After what felt like a week, but was probably not much more than a minute or so – two young guys suddenly walked over and approached us. They looked to be in their early 20's.

One guy was very tall and lanky, with a narrow face and thick, wavy, black hair. He was wearing black pants and a dark shirt. The other guy was very short, much shorter than his partner. He was also wearing western clothes; old jeans and a white t-shirt that appeared to have blood-stains on it. He had a wide, dark face and a few whiskers covering his chin. Also covering his one eye was a large, bloody bandage with fresh blood on it.

I was very surprised to see them walk up to us. Their unexpected appearance was a little unsettling. They looked like the 'odd couple.' The two guys were such a mismatch, with the one guy so tall and lanky, and the other so short…And then the short guy, having a large bandage with fresh blood oozing from it. It made for an odd and disturbing image.

The two young guys looked over at John and me and with a little body language and few words asked us what we wanted. We communicated that we wanted train tickets to Tangiers. The two guys seemed to understand.

The tall lanky guy then turned to the glaring bus clerk behind the counter, and speaking in Arabic demanded tickets for us. He spoke in a very loud, angry voice that broke up the silence in the station and reverberated through the large room. At first the bus clerk didn't react. But the tall guy and his partner both spoke very harshly in Arabic again, demanding tickets.

Finally, the bus clerk nonchalantly walked over to the counter and with a look of dissatisfaction prepared two tickets for us. The tall guy gestured the price to John and I, and we quickly paid for the train tickets. I learned much, much later that our tickets were actually to a town called Sidi Slimune, and were not really to Tangiers. But, hey, it was a train ticket.

With the silence and drama broken, people in the vast station started going back to their business and eventually the commotion and noise in the huge room picked back up to the same noisy level as when entered. The attention was off of us. It was a relief to have the unnerving silence broken and the intense stares gone.

But now, John and I were with the 'odd couple', the tall lanky guy and the short, bloody guy. I didn't trust either of them and wasn't sure why they stepped up to help us out of our jam. I certainly didn't think it was out of the goodness of their heart. I was very alert and on guard.

At any rate, John and I were now with our two new 'good friends' whether we liked it or not. They led John and I back over to a corner of the station where a group of young guys were sitting together. There were about a dozen guys, sitting and lounging haphazardly on the floor, talking and smoking cigarettes…as well as other things, which I assumed to be hash.

They were quite a rugged group, mostly unshaven wearing a mix of western clothes and a few in robes and turbans. Several of them appeared to not be quite all there.

As we sat down with the group, I whispered to John, "Man this is a pretty ragged bunch. We gotta be real careful."

"No kidding." Looking over at a couple of the young guys leaning against the wall, John said, "Those two guys are as high as a kite. They're pretty much out of it."

"Yeah. They sure are."

Sitting down with my back to the wall and my backpack under me with its strap hooked on my leg so that it could not easily be pulled away from me, I scanned the group, instinctively making a note of any potential threats. There were several.

I nudged John, nodding in the direction of one of the guys sitting with us and said, "That guy with the torn shirt has gotta a knife in his belt. I think the guy next to him has one too and that big buy with the beard has some brass knuckles. We gotta watch each other's back."

"That's for sure. Just stay alert and keep your guard up."

And that's exactly what I did all night long - for the next dozen hours. I didn't know it at the time, but I had an extraordinary, draining night ahead of me. It was the strangest night of the trip, with an incredible 9-hour train ride that was unlike any I've ever taken…and I've taken some awfully strange rides. The experience was like something out of a Fellini movie.

CHAPTER **28**

A Tight Spot

John and I ended up sitting in the big train station with the 'odd couple' and their buddies for over two hours waiting for the train to pull in. The train was late getting in, and it was a very tiring wait because I was constantly staying alert and on guard.

A short while after we sat down a very strange thing happened. Three crisp uniformed soldiers with side arms and long, black nightsticks suddenly entered the station. They arrogantly strutted into the train station from the same doors John and I had entered earlier. They marched directly to the middle of the huge room and stood with their backs together facing out at the crowd in different directions.

The three soldiers stood there for a good five minutes menacingly pounding their sticks in the palms of their hands, glaring out at the crowd. It was a blatant act of intimidation. The noise and activity ceased immediately and the crowds cowered and huddled together against the walls with a look of obvious fear. Even the guys we were with looked scared stiff and leaned back against the walls, avoiding eye contact with the soldiers. No one spoke or dared move while the soldiers were in the building.

After about 5 minutes, the three soldiers marched out of the huge, crowded station and the activity and commotion picked backed up and the fear faded. Then about an hour later the exact same thing occurred again. Three soldiers marched into the room, assumed the same intimidating pose, pounded their sticks and menacingly glared out at the crowd. The crowds cowered in the same state of fear again until the soldiers left.

The soldiers later came in a third time and did the exact same thing. It was really strange. The soldiers never said a word or made any threats or commands. They never attempted to arrest anyone for drugs, or other offences, or to even confront anyone. It was just a blatant act of intimidation… It definitely worked. You could feel and taste the fear when the soldiers were in the room. The sense of fear was so thick nobody dared move while the soldiers were present.

After the first time it happened, John leaned over close to me and said, "Man, what was that about? That was strange. You believe how scared everyone was."

"Yeah." I replied, glancing around at the rough group of guys we were sitting with. "I thought some of these guys were going to piss their pants. They looked scared to death."

"No kidding. They've got enough drugs on them to service a small town. They could probably be put away for a long time. You have any ideas of the drug laws here?"

"I'm not sure, but my one Moroccan classmate from Harlaxton said they were 'very harsh'."

"Well, we gotta lay low." John said, "We were lucky the soldiers couldn't see us over here with these guys. Who knows what they would do if they saw a couple of Americans?"

"That's not something I want to find out."

"I hear ya." John replied.

"Yeah. We gotta stay out of sight, as best we can, until the train gets in."

And that's just what we did. We sat with the group of young, unruly guys huddled in the corner for a couple of hours, trying to blend in and avoid any attention. It was a long, tiring wait. Though I was exhausted, it wasn't a safe enough situation to sleep and close my eyes, even with John nearby. Not with these guys around us. They were pretty erratic and not exactly the most trustworthy bunch. They were continually doing drugs, getting up, moving about near me, occasionally pushing and arguing with each other.

During the long wait, I started getting really drossy and had trouble keeping my eyes open. I forced myself to stay alert, and to keep up the strong, confident attitude. I didn't feel safe sleeping, but, man, I was getting tired.

After a couple hours of sitting and waiting, a train finally pulled into the station, and immediately the masses of people in the station just exploded into a frantic race to get on the train. It was like a stampeding herd of cattle pushing and shoving, fighting their way to get a space on the train.

The 'odd couple' (the tall guy and the short bloody guy) along with their buddies joined the stampeding crowds and raced toward the train, pulling John and me along with them. We pushed and fought our way through the rushing crowds onto one of the train cars.

After climbing our way on one of the packed train cars, I looked over at John and said, 'Man, it's dark and dirty in here. Do you see any seats?"

"No, there's nothing. No seats or benches to sit on. Nothin."

"Man, it's filthy and stinks." John said as we pushed our through the crowds to find a little space on the floor to sit.

"Smells like a mix of urine, sweat and drugs. Quite a combination." I said as we quickly fought for a little space to sit among the masses of people cramped in the dark little train car.

The train seemed almost to be designed for transporting cattle. There were no seats and only a few scattered benches, with no lights, the floor was filthy and the windows were cracked and dirty. It was very dark, with very little light filtering through the smeared windows into the train car. The air had a musky feel and stink to it.

John and I quickly claimed a tight space to sit on the floor with our two 'new friends' and their buddies. As we sat down in the darkness and got our backpacks situated, there was mass confusion all about us.

People were yelling at each other, little kids were screaming and running by, somebody was playing the bongo's, men were arguing, some of the drugged out guys were shouting, talking incoherently and stumbling back and forth, an old man in the corner was curled up sleeping, a guy sitting across from me was smoking a big wad of hash and mumbling, some other guys were chanting, and on top of everything else it was freezing cold.

Not exactly your typical train-ride…But actually like almost everything else that happened on the trip; whether it was good, bad, dangerous, difficult, frightening or fascinating – I loved the experience. I just soaked it all up.

Shortly after getting situated on the floor, the train started shaking and rumbling as it picked up speed and started rolling its way down the tracks. Sitting cramped on the grimy train floor in the darkness surrounded by a group of at least a dozen guys, many of whom seemed slightly crazy and some of whom I perceived to be a potential threat - made for a long ride, and an interesting night.

John and I were definite potential targets. I didn't want to doze off and get knifed, or wake up with my money or passport gone or worse. For the entire nine-hour ride I was continually on guard and tried to stay focused and alert maintaining that strong posture to look down any potential threats. It was very draining and tiring.

Several strange things went on during the long train ride, but the one thing that stood out the most - is a couple of hours after we pulled out of the station, one zonked-out skinny guy with a scruffy beard, dirty jeans and long curly hair staggered over in front of me where I was sitting cramped on the floor. The guy looked directly down at me through the dim light and with a frantic, glazed-over look in his eyes, spread out his arms and started crowing liking a rooster.

"Cock-a–doodle-do!!…Cock-a-doodle-do!!" He screamed in a high-pitched voice.

Then he stopped for moment and just stared down at me with his frantic expression.

After a moment he flayed his arms out and screamed again, "Cock-a-doodle do!!…Cock-a-doodle do!!…Cock-a-doodle do!!"

The guy did it for a good five minutes with no let up, before finally stumbling away into the darkness. He went away but not for good. He repeatedly came back over to me for the next 3-4 hours, and did the same rooster-crowing bit. It was incredibly irritating.

I was exhausted. The last thing I wanted was to put up with this lunatic and his manic screaming. I felt like picking him up and throwing him into the next train car. I'm sure it would have been easy enough to do, and in his condition he probably wouldn't have even noticed.

I seriously contemplated it at one point, but decided against it. I didn't want to call any attention to myself. Also, John and I were seriously outnumbered in the enclosed, dark, cramped train car. If the crowd ever turned on us, there would be no place we could go and little we could do.

"Man, this is like the train ride of the bizarre." I leaned forward and said to John, who I could barely see sitting a ways from me in the darkness. We had been separated when we hurriedly sat down with the crowd.

"More like 'One flew over the cuckoos nest,' if you ask me." John replied.

"Yeah…It's gonna be a long night. Watch your back."

"It's like a circus scene from a Fellini film or something around here. But I swear if that crowing rooster guy comes back over to me one more time, I'm gonna toss him off the train."

"I hear ya." John said with a chuckle, "He seems to be quite taken with you…Must think you're a farmer or something. Wants to wake up the cattle and chickens."

"Yeah, something like that. Or maybe he's just high as a kite…Or maybe he's just plain crazy."

"Who knows? Just keep your cool, Dennis. We're way out numbered in here. We just gotta ride it out tonight. Make some miles."

We ended up sitting on that cramped floor for almost 10 hours with no break. After about 4-5 hours on the rocking train, there was still a lot of activity and commotion, but it had quieted down some. I started getting really tired and had trouble keeping my eyes open, but I still didn't trust closing my eyes and sleeping.

Several of the young guys around me were still awake and stumbling about and I had a strong gut instinct that a couple of them were eyeballing me, waiting for me to doze off to make some kind of move on my money or backpack. But I knew sooner or later I was going to doze off no matter how hard I tried to stay awake. John had already fallen asleep a short while earlier and was dozing off and on. I needed to do something to get some zzz's without making us vulnerable.

What I came up with was I had a kind of winter stretch, skull-cap in my backpack that I had used in the snow and cold of Europe. I pulled it out of my backpack and put it on my head. Then I pulled and stretched it down over the top of my face. It covered my eyes, but I could still faintly see through it. I could see out, but no one could see my eyes through the stretched cap. With the cap down, no one could know if my eyes were open or closed.

I pulled the cap down over my eyes and leaned my head back resting against the wall behind me. I then made a point of watching and moving my head following people as they walked and moved about the train. I made it very obvious that I was watching and could see through the cap covering my eyes.

After a while, I would allow myself to doze off for a few minutes. Then I'd wake back up and keeping my head pressed against the wall – I'd make a point of turning my head to watch someone walking or moving about near me, so that anyone watching me would know that I was awake and alert.

Then I would close my eyes again and just relax for a short time, then wake up and do the same thing again. It made it really tough for anyone to know if I was awake or not at any given time. I did that continually during the tiring, all-night ride. It was draining, but it got me through the long night.

A TIGHT SPOT

One time after a short doze, I opened my eyes back up to find one guy leaning over toward me tentatively stretching his hand toward my backpack. I very suddenly jerked my head in his direction and aggressively reached at him. He jumped back in complete shock, practically doing a somersault. He quickly moved far away from me and I never saw him again.

Finally, after the strange, tiring all night ride the morning sunshine started slowly filtering in through the train windows. The long ride was soon coming to an end. Most of the other people on the train had woken back up, and thankfully much of the noise and commotion had died down as people were finally resting.

The tall, lanky guy, who had helped John and I get our ticket back at the Oujda train station, wandered back over to where we were sitting and sat down next us. I don't know where he or his short bloody friend had had disappeared to during the long night ride since it was dark and guys were wandering and moving about on the train all night long.

We found out his name was Chancour. He started trying to explain that he would be leaving the train soon. The next stop was his hometown and he would be getting off the train there. His family would be waiting for him at the next train station, and he wanted us to meet his family. He also explained that John and I would have to get off at the stop after his. It was the last stop on the line.

"Where is your friend?" John asked.

He didn't understand. So John gestured, about his friend with the bloody bandage over his eye.

He understood and communicated that his friend got off at the previous stop, about half an hour earlier. It was where he lived with his family.

We spent the next hour or so until we pulled into his train stop, communicating with Chancour. Although I hadn't trusted him or his motives when he helped us out of our jam the previous night, he turned out to be a good guy.

While sitting with him we exchanged addresses. When the train pulled into his stop, John and I quickly got off the train for a minute and met his mother, and sister. They were waiting for him out on the train platform.

In contrast to Chancour, they were both heavyset but with the same dark features – at least the little I could see of them behind their veils and long robes. They were shocked, but seemed thrilled to be meeting John and me.

Although they didn't actually speak back to me, they were the first women I had said a word to in weeks.

After a quick greeting with Chancour's family, John and I jumped back on the same train and waved goodbye as the old train pulled out and chugged down the tracks.

"Whatta you know! He turned out to be a real good guy." I said, pointing in the direction of the train platform where the Chancour was still standing.

"Yep, he was." John agreed. "That was a tough jam he got us out of last night at the station…Stepped up and got the tickets for us. Never tried to make a move at our stuff or ask for any money…A good guy."

"Can't say the same for some of the guys he was with, though" I replied. "They were a wild crazy bunch, weren't they?"

"That's for sure. What a night, huh?"

"Yeah, it was a long, cold ride but, man, what an experience." I said grinning.

It was some kind of ride all right; a train-ride of the strange and bizarre…quite tiring and irritating at times, but a fascinating experience.

Chancour, that same guy who got us our tickets, later sent a long letter addressed to John and me at my address at Harlaxton University in England. I received the letter about a month after I returned to my university from the trip. It was an extraordinary letter.

The letter was written in French in elegant handwriting, using incredibly refined language. I had it translated word for word by a university friend who was a French linguist. She couldn't believe how eloquent it was. She assumed the letter had been written by some French poet or writer friend of mine. She was shocked when I showed her the picture of the guy who sent it, and I explained how and where I met him.

I still have his original letter with the English translation, along with the small picture of Chancour that he enclosed with it. This is the actual first line of the letter that John and I received from him, translated from French.

'Dearest friend John:

I see absolutely no way in which I am able to express to you and Dennis my joy and my character at the moment that I put the pen between my fingers to write you this letter, and I hope very much that this letter arrives finding you in good and satisfying health…'

A TIGHT SPOT

The letter continued in the same vein for two full handwritten pages. Who knows if he actually wrote it?…and if not him, then who? For me it's a reminder of one of the strangest rides I've ever taken and the good guy who got us out of a huge jam.

After seeing off Chancour, John and I took the train for about another hour to the next and last stop on the line. We arrived at the station at about 8AM.in the early morning as the long ride had finally reached its end.

As soon as the train came to a slow grinding halt, John and I tiredly trudged off the train. It was a cool morning, but was quickly warming up as a bright orange, blazing sun rose in the sky in front of us.

"Dennis, you have any idea where we are?" John said as he yawned and stretched on the station platform.

"Not really." I replied. "I thought we were going to Tangiers. But this town doesn't look like it. It's way too small."

"Yep and there is no sea around here."

"Yeah, it's tough to see much, but it doesn't feel or smell like were near the open Sea."

"Man. Where are we?" John asked looking around.

"Let's see if we can find out."

Walking down the station platform, I saw a station sign but it was written in Arabic, so I didn't have a clue what it said. It took us a little while checking around the station before we understood that the town train station we were standing in was called Sidi Slimune. However, that didn't do much for us. We now knew the name of the town, but we had no idea where it was located and we had no map to find out. We never did find out. The only thing I knew was that we were still quite a ways from Tangiers.

Like during much of the trip, I didn't really knew where I was…Heck, for much of the time I didn't know where I had been or where I was heading either..

CHAPTER **29**

Out of Money – Out of Time

John and I walked out of the small train station into the morning sunshine to try and find some food. The station seemed to be somewhat isolated and a ways from the actual town. There were some rolling, sandy, grass hills and a few low buildings in sight, but not much else. Sidi Slimune seemed to be a small or mid-sized town, at least as best I could see from the train station. That was about all we knew. Fortunately, near the train station we did come across a small food stand with an older, bearded Arab man selling some bread. We each bought a loaf and quickly ate it, along with a few swigs of good ol' Coca-Cola that we bought as well.

Getting a little food in my stomach took the edge off of my hunger, although I wasn't anywhere near full. But money was really tight now and I couldn't afford any more food. I knew any money spent now was money we would have to somehow make up later on the trip to make it back. We were seriously running out of money.

It now wasn't a matter of *if* we would run out…It was just a matter of *when* and how far we could get before we did.

"Well, whatta we do now?" John said as he sat down in the sand alongside the dirt road leading away from the train station.

I was still dead tired from riding the rails all night. I was too tired to answer or think much about anything at the moment. I just laid down in the sand next to the road with my head on my worn backpack and closed my eyes.

Finally I said wearily, "I don't know. Whatta you think? Whatta we do now?"

John then also stretched out with his head on his backpack and stopped talking. We both just relaxed and dozed for a while out in the open under the rising sun. The sun felt good on my face and skin, warming me and brightening my spirits after the freezing cold ride the night before.

After getting a much needed rest, John and I got back up and decided to head back to the train station to see about getting a train into Tangiers. It took us a while but we found out there was a train leaving soon going to a town I thought was called Algers, which we believed was in the direction of Tangiers. We decided to buy tickets, so we spent some more of our dwindling money, got our tickets and boarded the train.

The train left shortly after we boarded. Fortunately it was not as crowded as the long ride the previous night, but we still didn't have seats. At least we did have enough space to stretch out a bit on the floor rather than being jammed in crossed legged with no space to move. So it was an improvement from the night before. Also with the bright sun warming up the day, the train wasn't freezing and was actually quite comfortable.

We rode the train for a few hours, as I occasionally dozed until we reached the end of the line. We were now finally getting near Tangiers. It was mid afternoon and the day had heated up by the time we were told we had to get off the train. We jumped off the train and made our way through the small, wooden train station.

"Well, we must be close to Tangiers." I said.

"Yep."

"So, whatta ya think?" I asked, "We keep moving and try to make it into Tangiers today, or hole up here in this little town?"

John thought for a moment. "I'm really beat. I could use a break, but I think we gotta keep making time."

"Yeah. We gotta keep moving as fast as we can, without burning any extra money. We can't really afford to pay for any more hotels or lodging."

"Nothing new about that. I think we've only paid for lodging 2 or 3 times on the entire trip."

"Yeah." I answered. "But now we got no choice."

"Uh-Huh."

"We also can't really buy any more food unless absolutely necessary." I continued. "Any money we spend, we gotta make back later on the road somehow."

"How we gonna make some money?" John asked annoyed. The idea of going without food didn't set well with him.

'I don't know...We'll have to come up with something. We always do."

"Uh-Huh. We always do." John said, nodding.

While we were thinking over our situation and what we should do, I asked John, "Your ticket from England to The States has to be used by January 3rd, right?"

"Yep. The 3rd. My flight leaves from London, the morning of the 3rd." John replied.

"So we got, what, maybe 4 or 5 days to make it back and be in London."

"Yep. That's it. Not much time."

"Man, it's gonna be tight." I said. "Both the money and the time's gonna be tight. Especially, the money. We're gonna have to make some money somehow to get back."

"Yep. We are. Well, let's get going. We got no time to waste."

John and I looked around the mid-size train station trying to figure out where we were now, and how far we were from Tangiers. We asked a few people and tried to find a map around the station, but no luck. It was an antiquated, wooden station with a few benches, a little ticket counter and the wind blowing through from outside.

As we walked around the cramped station, a few Arab men were standing about staring at us with intensity. It was hard to read their expressions. They weren't exactly hostile, but they sure weren't friendly either. We kept to ourselves. We decided to pass on the train. We walked out of the station into the late afternoon sunshine to see about hitching a ride along the small, single-lane, paved road that led through the sandy, little town lined by single story buildings. The town was spread out and even though it wasn't real big, the streets were winding and confusing.

We ended up doing a lot of walking, wrong way hitching and backtracking for the rest of the afternoon and evening. It was frustrating. We seemed to spend as much time going the wrong way, as we did going where we needed to go. We spent more time walking than we did riding in cars, with about 4-5 short rides between the walking and mistakes.

We never did make it to Tangiers that night. We got very close, but ended up sleeping along the roadside under some trees in the outskirts of Tangiers. We just planned to rest for awhile and then continue hitching. But once I fell asleep, I didn't wake up until the early morning sunrise rolled over the horizon and the sun was shining bright in my eyes waking me from my slumber.

We sat in the dirt getting our backpacks situated and our clothes rearranged. I had taken out most of my extra clothes and laid them over me the night before to try to keep warm. It didn't help much. I was still cold, but I was too tired to notice much. Slowly we got up and headed back out to the road. I was really hungry and I'm sure John was too, but we didn't talk about it. Money was really tight. It was too early in the day - we'd eat later after we made it to Tangiers. We had to ration our money as best we could.

It took us a couple hours of walking, hitching and one bus ride before we made it into Tangiers. The bus ride was really crowded and we planned it so that when we got on the bus John paid for one ticket, while I snuck on behind him. It only saved us a buck and half, but it was still critical for us. Every dollar we spent now was money we needed to make back somehow later.

We made it into Tangiers by mid-morning. We had now made it all the way across Tunisia, Algeria and Morocco; all the way across northern Africa and a chunk of the Sahara to Tangiers, just like we had set out to do when we first reached Africa all those days and miles ago. We had come a long, long ways and had crossed the northern tip of the continent…But in reality we were nowhere near home yet, not even close and with no way of getting there.

Tangiers was very big and busy. It looked like a real city, after our past few weeks of desert travel, Tangiers seemed absolutely huge. Everything was wider. The roads were paved and spread out and there were many older, tall buildings lining the seemingly disorganized, winding streets. There was all kinds of activity and commotion, with more cars rumbling by than I had seen in all of the past two weeks, many men hustling, selling goods and food, women covered with the hijab and others without it out shopping at the busy market areas, men on corners smoking and in hushed discussion, a lot of buildings over 3 stories tall lining the busy streets, with several small shops and outdoor markets scattered in among the taller buildings.

As we started wandering the streets of Tangiers, John and I discussed our situation. We had finally made it all the way across northern Africa… But having finally made it to our long sought goal of Tangiers; the sheer distance and the impossible obstacles we still had to somehow overcome started to sink in. It hit us hard. We had maintained such a relentless focus on making it across northern Africa for so long - now that we had actually made it and had time to think, the reality of our situation hit us head on. We knew that despite all our efforts, we weren't even close to making it back to England. Not by a long shot.

"We've made it this far, now what?' I asked.

"Well, there's no way we can make it back overland. We really made a go of it…But to make it overland, we still gotta cross the Mediterranean Sea here, make it all the way across Spain and France and then cross the Channel to England. No way we can make it."

I just wearily nodded my head.

"How much money you got left?" I asked John.

Without checking, John said, "I got about $58, and a few dinar. How about you?"

"I've got a total of 63 bucks, plus some Moroccan dinar."

"Man, it's really getting tight. It's not possible, no matter what we do. No matter how little money we spend, we're not gonna make it back by land." John said dejectedly.

The realization hit us like a Mike Tyson uppercut…Real hard.

Now that we had finally made it all the way to Tangiers, and knew for certain we couldn't make it back overland with the money we had, I felt just totally worn out and defeated.

I had known in the back of my mind that we couldn't make it back for some time, but I never had to face it head-on. There's was always some outside chance we could somehow do it, and during the trip I was always focused on the challenge of making it across northern Africa.

But now that we had actually made it all the way across northern Africa and achieved our weeks long objective of crossing Tunisia, Algeria and Morocco - We had hit the end of the road in Africa. We were blocked by the sea. There was no more road in Africa to travel.

We had overcome so many challenges and difficulties to make it here… But *here* wasn't even close to where we needed to get to - to make it back. We had reached a dead end facing the Mediterranean Sea, and still had to somehow cross the Strait of Gibraltar and travel another 1,500 kilometers overland.

We were desperate and we knew it.

John and I took a few minutes to sit in the shade alongside some buildings to try and get our wind back and get refocused. For the first time on the long trip, I had lost my nerve and relentless drive. It was just gone.

We had both been intensely focused for so long with no let-up, that we just lost our wind. I just had no get-up-and-go left; kind of like I had been hit hard in the gut, and knocked down with no will to get back up and continue. I felt defeated, beat.

It was the first and only time it ever happened on the month long trip.

OUT OF MONEY – OUT OF TIME

It didn't last long though. We spent about 30 minutes just sitting in the shade feeling dejected, before John looked over at me and kicked my leg, "Hey. We're burning daylight. It's time to move. We're not going to make it back by sitting here in the dirt."

"Yeah. I guess your right." I said wearily.

"You *guess* I'm right?...Man, you *know* I'm right." John responded with a grin.

"Whatever you say." I said, now starting to smile myself.

"Your older brother is always right. Haven't you learned that after all these years." John said jokingly.

"No...Can't say I have."

"Well, it's about time you did."

"That'll be the day." I replied with a grin. "It seems to me...that except for doing a lot of snoring, and eating, and getting us lost – the older brother hasn't done much on this trip."

John laughed and said, "Well, little brother, at least my smelly farts didn't almost get us killed by a couple of cutthroat truck drivers, out in the middle of the Sahara."

I laughed as John continued, "Who ever heard of somebody's farts stopping a truck dead in its tracks. Those farts outta make it into the Guinness Book of World Records."

With our spirits raised and attitudes refocused, we continued joking and ribbing each other as we made our way through the city. After some walking and getting a little feel for the place, we got down to the business at hand.

"John, let's see if we can find a standby flight or some kindda discount flight back to London. Maybe we have enough money to buy tickets. Or maybe a ship direct to England. Maybe we can work on a ship to get passage."

"Uh-huh." John said listening

"Anything to make it back...And skip the overland travel."

"OK." John agreed. "I doubt we have enough money for a ticket, but it's worth a try."

"What else are we gonna do?"

We set out in the city to see what we could find out. As we started out on our way we were again approached by several men and soon surrounded by a group of rough looking, street guys trying to hustle us. They were dressed in a mix of western clothes and a few wearing the long traditional robes and turbans.

TRAVELIN' MAN ACROSS THE SAHARA AND BEYOND

We got the same "Hey Joe, what do you need?" routine with several guys offering us hash and goods or whatever we needed. This time John and I were more prepared for it, and being daytime, with a lot of other people out on the streets, we weren't so vulnerable. We were more aggressive in confronting the guys around us and telling them to back off, that we didn't need anything. We kept moving and making our way through the streets with the hustlers loosely following us. They were quite aggressive, but we just kept moving and ignored them. After a while they started dropping off, and John and I were left pretty much on our own.

We ended up spending the entire day and most of the evening, about 10 tiring and frustrating hours, wandering through the crowded city of Tangiers trying to find out information about transportation back to England; flights or ships. We tried to see if maybe we could get hired to work on a ship to England, anything to get us back. We were still stared at a lot, but nothing like the intense experience we had in the Sahara. There were also a few other Westerners that I saw on the streets.

It was now early evening and getting dark and cold. During the entire day, we spent no money on food, or anything else for that matter. We couldn't afford it. It was a tough day and tough going. We did a lot walking all day, and hadn't eaten anything, since the little bread we had the previous day. My stomach was growling most of the day in an angry, hungry outburst, but I tried not to think about it, and we didn't talk about it. We were just back to doing what we had to do.

"Well, we've been to about 3-4 little travel agencies, a shipping line and two airline offices with no luck." I said disappointed. "We just don't have enough money for a flight or ship from here to London. No matter what we do, we can't buy a ticket."

"Yep. We're not even close. With the best price that one guy from British Air quoted us for a discount seat - we still don't have enough money."

"Man, even with all our money added together we can't even buy <u>one</u> ticket, let alone tickets for both of us." I said.

"How we gonna get out of here?" I wondered.

"I don't know. We're stuck here, unless we get some more money."

"Yeah. We gotta get some money somehow…and soon."

We both thought for a few minutes, and then John said, "Let's see if we can sell something on the street."

"Sell something? Like what? We don't have anything."

"How about something we're carrying? Maybe we have something somebody would want."

"I doubt it." I replied. "But OK. Let's see what we got."

We stepped off the busy street into the shadows and took off our backpacks, hoping maybe there was some little trinket or something we had forgot about that would be of some value on the street. After thoroughly looking through every part of our backpacks, pockets, wallets, money belts, and bags we came up with very little; Mostly just some smelly, old clothes.

John looked at me, "We don't have much."

"No kidding."

"But who knows," I said hopefully, "maybe somebody would buy something from us because it's from the US, or it's unique here or something."

"Yeah. It's worth a try. We got no choice. We gotta sell something and we gotta get some more money."

"That's for sure." I said grimly. "If we can't get some more money soon, we're dead."

It was dark and getting cold on the congested city streets, as we set out to sell something and to try and make some money. The air turned cold as the night came on, but the city was still full of people, activity and commotion. There was a kind of noisy chaos taking place all around us.

As John and I headed out onto the dark streets of Tangiers that night, we had no idea what we were walking into. I didn't know it at the time, but the next 24 hours would be some of the most eventful, difficult and dangerous of our trip.

With our backpacks on our back, as always, we only walked a short ways down the street before we were surrounded by about a half a dozen hustlers all aggressively vying for our attention. A couple of them were openly showing us bags of hash or other drugs and all of them were incessantly tugging at my arms and bantering away, "Hey, Joe what do you want? I got what you need. Come with me, Joe."

With the crowd pushing around us, John and I stopped in our tracks and scanned the group of men. We both made eye contact with each other and shrugged, as John looked into the crowd and pointed at one guy with a shaggy beard, wearing dirt-stained pants and a grimy, long brown coat.

"You. We'll deal with you. Only you."

The guy with the scraggly beard stepped forward somewhat surprised. We quickly pulled him aside and again said, "We'll deal with you…Only you."

He quickly understood, turned back toward the other men and started speaking harshly in Arabic. There were some taunts and apparent threats made back at him by the group of men, but he spoke in again in a very angry voice and raised his fist at them.

John and I just stood by and watched for a few moments as it appeared a small riot or fight might break out. But eventually, after some more shouting and heated exchanges in Arabic, the other men started wandering away into the shadows to find some other prey…until we were finally just left with the scraggly bearded hustler.

John and I had picked him out of the crowd merely by gut instinct. We needed someone to deal with, to try and get some money, and he was the guy we chose.

Standing in the shadows of the wide paved street, John and I explained to him. "We need money. We will sell our goods for money."

"Drugs, Ok, I get drugs. Much drugs. Good hash." The scraggly bearded guy responded motioning like he was smoking some hash, not understanding anything we said.

"No. No. We want to sell our things for money." I repeated. "Sell our things - get money. We need cash, not hash."

Ah…Yes. Yes. You want woman. I get pretty woman." The bearded guy said smiling still not understanding anything we said.

"No. No we want to sell our things for money…for cash." John said loudly.

"Ah…Yes, yes, ok. My friend buy things, you many money." The hustler said, finally understanding us.

John and I both nodded our head repeatedly. "Yes."

"OK. Come now." The bearded hustler said pulling at us to follow him. "I take you. Come. Come. My friend clothes store, he buy, you many money."

CHAPTER **30**

Trading for Money or For our Lives

With an understanding finally reached with the street hustler, we started following the guy through the winding, busy streets of Tangiers; crossways, down and around several wide paved and marked streets, through market areas and over a few hills.

Once he started out, the bearded guy just kept moving at a fast clip as John and I walked along behind him trying to keep up. There was a lot of night-time action taking place on the street, as we cut in and among the crowds of hawkers and hustlers selling their goods, smoking, shouting and talking. We walked behind the guy for quite some time, as he made several quick, sharp turns down different streets. I'm usually quite good at directions and finding my way around, but even though I tried to pay close attention to the turns we made, the streets and some landmarks, very soon I was completely lost in the city.

Tangiers was a really large city. It was an interesting place with some beautiful mosques and landmarks here and there across the landscape. But it was slightly haphazard with a kind of twisting, winding grid to it that was difficult to grasp without stopping occasionally to take note. And this guy seemed to be leading us on an aimless, incoherent march through the city.

As we were following along, I said to John between breathes, "Man, I'm lost. How about you? You got any idea where we are or how to make it back to where we were?"

"Not a clue. He's taking us for quite a ride."

"You trust this guy?" John then asked nodding to the tough looking, bearded street hustler in front of us.

"No, I don't. But what can we do? We gotta get some money tonight somehow."

The street hustler continued at a fast pace and we continued following along. We had followed the guy for at least half an hour all through the city, when he suddenly turned off the wide street we were on, cut around a sharp corner and started heading down a dark alley.

In an instant, we were walking into an almost deserted kind of narrow pathway, with only a very few shady characters leaning against the walls in the shadows or sitting in the small rooms off the alley. It had a real bad feel to it.

It was a single, narrow, hard pathway winding between an endless line of low, rock walls with some little entrances, rooms and small shops leading off it. The narrow pathway had several slight hills and winding turns, and only had enough space for about 3-4 people across. It was narrow and dark; with only a little light breaking up the darkness from small, rudimentary, light poles scattered here and there.

The moment we made the turn onto the back alley, I came intensely alert. I had an immediate bad gut instinct. Set-up! He's leading us into a set-up. I looked over at John. We made eye contact. We didn't have to say a word. We both knew what the other was thinking.

John just shrugged, and said quietly, "Let's give it a little further."

"OK." I nodded back.

"Hey! How much further? Where's your friends shop?" John shouted at the bearded hustler ahead of us.

The bearded guy turned, waved us on and said, "Soon. Joe. Soon. Friend clothes shop. Soon. He buy. You big money."

He then continued walking on, but it was now at a slower pace.

I looked warily over at John and we made eye contact again. I slightly nodded in the direction behind us and said evenly, "You watch our backs. I'll cover the guy. OK?"

"OK."

We had put ourselves in an extremely vulnerable and unprotected position. John knew it. I knew it…

Letting myself be led late at night, down a dark, confined, isolated alley with no exit points or means of escape, to an unknown destination, with a hustler from the street that we had just met, to meet some unknown trader… It went against every instinct and travel habit I had.

There's no way John or I would ever knowingly allow ourselves to be put in such a defenseless position, unless it was absolutely necessary. And at this point, we both felt it was necessary. We had to get some money and soon. We needed to get some money that night. Every day or hour we went without getting some money, put us further and further from making it back.

We were truly desperate.

As we continued following the bearded hustler down the narrow, shadowy pathway, it became more and more confined and deserted. We were now completely isolated from the main area of the city. After walking another couple hundred meters, the guy abruptly stopped.

I immediately looked around, expecting to be jumped from the shadows. Nothing happened.

The guy pointed up ahead a little ways and said, "There. Friend shop. Now he buy. You sell. Big money. OK?"

The bearded guy then gestured like 'Shh. Shh. Be quiet.' With a nervous glance ahead, he signaled again like 'Be careful. Be careful' and said, "Friend. Power man." And motioned like bowing, meaning we needed to show respect to the guy.

The bearded guy's demeanor had quickly changed. He lost his confident, calculating manner and suddenly become quite hesitant and even fearful.

"He's getting scared." John said quietly. "Who's he taking us to meet? What the heck is 'power man' anyway?"

'I don't know. But we gotta be real careful."

We walked up a little further and came to a garage size, single room leading directly off from the clay walls that lined both sides of the alley. The room had a large, open entrance and when I looked in, it did appear to be some kind of clothing shop.

There was a single light bulb hanging from the ceiling brightly lighting up the room. It was a single rectangular room about 15 meters deep and 10 meters wide. There were some clothes hanging on the walls throughout the room, with a mix of long coats, shirts and pants. The room was mostly open in the middle area. I didn't see anybody in the room or anywhere in sight.

The street hustler pointed into the room, started hesitantly walking in and signaled for us to follow him. The room wasn't that big. I wondered where he was going.

I looked over at John, "Where we were suppose to go?"

"I don't know. And where's his friend?"

John then looked at the guy and said, "Hey. Where's your friend? When do we meet your friend?"

The street hustler turned slightly and just waved for us to follow him into the shop. As John and I were walking in, he moved over to the back wall of the shop. At the back wall, he reached out and pulled up a big, heavy rug that was hanging on the wall. Behind the rug was an opening about 2/3rds the size of a normal doorway leading into some kind of hidden back room.

While holding the rug up, he pointed into the little back room, motioning for us to go in. John and I looked at each other for a moment. We didn't have to talk. I just looked at John with a 'Man, what are getting ourselves into?' kind of look.

After a moment, John just shrugged with a kind of 'What can we do?' gesture. I shrugged back.

A single word was never spoken, but we had said volumes. We had made our decision. We were going in.

John walked up to the opening in the rear wall, bent down and pushed in through the small entrance into the back room. I immediately followed. The bearded hustler followed right after me. The room was small and completely empty, with nothing but scraped and decrepit, clay walls enclosing the room on all sides. While it had a light, it was much darker than the larger outer room.

I quickly sat down cross-legged on one side of the room, nearest the door with my backpack under me. John sat next to me on my left, leaning back with his backpack behind him against the wall. The street hustler sat further back in the room against the rear wall facing the little opening that we had entered from.

Almost immediately after we entered the room, unexpectedly, a man bent down, entered the room and quickly stood to his full height. He was a big guy. He just stepped into the room and took a dominant position standing next to the small opening. It was the only way in or out of the room. He stood right next to the doorway with his hands clasped in front of him, ignoring us and staring straight ahead.

He was a big, dark haired, whiskered Arab guy with a large blunt nose and a full belly. But kind of barrel-chested, with a belly that looked like more muscle than fat. He was wearing western style clothes, nice clothes; a dark shirt, black pants and dress shoes.

He looked like hired muscle, like intimidation. Our situation and position was going from bad to worse. Things had been going south ever since we started following the bearded hustler off the main roads and entered the isolated, back alleyway. My gut and instincts were ringing warning bells off the hook.

I was shocked to see the big guy. I didn't know where he came from, and how he got to the back room so fast. I was thinking maybe there was another hidden room somewhere in the shop that I didn't see.

I leaned over to John on the floor next to me. "What's up with this?"

"I don't know. This is something else. Where did that guy come from so fast?"

"I have no idea."

We waited nervously, sitting on the floor of the back room for several minutes with nothing happening. There was a definite tension filling the air. The big guy just kept his position next to the door opening, and we sat on the floor with the bearded hustler waiting and watching.

Finally, John looked over at the street hustler, who had been sitting silently on the floor, and said, "Where's your friend? You said your friend would buy some of our stuff. We're not going to wait all night."

The hustler who had brought us here looked at John quizzically, like he didn't understand what John said.

So I repeated slowly, "Where…you friend? When…we meet?"

The hustler smirked coldly, and signaled with his hands like, 'Wait. Wait.'

I nudged John, and said under my breath, "This is not good. Not good at all."

"You got that right." John replied quietly. "We might be getting set up for a bad fall. Keep ready. We'll have to see how it plays out."

John and I continued sitting on the floor for what was probably another 10 minutes, but it seemed like a couple of decades.

It was dead quiet and tense, with a palpable feeling of danger filling up the air around us. Time seemed to slow down for me. It was like everything moved in slow motion as we awaited our fate.

Finally, very suddenly and swiftly, a head and then a man swept into the room from the small opening. The big guy standing guard and the bearded hustler on the floor both immediately came to attention with a look of fear or respect. I wasn't really sure which, maybe both.

The man who entered the room was a tall, slim, dark-featured Arab of about 35. He was very distinguished looking with a full head of jet black hair, refined features and a trimmed beard. He was wearing an exquisite, full length robe or coat with the hood pushed back from his head. The robe he was wearing looked absolutely magnificent and appeared to be made of some kind of animal skin. He looked liked an idealized version of a mystical Arab sheik from the 'Nights of Arabia' or something. He made a very strong and stunning impression.

It took me a moment to absorb and to adjust to his presence in the room. He was about the last person I expected to see enter this small hidden back room, in the shadows of this remote shop, in the very back alleys of Tangiers.

John and I both just sat on the floor for a few moments looking up at him mesmerized, while he stood over us calmly staring down at our faces. Then before we could say anything, and without any kind of introductions being made, the 'Arab sheik' started talking.

Not really talking…Actually, what he did had no resemblance at all to 'talking.' He just started flat-out ranting. And I mean a bitter, manic, vicious rant. It was like a switch had been flipped, and he went psycho as he started frantically pacing the floor directly in front of us.

While pacing and looking down at us, the 'sheik' took off on a vicious rant directed at John and me, practically spitting the words, as he screamed at us and jabbed his finger at our faces. He started ranting about Americans and how 'hates all god damn Americans,' and how he wished he could 'kill all Americans', and how Americans do this! and this! and this! to harm him and his country. He continued to rage on and on and on about how he wanted to kill Americans…With each point, he would momentarily stop pacing and angrily look down at us, while menacingly jabbing his finger at our faces. Then he would continue his pacing and rants, stop, get back in our face and angrily jab away again.

Needless to say I was absolutely stunned and taken-a-back by his outburst, and if I had more time to think about him and the situation I was in, I probably would have been petrified, too. He was making some very direct threats against us, and I had no idea if he was crazy enough to carry them out. And John and I were in a completely unprotected position, alone and totally isolated with no means of escape.

But as it was, it happened so quickly and unexpectedly that I didn't have time to react or think of anything much more than 'Man, this guy is absolutely crazy. He's nuts.' John and I just sat on the floor motionless, absolutely bewildered, looking up at the guy as he continued his ranting.

After several vicious rants about his hatred for America and his desire to kill Americans – He suddenly, in almost mid-sentence, changed topics and went off about how he knew we had some guns… and how if we could get him some guns, he would give us lots of money. He said he knew Americans always had guns and if we got him some guns, he'd pay us big money.

John and I were just dumb-founded and shook our heads, gestured strongly, saying, "No. No. We don't have any guns."

It didn't deter him.

He angrily raged that he was sure we had some guns and continued his pacing and rant about how he needed us to give him our guns, and how he knew Americans always had them, and how he would give us lots of money if we did.

We kept saying "No. Sorry. No. We don't have any guns."

Pulling back our jackets and shirts and pointing to our backpacks we continued, "Look. We don't have any guns. They're not here. There's no place we have them."

It took a while and a lot of convincing, but he finally seemed to believe us that we didn't have some guns with us or hidden somewhere.

Then, in the flick of an eye; after his threatening, spitting torrent of rants against us - He went completely calm, sat down cross-legged across from us on the floor and in an even, composed voice said, "OK. Now we deal. Let me see what you have to trade."

It was strange and unnerving. In a moment's time, he went from being a raging, ranting lunatic to a calm, composed trader ready to do business. Again, I was completely taken-a-back and caught off guard. It took both John and I a minute to regain our focus.

I also was thinking at the time, even as he was making his vicious rants and threats against us, that 'Man, he really speaks fluent English.' He spoke English extremely well. It was the first time in weeks I had heard anyone actually speak English that I could effortlessly understand. The perfect English he was speaking during his rants also seemed so disconnected to the situation and to what he was saying. It added another layer of disbelief to what was occurring.

As John and I were trying to return our attention back to the business at hand, the 'sheik' unexpectedly reached across and pulled my backpack out from under me, and started going through my things. I was sitting closest to him and, again, I was caught off guard and didn't really react.

I had rarely been caught off guard on the entire month long trip. Now within a few minutes of meeting the crazed sheik, I had been taken by surprise three times…I didn't like the feeling.

The 'sheik' opened my backpack and roughly started pulling things out. He made a disgusted face as he went through my limited supply of smelly, dirty underwear and t-shirts. He started taking stuff out and throwing it on the floor. As he was going through my things, he glanced at the big guy guarding the door and said in English. "Look at this. This is crap. What's this? Oh, this is crap."

He was not at all impressed with what I had to offer in my backpack. Actually, he seemed downright offended. I can't say I blame him. Most of the dirty, smelly stuff in my backpack hadn't been washed in almost two months, since well before I left to go to the Soviet Union, which was a couple of weeks prior to the start of this trip across Africa. My stuff wasn't really fit for human use, let alone something that anyone would want to pay good money for.

After the 'sheik' finished going through my things, he just tossed my backpack back over to me and pushed over my clothes from the floor. I quickly stuffed everything back into my backpack.

The sheik then started looking over the clothes John and I were wearing. In my case, I had been wearing the same pair of pants for every day of the trip and most of the clothes I had with me I was wearing at the time. It was a cold night and I was wearing more things than I was carrying in my backpack. As I said before, I like to travel light.

At the time I was wearing a long windbreaker jacket with my old high school letter jacket underneath, a plaid shirt, a torn T-shirt, and the same rugged corduroy pants that I had worn every single day of the trip, with a thick leather belt that had a chain attached to my wallet. I only had one pair of pants with me for the entire trip.

Basically, I could put almost everything on at one time that I had with me, except for a few extra pair of socks and underpants. So there wasn't really much in my backpack of any value at all.

The 'sheik" started looking over at what I was wearing and noticed my high school jacket with the varsity letter on it. It was a traditional American high school jacket, which were quite popular at the time and often featured in American movies.

He became quite smitten with my jacket. Like a lot of people I met traveling over the years, no matter what their political views of the US, they often were quite taken with American culture and followed it closely - Whether it was American music, movies, products, personalities, trends or sports.

The 'sheik' looked at me and gestured toward my high school jacket, "Let me see that. I like that."

"What? This? It's my high school jacket." I answered.

"Yes? It's a true American school jacket. Is it not?"

"Yeah. It's from Brother Rice High School in Michigan, my school. It's a great school."

"Give it to me." The sheik demanded. "Let me see it. I like that."

Before I had a chance to answer, the sheik leaned over and started pulling at my outer windbreaker and grabbing at my high school jacket. I pulled away saying, "Just a second."

I leaned back away from him and pulled off my windbreaker. I then undid the high school jacket, took it off and handed it to him. He held the jacket in his hands feeling the material and running his fingers over the varsity letter that was sewn onto the front of it. He smiled brightly, stood up and took off his magnificent animal skin robe and put on my old, worn-out high school jacket. He then started strutting across the small room pulling the jacket tight around him when he barked in Arabic some kind of command to the big guy standing next to the entrance. The big guy immediately jumped to attention and hustled out through the small opening, bending deeply to get his bulk through the little doorway. He reappeared very quickly carrying a full length mirror that he set against the wall next to the doorway.

The 'sheik' stood in front of the mirror admiring himself, smiling smugly. He then turned back to the big guy and said something in Arabic again. This time he spoke longer and seemed to repeat himself to make sure the big guy understood.

The big guy left the room again, while the 'sheik' continued looking in the mirror, admiring how he looked in my beat-up high school jacket. It was the first time since the 'sheik' had entered the little room that John and I had a chance to collect our thoughts. Things had been moving very fast, out of our control, but things had now slowed as the 'sheik' waited for the big guy to return

John leaned toward me and said very quietly under his breath, "This guy is really a piece of work, isn't he?"

"Sure is."

"Maybe if we're lucky, though, we can still get some money out of this."

"I'll be happy if we get outta here with our lives. This guy is crazy." I replied grimly.

"Yeah, he is. As long he stays focused on business and making a trade, we might be OK."

"Maybe…But if he turns psycho again, we could be in real danger." I whispered back genuinely concerned.

"There's no way outta here, except through that opening." John said, slightly nodding in the direction of the small doorway.

"Yeah. That's it. It's the only way outta here. We might have to make a run for it."

"Yeah, and we gotta be ready to move. I mean really move!…At the very first sign of trouble."

"You got that right. Get in position." I said. "We might not get a second chance."

As we sat on the floor watching the sheik admire himself in the mirror, John and I both subtly and slowly changed our sitting positions and adjusted our backpacks. So that we were now in a stance that we could spring up and begin moving forward very quickly, with no hesitation.

In the few moments that we waited for the big guy to return, I also quickly visualized in my mind what I would do if I had to make a run for it; How I would carry my backpack, which way I had to step first and move, and where I had to go to get out of the room, out of the shop and out of the back alleys we were lost in. It's something I often did in critical or pressure situations – Take a quick moment and just visualize in my mind exactly what I had to do, step by step, so that I wouldn't have to hesitate at all when the time came to act.

Shortly, the big guy came lumbering back into the cramped room. When he did I was very surprised to see what he had with him. He was carrying a beautiful, exquisite full length robe, similar to the one the 'sheik' had been wearing before he discarded it to try on my jacket. The robe was absolutely stunning and, like the sheik's, it was intricately designed and tailored with a cool looking hood attached.

The 'sheik' directed the big guy to hand it over to John and me.

As the big guy did, the sheik said in a commanding voice, "I will give you this robe for your school jacket. It is a very fair trade!"

And it was…It was an extremely fair trade in my eyes. The robe was simply magnificent and I'm sure much more valuable, at least in the US, than my old high school jacket.

John and I were momentarily speechless, and just held the beautiful robe in our hands looking at it. I would have loved to have been able to keep it. It took us a minute to regain our senses. Finally, John looked over at the bearded street hustler, who had brought us here and motioning toward him, said to the 'sheik,' "Your friend said we could trade for money. We only came to trade for money."

I quickly added, "This robe is great and a fair trade, but we told your friend we only trade for cash. We need money, not clothes."

The 'sheik' reacted with a flash of anger and a bitter look. He then hissed a command in Arabic to the big guy, who quickly grabbed the robe from us and took it away. As the big guy did so, the sheik took off my high school jacket and angrily flung it back at me. I took the jacket and quickly crammed it into my backpack to free up my arms. I didn't want to have to carry it or take the time to put it back on.

The 'sheik' then sat back down cross-legged on the floor across from us and seemed to ponder the situation, as he seethed with anger. I don't think he was used to being turned down.

As we were all sitting on the floor, the big guy returned and took his place standing next to the doorway. While the sheik continued sitting, I could see him glaring over at John and me. After a moment he started focusing his attention on my right hand. He then reached toward my right hand, but I instinctively pulled it away.

Still looking at my hand, he said to me, "Let me see your ring. What is that stone? What does the English writing on it say? I like that."

I held my hand out and looked down at my fingers. "It's my school graduation ring. It's got my high school name – 'Brother Rice High School' and the year I graduated, 1977"

That information seemed to really impress the 'sheik.' (Like I said, no matter what the political views, having a piece of Americana carried a special appeal with a lot of people on my travels.) The sheik was now even more interested in my ring, and began grabbing at my hand again. With his two hands he grabbed my right hand and started to try to pull the ring from my finger.

I closed my fingers into a tight fist, and said strongly, "No deal. I don't trade my ring. It's special."

He didn't back down. He continued trying to open my fist to pry the ring off my finger. "I want it. I will make good trade for the ring."

I continued, "No. It's not for trade. No chance. It's special to me."

A slight tug-of-war ensued for a couple of minutes as the sheik tried to get the ring from me.

"I will give money for the ring." He finally offered. "I will give good money."

"No deal." I shot back. "It's special. It's my school ring. It's not for trade…not for sale."

Even in my desperate situation, when it came right down to it, I wouldn't give up my high school ring for money. The jacket I would have, but not the ring. My time at Brother Rice High School was a great time in my life, and a valuable experience for me. My four years at Brother Rice imparted life-long values and habits that have served me well throughout my life. It was a very special experience for me and like I said to the sheik, my high school ring was also special. I wouldn't sell it no matter what the situation.

Also at this point, I didn't really trust him to pay over any money once he had the ring in his possession, but that was secondary. Even if I believed him, I wouldn't have given the ring up.

When it became obvious that I wouldn't budge about selling the ring, the sheik finally stopped trying to pull it off my hand and gave up. He leaned back, glared at me with a bitter, angry expression; quickly stood up and menacingly shouted something at my brother and me. He was, apparently, so angry that he used Arabic, forgetting we only spoke English.

After pausing a moment he then coldly looked back directly at us, leaned in close and using Arabic in a low, seething voice, he hissed some kind of threat at us. I don't know exactly what he said, but it sent a cold chill down my spine.

The sheik then abruptly turned and stormed out of the little doorway and left the small room.

Sitting in a forward position on the floor, John and I made one quick glance at each other, and without hesitation we both instantly grabbed our backpacks, bolted from the floor, and made a dash straight to the small doorway leading out of the confined room.

The big guy, who was still maintaining his position standing next to door, was taken completely by surprise. He had no time to react. We were up off the floor and out of the small room in a couple of heartbeats. Being closest to the door, I was the first out. When I got out of the hidden back room, without looking or hesitating, I just kept going at a dead run straight out of the little shop into the dark narrow little alley. It wasn't until I was out of the shop in the alley way that I even glanced back to see what was behind me. Fortunately, what I saw was John racing toward me. So I kept running. I turned right out of the shop, which was the way we entered the shop and took off at dead run down through the shadowy, winding pathway.

I kept running and running as fast and as far as I could along the narrow rock alley between the clay walls lining both sides. Finally, we made it out of the little side alley and got back onto some of the main streets of the city. I still didn't stop, but just kept running through the streets, weaving in and out of the street activity. I didn't stop running at full speed until I heard a puffing John shout, "Dennis, slow up. Slow up!"

I slowed up and John caught up, motioning for me to stop. So I did.

John bent over huffing and said, "I think were safe now. We're good. We can take a break."

With the adrenalin rush fading, I, too, bent over and started gasping for breath.

After catching my breath I looked up and took a look around. "Yeah. We should be good. This is a big city. If he does send someone out after us, it'll be real tough for anyone to find us."

"Yep." John agreed. "Let's just keep moving and put some more distance between us and the psycho sheik."

That's what we did. We just continued walking at a quick pace, in a meandering way with no set destination, just trying to put some more distance, streets, and turns between us and the threatening guy we left behind.

It was quite late at night now, nearing midnight, but in many of the areas that we walked on our meandering trek through the city, there was still a lot of activity and people out and about. We were still occasionally approached by guys with the 'Hey Joe' routine, trying to hustle us or sell us something. We kept our distance and kept moving..

Finally, after a good 30 minutes of fast paced walking, we stopped and sat down in an isolated, dark, market area. It looked like the market had closed and everyone left for the night. We found a secure place to sit in the dark and take stock of our situation.

"Well, that didn't really go so well, did it?" I said.

"I guess you might say that." John replied, "Considering we wasted half the night, nearly got beat up or killed, haven't eaten, and are still no closer to getting back than we were when we first arrived in Tangiers."

TRADING FOR MONEY OR FOR OUR LIVES

"Yeah. But at least we had such pleasant company this evening at the little clothes shop." I said grinning sarcastically.

"Sure. We oughtta go back and see the psycho sheik for tea and crumpets in the morning. I'm sure he would be thrilled."

We both just laughed for a moment as the tension faded, before I continued, "Man, that guy was something. He was either stone crazy or that was just his negotiating style to put us on the complete defensive. He didn't act like many people had said 'no' to him before."

"Yep." John agreed. "I think that might have been a new experience for him."

"Uh-Huh. He sure didn't take too kindly to it."

"I don't know what threats he made there in Arabic at the end. But, man, I'm glad we didn't stick around to find out."

"No kidding. He looked ready to kill us. For real." I said.

"He was really set on getting your ring…No matter what."

"Yeah, he sure was." I answered, "But there was no way I was gonna give it up."

"Yep. So I noticed."

I had several different incidents with that same ring over the years on my travels, with people trying to steal it, buy it or hustle it from me. As I said it was my high school graduation ring from Brother Rice High School in Michigan. My years at Brother Rice were special to me, and the ring was special to me.

I ended up usually wearing the ring upside down, so that the stone and writing were facing down into my palm, and could not be seen. It was not a real expensive ring, but its size and the writing and the Americana aspect I guess made it a magnet to a lot of people on my travels. I had so many people try to steal it, buy it or hustle it from me.

Probably the strangest incident involving that ring was one time when I was on a small shuttle train on a fairly remote Malaysian island. I was traveling alone through Asia, sitting in a window seat on the crowded train with my right arm resting and hanging over the open window ledge. I was just kind of dozing waiting for the train to pull out of the small station.

TRAVELIN' MAN ACROSS THE SAHARA AND BEYOND

There were several local people milling about selling food and drinks, and hawking trinkets as the train was getting ready to get on its way. Finally, the old train fired up with a loud squeal and hiss from its engine, and the train started to slowly chug out of the station.

As soon as the train lurched and started moving, I felt something tugging and pulling at my arm. For a quick second I thought maybe my arm was caught on a station sign or wire or something. I was very alarmed. When I quickly looked out the window to see what the problem was, I got quite a surprise.

Outside my window, running alongside the old train was a well dressed, dark haired, guy with a mustache and about 30 years old. He was desperately trying to pull my school ring off of my finger and he had a strong grip on my hand. He was running and stumbling along the tracks, trying to pull and slide the ring off my finger, before the train picked up too much speed.

However, that was not the most surprising part of this little story. What he did next was. As I looked out the window and started to try and pull my hand back inside, the guy looked up at me with a bright, cheerful smile and said in English, "Oh, hello. Good day! I'll be finished in just a moment."

He then went back to desperately trying to pry my ring off before the train got going too fast. He acted like it was the most natural thing in the world - to be trying to steal my ring.

And he almost did. He was very good at his apparent job. He had a very strong grip that made it very difficult to pull my arm back in the train. He also had some kind of ointment that he somehow gotten on my finger, making it easier for a ring to slip off. The only way I kept my ring that day was because the train got going too fast before he could pull it off, and he couldn't keep up. When the guy finally gave up and stopped running along with the train, he bent over to catch his breath as the train pulled away. But not before smiling warmly at me, and giving me a big friendly wave.

He might have been a thief, but man, he sure was a cheerful, polite one.

The final bit to the story of my high school ring…I ended up losing that same ring in the Atlantic Ocean a few years later. I was body surfing in some strong waves with a girlfriend in Atlantic City, and I came up after crashing in the surf from a bad wipeout and the ring was gone…Just like that it was gone.

CHAPTER **31**

No Matter What!

It was now the middle of the night and our situation was getting more critical by the hour. We had already been in Tangiers for about 20 hours, and despite spending the entire time trying to find a way to get back, or a way to get some more money, we had made no progress at all. We had spent 20 hours of hard time and effort, and had nothing to show for it.

"Man, we gotta get some money or find a way out of here soon. Real soon, or were gonna run out of money and never make it." John said, as we sat in the empty market and continued discussing our situation.

"Yeah." I agreed. "Time is critical for us."

"Yep. We gotta get something done fast."

"We can't spend any money unless it's getting us back to England."

"I know. And I'm starving, but if we spend money, we gotta make the money back somehow."

With the money we had left, we did not have enough to buy a ticket to get back to England. From where we were, in Tangiers, there was no ship or flight we could afford to pay for; even with both of our money combined we didn't even have enough to buy one ticket, let alone two. And there was no way we could make it back overland with the money we had. We were also now blocked by the Sea. To move forward, the only way was by ship - To take a ship across the Straight of Gibraltar either to Spain or to the tiny rock peninsula of Gibraltar.

We had hit a dead end.

We sat for a while longer, contemplating our options. There wasn't any specific plan or idea that we could think of to get us back to England. It didn't look good. It was real late, maybe about 1 or 2 AM but we couldn't afford to sleep.

Finally, I spoke up. "Well, sitting here isn't going to get it done for us. I don't know what we can do. But we gotta come up with something...we gotta keep searching."

"You got that right." John agreed.

"You wanna take a look around the city? See what we can find out on the streets."

"Yep. Let's go. See if we can get some info. We gotta come up with something and soon."

So we picked up our backpacks and wearily headed out onto the dark streets of Tangiers. It was late, and it had already been an incredibly long, eventful night for us, but the night was far from over. Actually, it wouldn't end for us until after the rising of the sun.

We were dead set determined to find a way back and we wouldn't rest (or eat for that matter) until we did. We had to find some way to get the job done. By this point we were exhausted, filthy dirty, hungry and running out of money – But we just kept our relentless focus.

John and I walked the dark streets of Tangiers for hours getting pieces of information, trying to find a way back. We walked over many areas of the city; including beautiful scenic areas, as well as sleazy and the off-beat. Tangiers was a city with a lot of night action, if you looked for it. And we were looking for it.

We tried talking to some of the street hustlers, men at the late night cafés, back street clubs, hostel owners and strangers on the street. Anyone. After a few hours, we hadn't come up with much.

As we were slowly walking along another one of the endless streets we had been down during the course of the long night, John said, "Man, we've talked to a lot of different people, but we haven't got much new info."

"Yeah. It's tough." I replied.

"Especially, with the language barrier, and a few of the guys we tried talking to looked at as like we were crazy."

"Can't really blame them…A couple of Americans approaching them on the street, in the middle of the night, asking for help to get back to England. Whatta ya expect?"

"Good point." John said nodding his head.

"But still, some of those guys really tried to help us."

"True. Like that tall Moroccan guy at the outdoor café on the side street." John replied. "He was a nice guy."

"Yeah, he was. But it still seems the only way out is by flight, and we can't afford a ticket."

"Nobody knew of any flights or ships cheaper than what we found today." I noted.

"There's just not much we can do. We're running out of time, money and options."

We shuffled along for a while longer in silence, lost in our thoughts, trying to come up with something. It had been a long, long day.

Unexpectedly, John broke the silence and blurted out, "Where's good old Freddy Laker when you need him?"

It took me a second to catch what he said. After a moment I chuckled and said, "Yeah, where is good ol' Sir Freddy? We could really use him right about now."

We both just smiled and kept walking.

At that time, in 1977, Freddy Laker was something of a hero and folk legend to me, as well as to my brother and a lot of other backpackers and travelers like us. Sir Freddy had created 'Laker Air', his own independent airline. And with it, he had single handily created standby flights across the Atlantic Ocean…or so the legend goes.

At that time by flying standby; I could fly from New York, Chicago or other random cities in the US to London or Frankfort in Europe for $129. That's $129 to cross the Atlantic Ocean. That's not much more that it cost me to just get across Lake Michigan from Detroit to Chicago by air.

From the age of 18 until I turned 21 years old, I traveled to over thirty countries in Europe, Africa, Asia and the Mid-East. I never could have done it without Freddy Laker and the standby flights he created. When Freddy

◄ TRAVELIN' MAN ACROSS THE SAHARA AND BEYOND

Laker started his discount standby flights from the US to England, the other airlines soon followed suit.

I believe I had over twenty international flights during that three year period from age 18 to 21, and I paid for every one of the flights myself with the money I made at Peabody's restaurant in my home town of Birmingham. In all of my flights I almost always paid $129-$139 to fly to Europe. The most I ever paid was $329 to cross the Atlantic, and the $329 was for a flight all the way from Chicago with a stopover in Iceland and then to Frankfort. I almost always paid $129-$139.

Flying standby was very, very cheap, but also very haphazard in those days. On one of my trips back to the US from London, I spent three days in a row sleeping out on the street trying to get a standby seat. Backpackers and travelers in London would try Laker Air, or go to the British Airways, or TWA Airline offices in downtown London and just line up on the street waiting in line all night.

At that time there was no order to flying standby. Who ever got there first would just take a spot on the street nearest the Airline office door, and people would line up behind him and sleep out on the street. Sometimes as many as 200-300 travelers would be lined up by the next morning.

At around 8:00am the airline office would suddenly open its doors and start letting people in one at a time to buy a standby ticket. On any given morning no-one ever knew how many people they would call in. It depended on how many unsold seats the airline had that particular day. On some occasions, it was 7 or 8 seats, on others 30 or 40, and on real bad days it was none. Even if you were one of the lucky ones to get called in for a standby ticket, you didn't know where it was going until you were called in. It might be a flight to New York, Chicago, or Washington D.C. It was all hit or miss. On one occasion returning home from England to Michigan the seat available was to Wash DC, so I took it and then rode buses and hitched the rest of the way home.

As soon as one airline such as BA office closed its doors, there was usually then a mad stampede of travelers racing across the street to the TWA office to see what the standby situation was there. The TWA, British Air and Laker Air offices would all finish giving out standby tickets by about 9:00 – 10am.

NO MATTER WHAT!

(Irritated backpackers without tickets used to call TWA, the 'Try Walking Across' airline - You had a better chance of making it across the Atlantic Ocean by walking it.)

By about 10:00am if you didn't have a ticket, you were stuck. It was too late to try another airline flying to the US, and you had another whole day and night to wait in London and try again.

It was usually haphazard and chaotic, but the amazingly inexpensive stand-by flights created by Sir Freddy Laker made a lot of my travel dreams possible.

We continued walking the winding streets all night long until early in the morning still trying to find a way out of Morocco. It had been a long, tiring night for us. At around 5:00AM in the morning, just a while before the break of dawn, we came across a couple of other backpackers out on the street. We saw them across the wide city street from us walking alone along the road. John and I hustled over toward them.

"Hey, you guys speak English? Any English?" I yelled over to them as we crossed the street.

The two guys stopped walking and the smaller of the two guys answered, hesitantly. "We Spain."

"Great. You speak English." John said.

"Yes. A little."

"Whatta you doing here in Tangiers?" John asked.

"We visit for vacation from Spain. Our home Barcelona. We have one week vacation. How about you?"

"We're Americans. We've just arrived here after traveling across from Algeria and Tunisia." I answered.

"You travel across Algeria? Tunisia?" The second bigger guy asked surprised. "I thought cross Algeria and Tunisia not possible. I never hear of that before."

"I don't know about that, but, yeah, that's what we did. We just got here today…err, ah, I mean yesterday." I replied.

We then went on to explain our situation, about our difficulties getting to Tangiers and running out of money, and how we desperately needed to find a way back to England. After listening to us, the two backpackers spoke among themselves in Spanish for a minute, then turned back to face John and I.

319

The smaller guy spoke, "We think maybe you buy cheap plane ticket from Gibraltar to England. We hear flights much cheaper from Gibraltar. You take ship Gibraltar and then cheap plane to England from there."

"You sure?" John asked.

"No. Not sure. But we hear that before many times." The short Spanish guy answered. "Flights cheaper from Gibraltar."

"Do you know how we can get to Gibraltar?" I asked.

"Yes, The ship I know…There is one cheap ship in the morning."

"Uh-huh."

After talking to his buddy in Spanish for a second, he looked back at us and said, "The cheap ship leaves about 8:00AM. But it's very difficult to get ticket. Sold out very fast. Must get there early for ticket. There is a second ship later, but very expensive."

John and I both looked at each other with a flicker of hope in our eyes. It was the first bit of good information we had got since arriving in Tangiers and starting our desperate quest to find a way back. The Spanish guys then went on to give us directions down to the sea and the shipyard. John and I thanked them for the info and they headed off down the deserted street.

Finally, after all our relentless, but unsuccessful efforts to find a way back from Tangiers, we had found our first possible option for getting back. Like always, once we finally found it and made our decision, we didn't hesitate. We just became intensely focused on our objective of getting to Gibraltar and getting a flight back.

"Whatta you think?" I asked John, as we stood watching the helpful Spanish guys walking away.

"I say we do it. We gotta get to Gibraltar." John replied.

"Yeah. It's our best chance. We don't have enough money to buy a ticket from here. If we don't do something fast, we're gonna have to start spending money just to survive on the streets and we'll run out of money soon. We'll be stuck."

"You got that right." John said. "Even if we can't get a flight from Gibraltar, at least we'll be across the Sea. We can then cross the border overland from Gibraltar to Spain and continue making distance by land until we figure something out."

NO MATTER WHAT!

That's what we thought anyways. But like a lot of the situations on our adventure, we were highly misinformed and didn't have a clue what we heading into.

We didn't know it, but at this time, in 1977, the border between Gibraltar and Spain was closed. There were no border crossings of any kind. It was a completely closed border. The border wasn't opened until many years later.

It meant that once we crossed the Strait of Gibraltar by ship and arrived in Gibraltar, there was no way to leave the little 'Rock' if we didn't get a flight.

Without a flight out, the only thing we could do was to wait a night in Gibraltar, then take a ship and backtrack across the same Mediterranean Sea to Tangiers. Then wait a night in Tangiers and take another ship across the same sea, just slightly to the east to Spain. And only then, after the expense and time needed for 3 ship crossings, could we start moving forward overland through Spain. By then we would be flat broke.

We didn't know it until later when it was too late, but crossing the sea to Gibraltar was an all-or-nothing decision for us. If we couldn't get a flight out of Gibraltar, there would be no second option…No third or fourth option either for that matter. That would be it. It would be a done deal.

We <u>had to</u> get on a flight back from Gibraltar.

We picked up our pace and started hustling to get down to the shipyards as the night began to slowly fade into a hazy, early morning. Our long night out on the streets of Tangiers was finally coming to an end. We were dead-tired and hungry. We were now going on two days with no food, but we we're too focused on somehow getting on the ship to notice much.

For about the next hour John and I made our way along the confusing streets of Tangiers to the shipyard. The sun slowly burned off the darkness and the night faded, as the city started to come to life around us. A few people were now out and about starting their day and the city started to take on some energy.

"Hey, you know what day it is today, don't you?" John asked me as we walked along the street in the gathering light of the early morning sunrise.

"I don't know. What, maybe Thursday? Friday?...Why?"

"No. I don't mean the day of the week. I mean, 'What's the <u>date</u> today?"

"Oh, the date. Man, I don't know. I just know we got about four or five days to make it back to London for your flight to the US."

"That's true. But you know - Today is the 30th."

"What?"

"It's the day before New Years Eve. Tomorrow's News Years Eve!" John said, jokingly whacking me on the back of my head.

With the fresh start of the new day unfolding after the exhausting long night, I started to get my second wind. It was a good thing, too. I was going to need it. After walking over some winding hilly streets, I got my first stiff smell of sea-water and the expansive, blue Sea of Gibraltar unfolded before us. The Sea was a beautiful sight with a deep blue color covering the crashing waves.

As we approached the docks, we asked a grizzled dock worker about the ship to Gibraltar. He was a lean Moroccan guy about 40, with a weathered, dark face and he was wearing a ship mate's cap. He was very a friendly and helpful guy. He explained with mostly body language and some writing that there was a ship leaving in less than two hours.

"Two hours!" John said to me in a concerned voice, "I sure hope they still have tickets. We still gotta buy a ticket, clear customs and make it onto the ship. It's gonna be tight."

We asked about the price and the dock worker wrote it down for us. In US dollars it came to about $11.

We checked our Moroccan currency real quick. Fortunately, we had just enough Moroccan money left on us. It turned out to be a real smart move not to buy any food or spend any money the previous day and night. We cut it very close with the Moroccan funds we had. If we only had western currency there would no way to get on the ship, because we couldn't change money since the banks wouldn't be opening until after the ship pulled out of port.

Looking over at the helpful Moroccan dock worker, we asked through gestures, 'Where do we get tickets, and clear customs and board the ship.'

It turned out everything was done in the same, single building. There was a lone building right near where the ship was docked that we could buy our ticket, get our passports stamped to exit Morocco and then walk out onto the ship.

We thanked the helpful guy after he gave us directions to the ticket/customs/ship boarding building. John and I started urgently walking in the direction he showed us.

"Seems we caught a break." I said to John as we hurried along. "Everything's in one building. We might just make it."

"Yeah. Hopefully we'll have no problem clearing customs. We haven't exactly had the best luck clearing borders on this trip."

"I just hope we don't need a special visa for Gibraltar."

"Man, I didn't think about that." John said alarmed. "If we do, we're dead."

"Well, we'll find out soon enough."

It took us just a short time to find the wooden brown, building near the shipping docks where we needed to buy our tickets. As we approached the building we could see a big, old vessel docked out in the misty water near the building.

"Bending my head to take another look at the rusting, ancient ship I asked, "Hey, is a ship suppose to lean like that in the water?"

"Maybe in the middle of a typhoon, but not in calm waters. Not while docked in the harbor." John said with a laugh.

"I didn't think so. The old boy looks like its hanging its head from a hang over or something."

John just nodded and smiled.

As we neared the doors of the ticket/customs/ship boarding building, I could hear a loud, deep roar like an engine or something. It was coming from inside the building.

"You hear that?" John asked.

"Yeah. What is it?"

I just shrugged.

John shrugged back…

We did a lot shrugging on this trip. After a while, shrugging became one of the primary means of communication between my brother and me. They had a lot of different meanings and depending on the situation, a shrug could convey many different, sometimes complex thoughts.

However, in this case it just meant, 'I don't know.' We didn't have a clue what the low, loud roar was.

So we walked up and opened the doors of the old building...and we found out. Inside the building were masses of people crowding every inch of the single, rectangular room. There were men, women, children, and families crammed inside; many in western clothes, others in traditional robes, some carrying bags or cases, others empty handed. But all of them were pushing and straining to make their way across the room.

The people were pushing in waves, trying to fight their way to two different corners of the building. One wave of people was heading east to one side of the room, and another mass of people were pointing west, fighting to get to the opposite side of the room.

Upon opening the door, I was immediately hit by a musky, sweaty current of heat and noise, especially, the noise. Kind of like a booming roar. Almost like at a baseball game when the ump makes a bad call against the home team, and a loud, low angry roar sweeps over the stadium. That's what the entire room sounded like.

"Man, this is chaos. What's going on?" John yelled over to me above the noise.

"I don't know, but it's absolutely packed in here."

"Are all these people trying to buy tickets? There must be a several hundred people in here." John shouted over the crowds.

"At least.. So whatta we gotta do to get our tickets?" I asked.

"I don't know. Let's find out."

After carefully observing the crowds and asking several different people among the pushing, stressed out masses, we finally figured it out.

We had to go to one desk on one side of the room to show our passport and get an exit stamp, allowing us to leave Morocco. Next, we had to get to the opposite side of the room to pay for and get our ship ticket. Finally, we had to go to a neutral area of the room to a small doorway leading to the dock and then board the ship.

And we had to get it done within a little less than 2 hours, before the ship pulled out. Two hours to get to two different desks in a single, confined room. No problem, right? It wasn't like we had to go to one building to clear customs, and then go to another place to get our ticket, and then go across town to the shipyard to get on the ship or something. We were just talking about getting to two different areas of the same room. Easy...

Man, it was tough. And it was tight. And it was tiring. But we did it and not with a minute to spare.

We ended up pushing and shoving and fighting our way through the swelling crowds in that claustrophobic, windowless room for almost two full hours. First, to one side of the room where a very stressed, obviously overworked custom official took one quick glance at our passports and stamped them, without a question and without even taking a look at us.

Then, to the opposite side of the room, which was only about 30 meters away, but with all the masses blocking our way, it seemed like more of a challenge to get across than the Sahara had been.

But we did make it to the other desk and paid for our tickets, using more of our dwindling funds. We were then given our precious tickets and we pushed, bumped and stumbled our way onto the ship among the crowds just a few minutes before the first booming horn sounded, warning that the ship would soon be getting under way.

CHAPTER **32**

Rocking and Rolling

Finally making it on the ship, we soon discovered it was not much different than the building we had just fought our way out of. It was just as packed and just as chaotic. There were people everywhere; crammed together, standing shoulder to shoulder in every nick and corner of the deck.

There was no room to sit and very little room to move, without pushing and straining your way through the surrounding crowds. They had packed as many people on as humanly possible.

Soon the horn boomed again and the huge ship started lurching and squealing, as it pulled out of the harbor and headed out to the windy, open waters. John and I pushed our way up to the upper deck of the ship out in the open wind. It was just as packed as the lower deck.

There was no place or space to sit down, it was crammed shoulder to shoulder but at least we were in the open air. I felt, for the first time since entering the ticket building over two hours earlier, that I could finally breathe a little.

"Hey, we made it." John said with an exhausted nod.

"Yeah. We did. That was a tough stretch. I'm dead tired."

"It's been a long stretch of grinding it. We've been grinding it for two days straight with no let up."

"Yeah." I said. "But we're not out of the woods yet. We gotta get on that flight today when we land in Gibraltar. I wonder how long this ship journey is?"

ROCKING AND ROLLING

John didn't respond. He just shrugged and stopped talking. I knew he was too tired and hungry to want to think about the next challenge we had to overcome. I felt the same way.

At this point we had somehow made it on the ship, and we were slowly storming over the open sea on our way to Gibraltar. We had done what we had to do. Now, we finally had time for some rest and to take a break. We could start focusing on our next challenge later, when we pulled into Gibraltar. The only thing we wanted to do now was to try and get some rest. You would think that would be pretty easy; considering we were exhausted, we were on a ship, had nowhere to go, nothing to do and several hours to kill. But it wasn't.

Shortly after getting out into the open sea, the wind really picked up and huge walls of waves started crashing into the old tank of a ship sending us rolling one way and then the other. The ship started really rocking and rolling. Each time the massive waves crashed into the aging ship, a strong wind blew across the shifting deck with sea spray flying in the air.

It was the roughest and worst ship crossing I have ever taken. Hands down. No other ship ride I've ever taken has even been close.

Despite the apparent ancient age and dilapidated condition of the rusting ship, I didn't really felt too much in danger of capsizing or sinking. I was too tired to worry about it. Besides, the ship was built and had the feel of battle tested tank. Nothing was going to knock it out of the water…But, man it was a rough, rough ride.

Within about 5 minutes of hitting the howling wind and rough, open seas, a guy who was obviously getting sea-sick made a mad dash pushing his way through the crowds to the bathroom. A few minutes later a second, grimacing guy did the same thing. Then soon after another.

Finally, one guy started on a dash to the toilet, but didn't make it. He started vomiting out on the open deck in front of the packed crowd, actually <u>on</u> some of the packed crowd. As soon as he did, it was like an immediate chain reaction. People starting get sick, vomiting everywhere, one after the other.

I've never seen anything like it. Soon there was vomit covering the deck, eventually swishing and streaming back and forth, rolling with the waves. I got sick myself. So did John.

"I'm getting off this deck." I said to John between gasps of breaths. "I've gotta get away from all these sick people."

Looking back at me with a sickly, ghost-white face, John asked "Where you gonna go? We're on a ship. There's no place to go. There are only two decks."

"I don't know. But away from here."

"Well, I'm staying put. I'm too tired to go wandering round the ship."

"Alright." I answered. "I'll meet up with you later."

I trudged out on the ship, pushing my way through the mass of vomiting humanity looking for any little private space I could claim for myself. It took a while and I got a sick a couple of more times along the way, but eventually I found an isolated little supply area at the back of the ship, near sea level. It was around a couple of bends on the deck and past a couple of signs signaling 'restricted area.'

There were many old life jackets and life savers piled against the beams and walls of the small area, with some large open portholes allowing the wind and a smattering of sea water to blow in. It was totally secluded and private.

I thought I was in heaven.

I pushed some of the life jackets around and made myself a nice little bed facing the open portholes. I placed my backpack around my feet to protect it from being stolen, as well as to make a nice stool for my legs. I was sick, exhausted and had been pushing hard for about the past 50 hours with no let up. I also hadn't eaten at all in that time as well. I was ready for a break. And now I finally had it.

So stretching out on a bunch of life jackets on the bottom deck of a rocking and rolling ship crossing the open seas, I finally did nothing but sleep for a few hours. Despite the rocking ship and crashing waves, I immediately fell dead asleep. It was just what I needed and had been long overdue.

After waking, I still felt a little weak and dehydrated, but a lot better than before I went to sleep. I wasn't sure how long I had slept and looking out the porthole it was difficult to tell the time of day, because the cloudy, misty weather was obscuring the sun. The waves were still real rough, but not the same crashing walls of water that they were earlier before I fell asleep.

ROCKING AND ROLLING

I weaved back through the crowds on the ship to the upper deck to see where John was and to find out how close we were to arriving at the Gibraltar port. On the upper deck there were many people sitting on the dirty floor in cramped, small groups, with others leaning over the rails trying to hold steady on the still rocking ship, with the wind blowing sea spray.

It took some time but I found John standing out near the rails. As I took a position at the rail next to John, I asked, "You have any idea when we pull into the Gibraltar port?"

"Not too long."

"Any idea what time it is?"

"I'm not sure. I think maybe 1:00 or 2:00 o'clock."

We stayed on the upper deck just looking out over the water watching the waves of the sea. The salty sea and occasional sea spray felt refreshing and helped clear my head. We stayed out on deck for not too long before John nudged me and said, "I can see land. We're getting close."

"Huh?"

"Out there. Can you see it?" John said pointing out over the water of the rolling sea in front of us.

"Yeah. I see it."

As we sailed a little closer, the 'Rock' of Gibraltar came into view. The large, rock mountain protruded from above the port, dominating the landscape. We stood taking in the grand view of the 'Rock' from our vantage point up on the second deck for some time.

Finally, I spoke up. "It's time to move. We gotta get ready to leave the ship. Get ahead of all these masses of people departing."

"Yeah. Who knows what time the flight is to London from here? We need to get to the airport as fast as possible."

"OK. Let's get down near the plank. And get ready to get off."

We diligently worked our way weaving though the massive crowds of people on board and actually made it to near the front, where the plank would be let down to let us debark. It took a lot of effort, but by the time the ship slowly bumped up to the dock, we were just about the first ones to get off.

Once the plank was put down, both John and I took off at a dead run down the long wooded dock to the shore. Whatever tiredness or sickness we felt was completely forgotten. We were pumped. In our minds our long sought after chance to make it back was in sight.

But in reality, we didn't know if there actually were any flights leaving that day to London; and if there were, we didn't know if there would be any available seats; and if there were available seats, we didn't know if we had enough money to pay for them.

There were a lot of things we didn't know, but to be honest that didn't cross our minds. We were in Gibraltar and the only thing on our minds was we had a flight to somehow, someway get on today.

After racing up to shore, I momentarily stopped and shouted to John. "Hey, John, take a picture with the 'Rock' behind me."

I stopped running for just an instant, John whipped out the cheap, little camera he had in his backpack, and took one fast picture as I stood under the big 'Rock' with dark clouds blowing past, wearing the high school jacket that the crazy sheik tried to trade me for in Tangiers.

We then took off running again, hardly even breaking our pace. We raced through the streets of Gibraltar trying to make our way out to the airport to see if there were any flights and any tickets available. We were running as fast as we could with our backpacks bouncing wildly on our backs. It was like we were on the home stretch of a grueling marathon race, and we were desperate to cross the finish line.

As were running through the well maintained streets of Gibraltar, I saw a sign across the street for a travel agency. It took me a moment to realize how I noticed the sign. It didn't hit me at first, but then I realized the sign was written in English.

I then started to take a better look around the street. There were actually a lot of signs and things written in English. The streets and shops and buildings also had the appearance of a British city. Gibraltar had a very different feel to it from what had been experiencing the past few weeks all across northern Africa and in southern Europe.

"Hey, John." I shouted over to my brother running alongside me. "This place feels like England. Look at all the English."

"It does, doesn't it?" John said looking around more closely.

"Let's stop at that little travel agency up ahead."

ROCKING AND ROLLING

"Where?"

I pointed up the street in front of us, "There."

We ran up to the shop and pushed through the door. It was a small travel agency with about 4-5 people inside. I looked at the Western man directly across from me, behind the counter. He was middle aged, balding, wearing glasses and a nondescript suit and tie. I was somewhat taken aback by his appearance. He looked so…so…usual…common, as did the other men and women in the little agency.

What happened next was even more surprising. He started speaking to me in perfectly fluent English, as did everyone else in the shop. In a few minutes, I heard more English spoken to me, than I had in all of the past month. It was almost like verbal overload.

The final and most startling thing was that no-one was staring at us. Nobody. Not in the least. Nobody stopped what they were doing to look at us. Nobody seemed surprised to see us. Nobody was pulling at us, or even mildly looking over at us with interest. Nothing.

It was quite the culture shock, actually, a kind of reverse culture shock. After the intense stares and attention we had experienced across the Sahara, it took me a moment to catch myself.

Finally, I urgently asked the guy across the counter, "Are there any flights to London leaving today?"

The balding travel agent sat down at his desk and opened a flight schedule book.

"Just a moment. Let me see…Flights to London today…"

As he scanned though his flight book, John and I glanced at each other. I gave John an intense look.

John looked back and then shrugged.

I shrugged.

We didn't have to say a word. We both knew what was the other was thinking. This was the moment of truth. Today was d-day. This was it. This was what we had been grinding, hustling and working so long for. We would find out if we could make it back…If we had made the correct decision in taking the ship across to Gibraltar.

After a few tense moments, the balding guy finally looked up and said, "I see there's one flight today leaving at 4:30, Gibraltar to London."

John smiled and I let out a sigh of relief.

"But," the balding travel agent continued, "All the seats are sold out. There are no more tickets available."

I felt like I had been sucker punched in the gut, and had the wind knocked out of me.

"No more seats! Whattdya mean, no more seats?" John asked with exasperation.

"I'm sorry." The man said, somewhat surprised at John's tone. "But we have no more tickets to sell. The flights been sold out for some time."

Then looking over to his co-worker, the balding agent said, "Debbie, BA flight 229 to London today is sold out, isn't it?"

"Why yes, Ian, it is. We have no tickets." She confirmed.

John and I just stared at the balding agent in disbelief and disappointment.

I think feeling bad for us, he added as a kind of justification. "You know, it is New Years Eve tomorrow. It's a small airport here and this is a very busy flying season. I believe all the flights are sold out for the next several days."

"New Years Eve..." I said quietly, nodding my head.

After a few moments of silence as we absorbed the disheartening news, John said to me. "Hey, let's get out to the airport. See what we can find. There's always something if you look hard enough."

"Yeah." I said brightening, "Maybe we can catch a seat at the airport. You never know. Just cause there are no tickets here doesn't mean we can't find something once were out there."

"That's for sure. There's always a way if you look hard enough." John agreed.

Looking back at the travel agent, John asked, "What time did you say the flight was leaving today?"

"It's at 4:30. British Airways flight 229." He replied.

"Great."

As John and I turned to run out the door, I quickly stopped, looked back and asked the travel agent, "So what time is it now?"

"Ah... It's 1:20. You've got a little over 3 hours."

"Oh, and how far is the airport from here?" I also asked.

"It's about 10 minutes by taxi." The balding travel agent said, pointing in the apparent direction of the airport.

ROCKING AND ROLLING

"How about if we run it?"

"Run it? You mean run to the airport?" He asked in disbelief.

"Yeah. Run it." I repeated.

'Well, I don't know…Gibraltar's a very small place, but the airport's some ways from here. I think it would take a little while."

"Thanks."

Before leaving the travel agency we quickly changed our last limited funds into British pounds.

John and I then stepped out of the travel agency onto the windy street with the grey clouds blowing over us.

"Whattdaya think?" I asked.

"Take a Taxi." John replied. "We gotta get to the airport as fast as we can."

"Uh-huh."

"It'll cost us some money, but we need time at the airport to check out the situation and to hustle up some tickets."

"Ok. Taxi." I agreed.

We ran out onto the quiet, well maintained streets and practically tackled the first taxi we saw coming by. After getting in the taxi, we told the young, ruddy faced driver 'Take us to the airport, Fast.'

With John and I urging him on, the taxi driver raced to airport in very little time. Along the way, John and I quickly told our story of traveling across Europe and Africa and how desperate we were to get on the flight to London today. When we came to a screeching halt in front of the small Gibraltar airport, we asked him the fare and started looking for some money to pay him with.

Speaking with a strong British accent, he said. "Cheers mate. It's on me."

Surprised, I said, "Pardon me."

The taxi driver replied, "No worries mate. I got it covered."

John and I were thankful and relieved; thankful for his kindness, and relieved because we really had no money to pay him with.

As we quickly jumped out of the taxi, I said, "Ta. Thanks for the help. Cheers mate." and gave him a thumbs-up gesture.

Without another look back, John and I raced into the airport terminal to find out about the flight to London. The airport was not so big at all, quite small actually. We ran through the airport looking for a flight counter or flight schedule board. We soon found a small ticket counter with a British Air ticket agent standing by. He was a heavy-set, guy in his 40's. The ticket counter area was basically empty of passengers since apparently the flights hadn't started boarding or checking in yet.

We quickly ran up to the counter out of breath, saying, "We need to get on a flight to London today. What flights are there?"

"There's one flight to London today at 4:30, but it is completely sold out." The BA agent replied.

"There's no seats? Are you sure?" I asked back.

"No. Nothing. This is a peak travel season. All flights to London are sold out for the next several days until after New Years. Sorry"

"Yeah, but there's gotta be something, some seats available."

"No. I can assure you there are no seats available. Everything has been sold out for some time." The BA agent replied politely, but also quite firmly.

"Everything? All seats?" John asked desperately..

"Yes. If you are traveling to Europe, the only way to leave Gibraltar is by air. Flights often sell out quickly. Especially now during the peak travel season."

"Wait. What did you say? Whattda you mean the only way to leave is by air?" I said surprised. "We can just travel overland across to Spain from here. Right?"

"No. You are mistaken." The agent answered. "There is no way through to Spain. Gibraltar has a completely closed border."

We were stunned by that bit of information. It was real bad news for us. Not only were there no seats on any flights for several days, but without a flight there was no way out of Gibraltar except by taking a ship back to Morocco and starting over. Despite all our efforts, we were blocked again from traveling overland. Our situation had already gone from bad to worse to desperate, and was now quickly approaching hopeless.

We had been burning time for a couple of days now without any progress forward and even more important we were burning money. No matter how tight or careful we were with our money, every day we spent without moving forward cut into our meager money supply and put us further from making it back.

ROCKING AND ROLLING

John and I stepped aside from the counter to talk over our situation.

"Man, we just can't catch a break." I said dejectedly.

"Yeah. What could be next?"

After a few moments thought I said, "We gotta get on that flight today. No matter what. It's our only chance. We gotta get a seat."

"Ok, but we don't even know the price of a ticket…if we even got enough money to buy tickets?"

"Ok. Let's check."

So we went back over to the BA counter and found out the price. Fifty-six pounds per ticket. ($85 each. $170 for two tickets) It was not good news. In fact it was devastating news.

We quickly scrounged together every bit of money we had and counted it. I was down to my last $53. We had a total of $96 between the two of us - Barely enough for one ticket, and not even close to enough for two tickets. So we scrounged together all our money again and counted again. Still $96.

It would seem our situation had now officially gone from desperate to hopeless.

"170 bucks for two tickets!" I said. "I thought those Spanish guys in Tangiers said there were real cheap flights from here."

"Well, they are cheap, much cheaper than from Tangiers." John replied. "But we still only got enough money for one ticket with…what, 11 bucks left over. It's not even close. And we each wasted 10 bucks on the ship ride over here."

"Man, whatta we gonna do now?" John asked.

"I don't know. But we still gotta somehow get on that flight today."

"Yeah, I agree. It's our only shot, but how?"

"I donno. Somehow." I replied unsure.

After a few minutes discussion John and I went back to the ticket counter. We begged and cajoled the BA agent until he acknowledged that there may be some passenger cancellations, and after more pleading he finally agreed to give us the seats if there were indeed no-shows. It took a lot of persuasion on our part, since there was already a waiting list with half a dozen names on it for any cancelled seats. But the hounded BA agent reluctantly wrote out our names at the top of the waiting list.

TRAVELIN' MAN ACROSS THE SAHARA AND BEYOND

Looking at the big airport clock, we could see it was now 2:50 and the flight would be leaving at 4:30, in 1 hour 40 minutes. We wouldn't know if there were any no shows until just before the flight was leaving. All we could do now was hope...and somehow come up with $74 for a second ticket.

The hoping part was no problem. We were desperately hoping and praying for no shows so we could get the seat the moment he said the flight was sold out...Coming up with $74, however, was quite another matter. Not so easily accomplished.

We first talked and pleaded with the BA agent; if there was some way we could pay for the second ticket *after* we landed in London.

We got a firm NO!

Then we tried to barter some of our goods in exchange for a ticket.

We got a firm NO!

Then I tried to use my university ID card as collateral for a ticket.

This time we got a firm and exasperated NO!

Before we could try another ploy, the irritated ticket agent told us we needed to pay *money* for the ticket. There was no other way and that was final!

John and I walked away from the counter dejected, but still not defeated.

"Let's see if there's a bank around here that we could get money from." John suggested.

"Ok. Let's go."

After a short walk around the small airport we found a single bank exchange office with a large window and two, young, female bank tellers standing inside. Putting on our best faces, we approached the bank tellers, and talking through the glass window we tried to negotiate an immediate loan of $74. Understandably, the bank clerks didn't find our proposals very tempting. Actually, they appeared to be quite flabbergasted by them. The longer we talked and the more they looked over our grimy, unshaven appearances, the more they seemed somewhat taken aback and a little frightened of us.

Can't say I blame them. At this point I had long hair, a slight beard, hadn't really eaten or slept in the past 40-50 hours, and for about 40 days straight had been wearing the same pair of pants, and had only one cold

ROCKING AND ROLLING

water wash with no soap. I'm sure I was getting pretty ripe and looking the worse for wear.

But we were persistent; we tried several different tactics and offered our Barkley Bank cards, ID's, backpacks, wallets, anything for the 74 bucks. The bank tellers finally got so frustrated by our badgering that they slammed the teller window shut and pulled down the protective steel curtain closing the bank in our faces.

At first I was shocked. I didn't know they could just shut down a bank office like that in the middle of the day. I assumed they would open back up after a moment. So we waited… but they didn't open back up. It was now 3:40. Our flight was leaving in 50 minutes.

"Whattda we do now?" I asked.

"Let's get back to British Airways and see about the ticket situation, and see if there are any seats." John replied.

"Ok. Times getting tight."

We hustled across the airport and pushed through the growing crowds of people now waiting for their flights. After working our way to the ticket counter, we asked the same heavy-set BA agent "Are there any seats on the flight for us?"

The agent looked over his flight list for few moments then looked up and said, "Right now there are 4 no show seats available, but I can't confirm them until boarding is almost concluded. Wait close by and I'll call you over if there any seats open."

John and I moved off to the side, keeping within direct eyesight of the BA agent. It was now 3:55…35 minutes until take-off.

John and I stood silently and anxiously among the crowds keenly watching the BA agent, and watching the minutes slowly tick off the clock. Shortly, an announcement was made for passengers to start boarding flight 269 for London. People started moving in the direction of the boarding gate and passport check. John and I waited, holding our breath.

It was 4:12, when the BA agent looked over at us and urgently waved us over to the ticket counter.

We ran over and the agent hurriedly told us, "I've got good news. There are exactly two seats available. You can get on the flight."

John and I looked at each other.

"Quickly, I need $170 for the two tickets and your passports right now." The airline agent commanded.

John and I looked at each other again.

John then said to the BA agent, "Please wait just a moment. We need to make a decision here."

I think understanding our predicament, the agent softened a bit and said, "Ok. But please hurry. The flight is leaving very soon and we'll be closing the gates in just a moment."

My brother and I hastily stepped aside as the final passengers began passing through the gate, and an announcement was made for the final boarding call for flight BA 269 for London.

"Whattda we do?" I asked. "We got enough money for only one ticket and eleven bucks left over."

"Ok." John quickly said, "I gotta use my return ticket from London to the US within three days or the ticket is wasted."

"Yeah, I know."

"So, I gotta get back to London. Otherwise I can't get back home to The States. How about if I take the money and fly back to London on my own?"

"Yeah, but what do I do." I replied anxiously. "I'll be stuck here in Gibraltar on my own with 11 bucks."

"Man, I don't know. Right now we got enough for one ticket, so we should we use it. What else can we do?"

"I don't know. We're out of options." I answered.

The BA agent standing nearby pointed to the clock, which now read 4:15 and said anxiously. "You've got to board right now! No more passengers will be allowed on."

I looked at John. John looked at me. I shrugged. John shrugged.

Finally, I said, "Ok. I'll give you the money. You go."

I quickly began handing over my money to John, as he gave his passport to the BA agent. We all counted up the money together, and the agent confirmed that we had $85 for one ticket and he hastily began writing out the ticket.

I stood motionless to the side holding the last remaining $11 in my hand.

After the agent gave John his ticket, John and I quickly shook hands and John said in a rush, "Ok. I…ahh…I think I saw some kind of American

ROCKING AND ROLLING

Express sign back in Tangiers. Remember, uhm…we walked past it after we got away from the crazy sheik. Remember?"

"Huh?"

"No…No…Maybe it was Barkley's. It was on the side of that one big street, near…ahh, near a market."

"Back in Tangiers? I have no idea what you're talking about." I said confused and alarmed.

"Yeah, yeah, when I get back to the US, I'll…I'll try to send money to you." John said hurriedly.

"When you get back to the US? In 4 or 5 days?" I asked.

"Yeah, yeah."

"Huh? It's not gonna work. I don't even know the place. I'm not even in Tangiers now"

"Well, there must be something else we can do…How about if I ahh…I…ahh…I'll..ahh…?"

At this point the BA agent interrupted us and pulling at John, strongly said, "You must board now! Right now!"

With that John and I stopped discussing any hair brain means to get me money and said a fast 'so long.' John was immediately hustled through the gate, down the airway plank and out of sight. In the blink of an eye he was gone.

I was now completely on my own.

I stood there, alone in the airport for a moment contemplating my situation and holding everything I had; $11, my beat-up backpack, a piece of stale bread and a mostly empty bottle of Coca-Cola. That was it. That was everything.

I was 19 years old. I had over a thousand miles ahead of me, portions of two continents, four countries and three ship crossings to cover in order to make it back…And I had $11.

In my mind I quickly evaluated my options…I was in Gibraltar, with no way out, no means of entering Spain overland, and no way to carry on. My only option was to spend a night in Gibraltar, then back-track by ship to Morocco in the morning, then spend a night in Tangiers before starting over and taking another ship to Spain. Then and only then could I begin traveling overland all the way across Spain and then across France before taking another ship across the Channel to England...

All with $11.

It would cost 10 bucks just to take the first ship back to Morocco. I'd get to Morocco with $1 and that's assuming I didn't eat or anything else...Then what?

The utter desperation of what I was facing quickly hit me, as a growing sense of panic seeped over me. I just felt an overwhelming feeling of 'I've got to get out of here now! Right now! It's my only chance...or I'll never make it back.'

With John gone and the plane already boarded, I thought I still might have a precious, few minutes to somehow...someway get on that plane and get out before it was too late.

I immediately sprang into action and started frantically going around the airport approaching anyone near me and asking them to give me $74 on the spot. With my unshaven and unwashed appearance, I must have been quite the sight.

I just walked up to anyone in the airport and gave a rapid spiel about 'my trip across northern Africa and the Sahara Desert, and how I needed $74 to get on the plane to get to England for university, and would you please give me the money right now!'

I quickly approached several people standing near me; an older couple, a middle-aged man, a group of tourists together, a trader, etc... Not surprisingly each person or group I approached quickly turned away from me with an offended expression and did their best to ignore me. It didn't deter me. I raced around the airport and asked anyone I came across to give me the money I needed.

I continued to get nothing but angry, cold reactions as the minutes ticked by and my chances for getting on the flight in time faded away. People were moving away from me with disdain even before I had a chance to approach them. It was like the parting of the Red Sea the way people hurried to move out of my path.

I soon looked at the clock. It was 4:38. The flight was scheduled for take-off at 4:30. It was now hopeless. It was too late. Time had run out. It was over...

ROCKING AND ROLLING

But…then…I approached a short, slim guy in his 30's with a mustache and a friendly, relaxed smile wearing what seemed to be some kind of airline uniform. I quickly gave him the same spiel I had already unsuccessfully given to over a dozen people.

He listened carefully, smiled, looked me dead in the eye and in a strong British accent said the words I've never forgotten, "Sure mate. I'll write you a check…It's gonna bounce, but it'll get you on the plane."

His name was Stephen Vella.

He worked for the airlines so he knew that they would have to take his check. He quickly dashed with me through the crowds over to the counter at the gate and told them he was paying the rest of the fare for my seat.

The two female airline agents standing at the closed gate said it was too late, that the plane had already taxied onto the runway and was awaiting take-off at any moment, and there was no way for me to board the plane. But we didn't have any of it. Stephen wrote out the check, set it on the counter with his airline ID, along with my remaining $11 cash and demanded for me to be taken on the plane.

The flight agents again insisted it was too late. But Stephen and I didn't budge. Stephen said, "If the plane is not in the air, it's never too late. Get this young man on that plane!"

At that moment the heavy-set BA agent who my brother and I had been hounding most of the afternoon appeared. He looked at the check and cash on the counter, looked at me, waved off the other two agents, quickly reached for the intercom and frantically called over the airwaves to the control tower. After quickly talking to the control tower, he yelled to me, "Grab your backpack and get your passport out! You're in luck, the flights been delayed a few minutes on the runway before takeoff. You might make it!"

I immediately turned to Stephen and thanked him profusely as he hastily jotted down his London address for me to send him his money. I then took off my high school ring (the same ring I had vowed never to relinquish), and offered it to him to hold in good faith until I repaid him his money.

He just smiled, shook his head and said, "No worries, mate. I trust ya. Have a good flight." He then turned and disappeared into the crowds.

I never saw him again.

And with that, the BA agent urgently pulled on my arm and we ran out the gate, down the stairs, out on to the massive tarmac and across the runway. We sprinted a long ways down the huge, paved runway to where my plane was waiting to take off. A small stairway was briefly swung out for me to board at the back of the plane as the passengers impatiently sat waiting. I was met on the plane by a pretty flight attendant who hurriedly ushered me to the last remaining seat, where I collapsed in relief…

Just moments later the big aircraft hurled down the runway and smoothly lifted off into the cloudy afternoon sky, heading undeterred on its way to London, England.

I had made it back after all.

Acknowledgements

This book was a labor of love. After years of telling people the story of the extraordinary adventure my brother John and I experienced traveling through Europe, and then crossing 1,000 miles of the Sahara Desert of northern Africa on just $6 a day…And after years of people telling me I should write a book about it. Finally, one day I decided to do just that. This book is the result.

When I wrote this book I made no notes or outline. It just flowed out naturally; while using my journal, travel documents and photos to piece together specific dates and events. The three objectives I set when I began writing was; to hopefully entertain as broad an audience as possible…to motivate people to follow their dreams and to not give up…and to inform people about different cultures, travel safety, surviving on the road, etc. Hopefully, in some small way I've succeeded.

This book would not have been completed if not for the great assistance and support of many people. First and foremost I want to thank my lovely wife Suzi for her continual encouragement in the long hours of writing this book, and for our many wonderful years together. I would also like to thank my step-daughter Jenny for her first-rate computer assistance which I badly needed. I'm very proud of her for the extraordinary person she is.

I also wish to give a heartfelt thanks to my mom and dad for their continued life-long love and support, and the strong foundation they provided me for my life. I was truly blessed with wonderful parents. They have always been there for me - no matter what. Any good that I have done or accomplished in my life is due to them.

Many friends also provided me with valuable assistance in completing this book. I wish to thank Tom Locke, Gus Swanda, Andrew Gamble, Kenneth May, Jeff Liebsch, Christine Park and professor Humes for taking the time to read the manuscript at different stages. Their keen insights and suggestions helped improve the storytelling immensely.

Additionally I need to thank Russell McConnell for helping put together the great cover design, along with Jeff Liebsch again; also Desiree Bullock for her suggestions for the cover.

In addition, I want to extend my gratitude to my brother Winston, Carrie, Pieternel and Jeannette for their support and encouragement, especially when I moved back to the US after so many years abroad. Also for the little guys, my nephews Sean and Jake, who I hope follow their dreams when they get older, whatever those dreams may be. I would like to thank Tinamarie Ruvalcaba and Elaine Simpson, for their assistance in preparing the book for publication.

I also want to respectfully acknowledge and thank Dr Tae-Chul Jung, Dr. Chul-Kyu Kim and Mr. Eui-Kang Kim at Kyungsung University in Busan, Korea for their friendship and support while I was working for them during the writing of this book… I would also like to give credit to Brother Rice High School in Birmingham, Michigan, which provided me with a great education and values for my life, and inadvertently plays a part in the story.

In addition, I wish to thank the deceased Mr. Peabody and his daughters Susan and Barbara, who gave me unlimited work at Peabody's restaurant during my high school and college years; which is how I earned the funds needed to pay for this travel adventure and for all my travels to over 30 countries before the age of 21.

I want to acknowledge the magnificent Harlaxton University in Lincolnshire, England where I was attending college during the time of this story. It is an amazing place and my time studying there was an important part of my

ACKNOWLEDGEMENTS

youth and plays a part in this story... I also want to express my gratitude to the Oxford Overseas Study Course Program at St. Peters College, Oxford University, England which was also a tremendous experience and influential in my travels and later life.

I wish to offer my sincere thanks to Bob Seger and the Silver Bullet Band and Gear Publishing, as well as Mr. Seger's associates Mike Biola and Tom Wechlar, for graciously allowing me to use Mr. Seger's lyrics in my book. I have been a life-long fan of Mr. Seger's music, especially his travel songs, and it's an honor to have his lyrics included in my book.

Finally, I need to give special thanks to my brother John, who shared the incredible adventure chronicled in this book with me, as well as many other adventures. This book is as much his story as it is mine. I owe a great debt to John as he is the older brother. A lot of what I did when I was young was because I was following in his footsteps... John is indeed a true travelin' man.

www.ingramcontent.com/pod-product-compliance
Lightning Source LLC
Chambersburg PA
CBHW070718160426
43192CB00009B/1239